Orpheus in the
Middle Ages

Orpheus in the Middle Ages

John Block Friedman

Harvard University Press
Cambridge, Massachusetts
1970

For Arnold Williams

Preface

Many readers of this book who were drawn to it by its title may find themselves offered both more and less than they had expected. More, because to talk about medieval Orpheus one must go back to the Orpheus of antiquity, and less, because once having journeyed there, the reader will find that the scope and method of this book necessarily exclude some of the most interesting and familiar aspects of the myth. Foremost among these is Orpheus' relation to the religious experience of the Hellenic world, a subject which has already been treated at length by W. K. C. Guthrie in his *Orpheus and Greek Religion* (1952), as well as by others more recently. Readers interested in the archetypal content of classical mythology may be disappointed that I have not chosen to discuss this subject. The speculative archetypal or mythic approach which has been so productively applied to the Orpheus of post-Renaissance literature did not seem suitable for a study of medieval Orpheus, whose development within the Judeo-Christian tradition is largely historical.

Readers whose special discipline includes classical legend and art might wonder at a medievalist's temerity in choosing to write about Orpheus at all. Certainly the hazards of an interdisciplinary study are obvious. I have borrowed freely from several different areas of specialized study, in which scholars better qualified than myself have written amply. Yet without recourse to tools and learning outside the usual limits of literary criticism, the student of the Orpheus legend would be left with little of all that was thought and said about this figure from Greek mythology. I hope, therefore, that those readers onto whose preserves I have ventured will look charitably upon my poaching. It has been undertaken in all humility, with the single aim of getting a better perspective on the legend of Orpheus.

In the interests of consistency and brevity, the spellings of the names of classical authors and abbreviations of the titles of their works are those given by the *Oxford Classical Dictionary*. Names of medieval authors are given in their shortest familiar form. In quotations from medieval manuscripts, spellings have been normalized and abbreviations silently expanded. Translations are mine unless otherwise indicated. I have taken the liberty of supplying the originals immediately following the translations when the original is unpublished, difficult of access, or necessary for stylistic comparison. Biblical quotations are from the King James version.

Acknowledgments

This book owes much to former teachers, William L. Alderson, Adolf Katzenellenbogen, and Lawrence J. Ross, who all, in one way or another, interested me in Orpheus. Special thanks are due to Robert E. Kaske for a wealth of suggestions and corrections of errors large and small, and to Miss Pamela Gjettum, from whose helpful criticisms I have tried to benefit in my translations of Latin authors.

Financial aid from Michigan State University enabled me to study at the Warburg Institute where Drs. A. A. Barb and J. B. Trapp shared with me their knowledge of magical gems and ancient music. I am greatly indebted to all of the libraries and museums who gave so generously of their time and resources during my research and granted me permission to publish photographs of objects and manuscripts in their collections. Some of the substance of this book has already appeared in *Speculum* and *Traditio*; the Mediaeval Academy of America and Fordham University Press have kindly allowed me to reprint this material.

My greatest debt is to my wife for her patience and her help in every way during the various stages of this book's composition.

Center Montville, Maine   J.B.F.
September 1969

Contents

Illustrations

xiii

Orpheus in the Middle Ages

I
Introduction

Few people need any introduction to Orpheus. The Thracian singer who charmed animals by his music and played his lyre in hell is a familiar figure to all who share in the heritage of Western culture. And yet he is not the same figure to us that he was to the Middle Ages, nor was he to them the same as the Orpheus known to the late antique world. Each age has fashioned Orpheus in its own image, giving him new attributes, emphasizing certain of his deeds at the expense of others, and even changing the course of the narrative to make the Orpheus myth conform to the values of the day.

The extent of this process first came to my attention while I was reading Pierre Bersuire's commentary on Ovid's *Metamorphoses*. Bersuire wrote that Eurydice, that is, human nature, had been tempted by a forbidden fruit while gathering flowers, that she had been bitten by Satan disguised as a serpent, and that Satan had carried her off to the underworld. Then Orpheus-Christus—for so he is called by the commentator—went down and took back his wife from the ruler of hell, greeting her with these words from the Song of Songs: "Rise up, my love, my fair one, and come away."

This medieval Orpheus, who was as unfamiliar to me as he would have been to Ovid himself, clearly reflected a fourteenth-century cleric's need to find Christian doctrine in the fables of the pagan gods. Yet the fusion of pagan and Christian imagery in the story seemed too apt, too resonant, and too unlike the more clumsy overlay of most of the other allegories in the book to have come unaided from Bersuire's pen. Intrigued by the very existence of a figure called Orpheus-Christus in the Middle Ages, and curious about the antecedents for this allegory, I turned to existing studies of the Orpheus myth for more information. It soon became evident that, though many books and essays had been devoted to the role of Orpheus in Greek religion, art, and literature,[1] little was known about the late antique and medieval forms of the myth, and that it would be necessary to look to the primary sources themselves.

There I came upon the track of Orpheus-Christus, in a book on late Roman art. On one page a mosaic of Orpheus among the animals was reproduced. Orpheus sat on a rock, his foreshortened legs dangling over the edge of it. His eyes were large and compelling, his hand raised as though to bless his lyre. This page slipped past and a manuscript illustration of Christ throned in majesty replaced it. Christ's pose was strikingly similar. The rock had become a throne; Christ's tiny legs needlessly dangled, though a footstool had been supplied for them. He stared out over the beholder, his right hand raised as though to bless the New Testament codex tucked under his left arm. The Christian painter had probably put the technical vocabulary of pagan art to the service of his new religion for lack of a better model and not from any conscious desire to identify Orpheus with Christ. Nonetheless, it was tempting to see this Christ in the pose of Orpheus as one step in a process of conflation

2

which would eventually lead to the Orpheus-Christus of the Middle Ages. As it proved, such pictorial details, especially in the late antique period, did indeed provide the impetus for portraits of Orpheus in literature, while literary portraits in turn gave rise to new details of his appearance in art. This process, however, was longer and more complicated than I had foreseen, and gradually resulted in a rich and various medieval figure, the study of whose history became in effect a study of the attitudes of antiquity and the Middle Ages toward pagan myth.

This book is about the changing conceptions of Orpheus and the different uses made of his myth in Western Europe, between the fall of Rome and the death of the Middle Scots poet Robert Henryson. Inevitably a history of Orpheus must be selective.[2] To discuss every appearance of his myth in art and literature from Hellenic antiquity down to our own day would be a Herculean task, and such a discussion would demand heroic readers. The method of this book is to group and consider materials according to what seem the most significant developments of the Orpheus legend, and to pay closest attention to materials which reveal changes, or which may have contributed to changes, in it. Actually, the works which manifest change also include the major sources of the myth by other criteria—for example, Clement of Alexandria's *Exhortation to the Greeks*, the Jerusalem Orpheus mosaic of the sixth century, Boethius' *Consolation of Philosophy* and its medieval commentators, the Paris Psalter, and a host of lesser known works. Every age, of course, was not equally interested in Orpheus. Some left us little or no evidence of change in his legend, while others simply left us no evidence at all of what they thought about him, and for these reasons are not discussed here.

The reader may wonder why, with some four centuries yet remaining after the death of Henryson until Jean Cocteau's "Orphée," he was not offered a complete history of the legend. There are two reasons. First, the history of Orpheus during the past four centuries has received a great deal of attention in recent years. Second, there seems to be a substantive difference between the treatments of Orpheus before and after Henryson's lifetime. This difference is hard to describe, but one way of putting it might be that later treatments of Orpheus are both more sophisticated and less serious.

To the early Christians the pagan gods were the symbols of a very real secular culture which had to be resisted and discredited, for they were, after all, the gods of the man next door. Justin Martyr, for example, may have scoffed at the fables of the Olympians, but he used the *Testament* of Orpheus, in which the musician rejects polytheism, to prove to the gentiles that one of their own philosopher-heroes had espoused monotheism. Whether or not Justin believed his own propaganda or knew that the *Testament* was a Jewish forgery, polytheism was enough of a threat to the spiritual safety of Christians in his day to make Orpheus' apostasy an important event for Christianity.

The Christian Middle Ages took the pagan gods just as seriously. They medievalized the gods' appearance, of course, and limited their power to that of planetary deities who acted as the ministers of God in matters of medical and judicial astrology.[3] Whatever the actual practice of Christians in conceding power to the gods, orthodox Christianity held that the stars could not exert their power contrary to God's will and that they could not force a man to sin against his will. As we shall see, too, medieval men continued the antique practice of seeing, in the stories of the gods, moral truths and allegories hidden beneath the surface. Thus Orpheus was just as valuable to Bersuire as he had been to Justin a thousand years earlier.

To postmedieval Europe, however, pagan mythology had quite a different meaning. The essential difference

4

between medieval and Renaissance treatments of mythology has been well expressed by C. G. Osgood. "The Middle Ages, with what one scholar calls their 'encyclopaedic grasp of the Universe,' found a significant place for mythology, as for all else, in their scheme of things. They assume a reality in the old myths, an essential truth variously reflected, but truth and reality nevertheless. The Renaissance, with its advance in classical scholarship, knew more and more about mythology, but took it less seriously. With the increase of knowledge the conviction of reality declines, at least in artistic use, and the old myths tend to become mere playthings, material of applied ornament and superficial decoration."[4] In a broad sense, then, it is the Middle Ages' view of the "reality" in the Orpheus myth that is the subject of this book.

A myth, according to the compiler of the *Suidas Lexicon*, is "an untrue story imaging truth." When we ask what the story of Orpheus and the truth it imaged was for the time treated in the present book, we find that the "untrue story" is almost as elusive and protean as truth itself. For the story was changed in shape and emphasis many time as it was passed down from the ancient Greeks to the medieval world.

A complete "original" version of the Orpheus myth does not, of course, exist, our information about Orpheus from the earliest Greek art and literature being extremely fragmentary; for purposes of comparison with later versions, however, it may be helpful here to attempt the reconstruction of an *ur*-Orpheus—the figure who would have been known to the Hellenic and Hellenistic world. Because so little literary or artistic evidence remains of him, this Orpheus of very early times may be said to resemble somewhat a broken antique statue, pieced together from scattered fragments and even then forced to face posterity without an arm or a nose. Yet without some such reconstruction it would be difficult for us to recognize or appreciate the changes wrought upon the myth by later hands.

What, then, was known about Orpheus by the Greeks up until the time when his legend was carried eastward and southward in the wake of Alexander's conquests? First, his parentage. To the Greeks, for whom a man's lineage was so important in defining his character, this was a matter of considerable interest, and it is not surprising that he was seldom mentioned without some genealogical comment. Orpheus was born in Thrace, the son of the Muse Calliope and the wine god Oeagrus, though Pindar seems to voice a common uncertainty when he refers to Orpheus in one place as the son of Oeagrus and in another as the son of Apollo.[5]

Second, Orpheus was an Argonaut. What may be the first literary reference to his presence on board the *Argo* occurs in the poetry of Simonides (b. 556), where we learn that "above [Orpheus'] head there hovered birds innumerable, and fishes leapt clean from the blue water because of his sweet music." Apparently Orpheus was chosen to make the journey because of his skill at the lyre. Euripides tells us that the musician played "the rowers a measure for their long sweep of oars," and his adventures are recounted in the *Argonautica* of the Hellenistic poet Apollonius Rhodius.[6]

Third, Orpheus charmed nature by his music. A Hellenistic poet, Damagetus, in the *Greek Anthology* is merely alluding to a feature of the myth well known in art and literature as early as Aeschylus when he writes an epitaph for "Orpheus . . . whom the trees disobeyed not and the lifeless rocks followed, and the herds of the forest beasts."[7]

Fourth, Orpheus was known as a man of powerful religious sensibilities, a priest of Dionysus who abandoned that cult to become a worshiper of Apollo; for his apostasy he was killed by the Bacchantes. This story was the subject of a lost play by Aeschylus, the *Bassarae*.[8] Certainly a change from the irrational, chthonic, and violent religion of Dionysus to the service of a rational, celestial, and legalistic god would be in keeping with Orpheus' pacific nature. We never hear of him fighting, and he was so opposed to bloodshed that he abjured the use of all animal foods.[9]

Fifth, Orpheus was a poet, writing songs of the creation of Earth, Sky, and Ocean, as well as of the ordering of the heavens. Plato quotes a few verses of poems he attributes to Orpheus, which were apparently well known in his time, but the poems associated with the name of Orpheus which have survived from antiquity are actually the productions of Neoplatonic writers, and date from the late Hellenistic and early Christian periods. These poems and earlier fragments are collectively titled *Orphica* in modern editions.[10] His cosmological poems gave Orpheus the reputation of a prophet among the Greeks. Euripides alluded to certain "tablets of Thrace" on which Orpheus set down his wisdom, and Plato named him as one of several prophets.[11] Given his literary interests, it is not surprising that Orpheus was also said to have invented the alphabet and to have first linked "verse in heroic feet."[12]

Sixth, Orpheus was renowned for his journey to the underworld to win back his wife, Eurydice, who had been killed by a snake. With lyre and song he petitioned the gods of the underworld for her release, and they granted his request subject to an agreement that he would not look back at her until he had brought her to the upper world. But love for her so moved him that he did look back and so lost her forever. This account is actually that given by the Roman poets Ovid and Virgil,[13] but their view of the myth appears to have been based on some lost Alexandrian intermediary. Considering that the trip to the underworld is the best known feature of Orpheus' myth today, it is rather surprising that so little was said about it in the Hellenic world. Early accounts of Orpheus' descent tend to be ambiguous about its outcome. Euripides, in the *Alcestis*, has Admetus say:

> But, were the tongue and strain of Orpheus mine,
> To witch Demeter's Daughter and her lord,
> And out of Hades by my song to win thee[14]

implying that the story he knew ended happily, with Orpheus returning with his wife to the world of the living. Isocrates (b. 436) speaks of how Orpheus "led the dead back from Hades"[15]—perhaps more of the dead than simply his wife. Since Eurydice was not even named as the wife of Orpheus until the third century,[16] we may conclude that the love story was not of as much interest to Hellenic authors as Orpheus' deeds in the male world of the *Argo*.

Seventh, Orpheus died at the hands of the Thracian women. The death of Orpheus was apparently a very popular subject among Hellenic vase painters since a good number of representations of it have survived.[17] Most of the more detailed written accounts, however, date from Hellenistic and Roman times. The reasons for his murder are not agreed upon by all the ancient writers. In addition to the story of his apostasy from the cult of Dionysus there are two explanations which deserve brief mention. One is that Orpheus was killed because he revealed the secrets of the gods;[18] another that Venus and Proserpine "came to Jove for his decision, asking him to which of them he would grant Adonis. Calliope, the judge appointed by Jove, decided that each should possess him half the year. But Venus, angry because she had not been granted what she thought was her right, stirred all the women in Thrace by love, each to seek Orpheus [the son of Calliope] for herself, so they tore him limb from limb."[19] Most of the Hellenic accounts, however, agree that after the death of his wife, Orpheus mourned her for a long time, spurning the women of Thrace who loved him. In these accounts it was anger at their rejection which caused the women to kill Orpheus. A Hellenistic poet, Phanocles (c. 225 B.C.), provides an alternative explanation for their wrath—an explanation which was to achieve some popularity. He wrote a long catalog poem, the *Loves*, of which only a few fragments remain, describing the loves of gods and heroes for beautiful boys. Orpheus appears in this curious work in a new role: "And Orpheus, the son of Thracian Oeagrus, loved Calais, the son of Boreas, with all his heart, and went often in shaded groves still singing of his desire, nor was his heart at rest. But always, sleepless cares wasted his spirits as he looked at fresh Calais. The Bistonides, sharpening their long swords, ringed him in and killed him because he was the first in Thrace to desire men and to disapprove the love of women."[20] Ovid offers this as a possible reason for the actions of the Thracian women, saying that Orpheus shunned women for three years after the death of his wife, and loved young boys instead.[21]

Eighth and finally, the fate of Orpheus after death befitted his life as a musician. The story is beautifully told by Phanocles. Orpheus' assailants, he says,

> cut off Orpheus' head with their bronze swords, and fastening it to his lyre with a nail, they threw it at once into the Thracian sea . . . and the head and lyre together were washed in the blue-green waves. And the sea put the head and lyre, still together, ashore at the sacred city of Lesbos. The sound of the clear-toned lyre reached both to the sea and the islands, and to the shore where the rivers flow into the sea, and there on the shore men buried the clear-toned head of Orpheus, and put into the tomb the clear-toned lyre as well, which had prevailed over both the dead rocks and the bitter waters of Phorcus. After this, the island had both songs and the lovely art of harping, and of all islands it is the most tuneful.[22]

From the third century comes a version of Orpheus' death, that offered by Philostratus in his *Life of Apollonius of Tyana*, which carries the sequel even further, telling how the Lesbians enshrined the head of Orpheus in a cave; its fame as an oracle caused people from as far away as Babylonia to visit the island, but Apollo, who already had a shrine at Lesbos, became jealous and told the competing head, "Cease to meddle with my affairs, for I have already put up long enough with your vaticinations."[23] Another story relates how, after the singer's death, the weeping Muses gathered up his scattered limbs and, to honor him, put his lyre, outlined with stars, in the heavens as the constellation Lyra, where it may be seen today.[24]

This, then, is the *ur*-Orpheus whose legend was to be transmitted, by both likely and unlikely means, from antiquity to the Middle Ages. Clearly, the earliest versions of his story contained many features that are not central to, or even relevant to, the highly selective myth of Orpheus we know today. Forgotten by post-Hellenistic writers, or at least subordinated to other concerns, were the Argonaut and pacifist, the vegetarian, the homosexual whose severed head was a noted oracle. The Thracian prophet, however, was to become the first link in a chain of portrayals which gradually brought the pagan Orpheus into the Judeo-Christian tradition, and thereby into the cultural experience of Western Europe.

The word portrait recurs frequently in this study to describe the appearances of Orpheus in art and literature. A great many literary descriptions—in effect, portraits—of Orpheus have come down from the antique and medieval world, witness to the influence of the rhetorical device of *ekphrasis*, while artistic evidence of the myth is, of course, almost exclusively made up of portraits in one medium or another. Yet just as much a portrait as any single piece of evidence is the collective view of Orpheus held by an age, the "compleat Orpheus" so to speak, who takes shape as we compare the various literary and artistic statements made about him. The chapters that follow attempt to arrive at these larger portraits and to account for their development.

The second chapter considers Orpheus the monotheist, as he was referred to by both Hellenistic Jews and, later, Christians, in their religious and philosophical controversies with their pagan neighbors. We find a poem attributed to Orpheus—then believed to have been a pupil of Moses in Egypt—in which he abjures the Olympian gods and speaks as a prophet of Mosaic law. The *Testament* of Orpheus is an example of the apologetic writing and apocrypha produced by Alexandrian Judaism and by a unique intellectual climate. It was taken over by the Christian apologists in their own arguments against the pagans, in order to prove that all pagan learning had originally come from the "philosophy" of the Pentateuch as revealed to Orpheus, Plato, and others of the ancient Greeks.

The portrait of Orpheus in Chapter III is that of a new being, Orpheus-Christus, who develops in the syncretistic climate of late antique art and hermetic literature. Orpheus, first adopted by the painters of the Roman catacomb frescoes as a figure type for the Good Shepherd, soon becomes identified with Christ in a much more profound sense.

In the fourth chapter we will see how the view of Orpheus and Eurydice as the complementary parts of man's soul—reason and passion—develops, first in Boethius' *Consolation of Philosophy* and then in medieval allegorical commentaries on the works of Boethius, Ovid, and other writers. At the same time another tradition, which saw the legend as an allegory of the arts, was developing out of the work of Fulgentius and the mythographers. This tradition, deriving the names of Orpheus and Eurydice etymologically from "best voice" and "good judgment," tended to view Eurydice in a more favorable light than did the clerical commentaries which saw her as a figure for the concupiscence of human nature. Both strains of commentary, however, helped to shift the emphasis of the legend away from Orpheus as an independent hero to Orpheus and Eurydice, the couple, and prepare the way for romance treatments of their relationship.

In the last portrait of this book Orpheus and Eurydice appear as a secular couple whose legend represents the power of the god Amor over the human heart. Orpheus has become, among other things, a knight, a model courtly lover, the wielder of magical powers and the writer of elegant love lyrics. This portrait develops out of many disparate images of Orpheus which seem to have converged sometime before the fourteenth century to form a unified and fairly consistent picture. The clerical commentaries contribute to it, as do manuscript illustrations and academic exercises in the use of the *ornatus* and other techniques of epideictic rhetoric. Perhaps most of all, the literary conventions of the romance impose their form upon the story. The results, which represent the flowering of the Orpheus legend in the Middle Ages, are the romance *Sir Orfeo* and Henryson's narrative poem *Orpheus and Eurydice*.

Even this brief summary of Orpheus' fortunes indicates that men found him to be of the greatest interest and utility in the main business of late antiquity and the Early Middle Ages: the propagation of religious belief. Only later when matters of faith were relatively settled do we find in art and literature a new concern for the human heart and a corresponding interest in Orpheus and Eurydice as lovers. Thus it is to the literature of religious controversy that we must go for our first portrait of Orpheus in the postclassical world.

II
Moses' Pupil:
The Orpheus Who
Came out of Egypt

About the middle of the third century B.C. a new and quite un-Hellenic story about Orpheus came into circulation—one which is seldom heard of today, but which was to be responsible in large part for Jewish and Christian interest in his legend during the next six centuries. This was the story of how Orpheus rejected polytheism. According to some Jewish and, later, Christian apologists, Orpheus traveled in his youth to Egypt where he received training in philosophy from no less a teacher than Moses himself. Having learned monotheism from its source, he remembered it throughout his life, though professing other, more Hellenic, beliefs. Then in his old age he recanted and left a testament to his son Musaeus, advising him also to reject the pagan gods and to believe in the God of Moses. This legend, alluded to by many authors during Hellenistic and early Christian times, owed not a little to the "discovery" of documentary evidence to support it, the testament itself.

The *Testament (Diatheke)*[1] *of Orpheus* is a poem in Greek hexameters, whose claim to the attention of the Hellenistic world lay not only in its supposed antiquity—Orpheus was believed to have died well before the Trojan War, which was thought to have begun in 1183 B.C.—but also in its philosophic significance, for in it Orpheus, the earliest of the Greek philosophers, accepted the God of the Jews. Here is the version of the *Testament* known to the Jewish and Christian apologists:

> I speak to those fit to hear. All you unhallowed, you who flee the ordinance of the laws (for God's law has been established for all), close the gates. Listen to me, Musaeus, son of the light-bearing Moon, for I speak the truth. Do not chance the loss of a dear eternity because of former opinions. Look to the divine word. Pay constant heed to it, directing there the inmost intelligence of the heart. Enter readily on the path, perceiving the single and eternal pattern of the universe. For an ancient tradition speaks of this Being. He is one, self-begotten, and all things are brought to pass by Him. He is immanent, yet transcendent. No man can see Him, though He can be known by the intelligence. And He, out of His goodness, does not ordain evil for mortal men. Strife, Hatred, War, Plague and tearful Grief attend them. Nor is there any other [God]. And He sees all with ease. You have not seen the track and sturdy hand of the great God upon the earth, but I have seen them and I will show you, my child. I do not, however, see the God himself. For He is above the clouds and ten-veiled to me and to all men for eternity. No speaking mortal can see this ruler unless it be the only-begotten branch from the Chaldean tree, for he [Abraham] knew the course of the planets and how the spheres rotate around the earth upon their axis. And this Being controls the winds of the air and the waters of the stream. And He makes the flame of His

self-engendered fire shine out. Moreover He dwells in the great heaven on a golden throne, and His feet stride the earth, and He stretches His right hand to the boundaries of Ocean. The base of the mountains trembles at His wrath; nor is it possible to withstand His mighty purpose. He is everywhere and He brings to pass all things on earth and in heaven and He commands the beginning, the middle and the end: such is the word of the ancients, such is the word of the one born of water [Moses], the opinions of God having been given to him in the double-folded Law. Nor is it lawful to speak otherwise. I tremble in my heart and body [before God]. From the heights He brings all to pass and makes all harmonious. O child, fix your thoughts on these matters, keep a rein on your tongue, and keep my words in your heart.

Φθέγξομαι οἷς θέμις ἐστί, θύρας δ' ἐπίθεσθε βέβηλοι,
φεύγοντες δικαίων θεσμούς, θείοιο τεθέντος
πᾶσι νόμου· σὺ δ' ἄκουε, φαεσφόρου ἔκγονε Μήνης
Μουσαῖ'· ἐξερέω γὰρ ἀληθέα· μηδέ σε τὰ πρὶν
ἐν στήθεσσι φανέντα φίλης αἰῶνος ἀμέρσῃ,
εἰς δὲ λόγον θεῖον βλέψας τούτῳ προσέδρευε,
ἰθύνων κραδίης νοερὸν κύτος· εὖ δ' ἐπίβαινε
ἀτραπιτοῦ, μοῦνον δ' ἐσόρα κόσμοιο τυπωτὴν
ἀθάνατον. Παλαιὸς δὲ λόγος περὶ τοῦδε φαείνει·
εἷς ἔστ' αὐτοτελής, αὐτοῦ δ' ὕπο πάντα τελεῖται,
ἐν δ' αὐτοῖς αὐτὸς περινίσσεται, οὐδέ τις αὐτὸν
εἰσορᾷ ψυχῶν θνητῶν, νῷ δ' εἰσοράαται.
Αὐτὸς δ' ἐξ ἀγαθῶν θνητοῖς κακὸν οὐκ ἐπιτέλλει
ἀνθρώποις· αὐτῷ δὲ χάρις καὶ μῖσος ὀπηδεῖ,
καὶ πόλεμος καὶ λοιμὸς ἰδ' ἄλγεα δακρυόεντα,
οὐδέ τίς ἐσθ' ἕτερος· σὺ δέ κεν ῥέα πάντ' ἐσορήσαις,
αἴ κεν ἴδῃς αὐτὸν πρὶν δή ποτε δεῦρ' ἐπὶ γαῖαν.
Τέκνον ἐμόν, δείξω σοι, ὁπηνίκα δέρκομαι αὐτοῦ
ἴχνια καὶ χεῖρα στιβαρὴν κρατεροῖο θεοῖο.
Αὐτὸν δ' οὐχ ὁρόω· περὶ γὰρ νέφος ἐστήρικται
λοιπὸν ἐμοί· <πᾶσιν> δὲ δέκα πτυχαὶ ἀνθρώποισιν·
οὐ γὰρ κέν τις ἴδοι θνητῶν μερόπων κραίνοντα,

εἰ μὴ μουνογενής τις ἀπορρὼξ φύλου ἄνωθεν
Χαλδαίων· ἴδρις γὰρ ἔην ἄστροιο πορείης,
καὶ σφαίρης κίνημ᾽ ἀμφὶ χθόνα ὡς περιτέλλει,
κυκλοτερές γ᾽ ἐν ἴσῳ τε κατὰ σφέτερον κνώδακα·
πνεύματα δ᾽ ἡνιοχεῖ περί τ᾽ ἠέρα καὶ περὶ χεῦμα
νάματος· ἐκφαίνει δὲ πυρὸς σέλας ἰφιγενήτου.
Αὐτὸς δὴ μέγαν αὖθις ἐπ᾽ οὐρανὸν ἐστήρικται
χρυσέῳ εἰνὶ θρόνῳ· γαίη δ᾽ ὑπὸ ποσσὶ βέβηκε·
χεῖρα δὲ δεξιτερὴν ἐπὶ τέρμασιν ὠκεανοῖο
ἐκτέτακεν· ὀρέων δὲ τρέμει βάσις ἔνδοθι θυμῷ,
οὐδὲ φέρειν δύναται κρατερὸν μένος. Ἔστι δὲ πάντως
αὐτὸς ἐπουράνιος, καὶ ἐπὶ χθονὶ πάντα τελευτᾷ,
ἀρχὴν αὐτὸς ἔχων, καὶ μέσσατον, ἠδὲ τελευτήν,
ὡς λόγος ἀρχαίων, ὡς ‹ὑδογενὴς› διέταξεν,
ἐκ θεόθεν γνώμαισι λαβὼν κατὰ δίπλακα θεσμόν.
Ἄλλως οὐ θεμιτὸν δὲ λέγειν· τρομέω δέ γε γυῖα,
ἐν νόῳ. Ἐξ ὑπάτου κραίνει περὶ πάντ᾽ ἐνὶ τάξει.
Ὦ τέκνον, σὺ δὲ τοῖσι νόοισι πελάζεο, γλώσσην
εὖ μάλ᾽ ἐπικρατέων· στέρνοισι δὲ ἔνθεο φήμην.

Little is known about the authorship and early history of this remarkable poem. Reports of its "discovery" as such have not survived, though one is tempted to imagine them as antique parallels to the publications of the infamous nineteenth-century Shakespearean critic John Payne Collier. Collier produced his own seventeenth-century documents in support of certain of his scholarly claims; the marked syncretism of this *Testament* suggests that its author likewise had designed a document to fit the particular proof he wished to make. The *Testament*, however, seems never to have been questioned as to its authenticity by Hellenistic or early Christian authors— partly no doubt because of a prevailing syncretistic climate of thought, and partly, one suspects, because of its usefulness in Jewish and Christian apologetic.

The text of the *Testament* presented here is to be found in the *Praeparatio Evangelica* of Eusebius (fl. A.D. 300),[2] as part of a fragment of the *Explanation of the Mosaic Law* by Aristobulus "the Peripatetic." Aristobulus, an Alex-

16

andrian Jew of the second century B.C., is perhaps best known for his view that there was a very ancient translation of the Pentateuch into Greek (made before the Persian conquest of Egypt in 525 B.C.), whence Orpheus, Pythagoras, Plato, and Aristotle derived all Greek science and philosophy. In the fragment which Eusebius preserves, Aristobulus attacks the originality of the Greek philosophers writing on cosmogony by showing their indebtedness to Mosaic history. He introduces Orpheus' *Testament* to bolster his argument that Pythagoras, Socrates, and Plato knew and recognized the one God of the Jews. It is unlikely that Aristobulus himself forged the poem; he says after quoting it that it was somewhat too Hellenic for his tastes: "Plainly, I think it clear that through all of this [the *Testament*] is the power of God. And accordingly I thought to myself I should remove the words Dia and Zena [forms of Zeus] which were everywhere in the poem, for the intention of the poem was directed up to God, on which account I quoted it."[3]

To understand the kind of sensibility which would go to the trouble of producing a poem like the *Testament of Orpheus*—and the kind of sensibility which would seize upon it and magnify it as an important adjunct to his legend—it is necessary to know something about the genre of works to which the *Testament* belongs. For this poem is not an isolated relic, but shares many characteristics with the pseudononymous works produced in abundance by Jewish writers, particularly in Alexandria, during the Hellenistic period.

There had long been colonies of Jews living in Egypt, and with the growth of Alexandria under the Ptolemies many Jews were invited to settle in the city, where they seem to have formed a privileged *politeuma* or community, possessing religious and social autonomy but not the civic rights of their Greek neighbors. There they followed their religion, built synagogues, perhaps with the right of

17

asylum, enjoyed their own courts of law and educational system, and from the vantage point of such security looked askance at the polytheism of their neighbors.[4]

Egyptian animal worship received the strongest Jewish contempt,[5] and we find little evidence that the Alexandrian Jews concerned themselves with the ideology of their onetime captors, aside from offering rebuttals to certain slanderous statements made by Egyptian writers about the Jews. Their Greek neighbors in Alexandria, on the other hand, posed a more serious cultural and religious threat. In spite of the fact that the Jews had their own social and religious community within the city, they became increasingly Hellenized. By the third century B.C. most had lost their knowledge of Hebrew and spoke and read Greek as did other Alexandrians. They had their own scriptures, to be sure, but the Law was translated into the Greek of the Septuagint for those who had lost their Hebrew, and thus when they read the Law they did so in the language of the gentiles. Philo spoke of Greek as "our language" and assumed that Abraham knew Greek etymologies.[6] Greek apparently was used in the synagogues of Alexandria, since Greek inscriptions were to be found there. Many of the wealthier sons of Jewish families were educated in Greek gymnasia where they learned the stories of the Hellenic gods and heroes. Some adopted Greek names like Alexander, Ptolemy, or Jason, or made up names containing the Greek word for "god" like Theophilos and Theodoros, while some even adopted the names of Greek gods, becoming Apollonius or Dionysus. Some Jews, quite naturally, wished to assimilate Greek culture in every way short of actually violating the Law, while others reacted strongly to such temptation and became increasingly eager to assert the existence of Jewish culture and its superiority to the culture of the gentiles.

It is interesting to note that the literature which grew out of this climate of thought did not consist merely of invective against the Greeks, but was frequently proselytizing in nature, attempting to show that the Hebrew civilization antedated and fathered the Hellenic, and to bring the Greeks to a greater understanding of the ties between the two cultures. A long tradition of Hebrew proselytism helped to give Alexandrian apologetic this direction, but perhaps equally as much did the nature of the charges leveled at the Jews during this time, and the well established Jewish bent for history.[7]

The charge that elicited the most heated response originated with Manetho, an Egyptian priest, and is summarized by Josephus. Briefly, Manetho claimed that the people of Jerusalem, in league with a group of Egyptian lepers, ravaged Egypt, destroying towns, temples, and images of the gods. Eventually they were given a "constitution and a code of laws . . . [by] a native of Heliopolis, named Osarsiph after the Heliopolitan god Osiris, and . . . when he went over to this people he changed his name and was called Moses." This parody of the Exodus was embroidered upon by Lysimachus (c. 100 B.C.) and Chaeremon (c. A.D. 50), both Greeks, who held that the Jews were a race of lepers driven out of Egypt, who went to Jerusalem, killed the inhabitants and installed themselves there. Related to these stories were others charging the Jews with having no culture, no real gods, and the like.

With regard to the cultural charges, it is true, the Jews of Alexandria could not compete with the Greeks on several grounds. They were not much interested in astronomy and mathematics—areas of science in which their Alexandrian neighbors had made great achievements—and for them Alexandrian lyric poetry was too closely identified with pagan myth and eroticism. Their religious restrictions, moreover, made it impossible to compete with the Greeks in temple ornamentation or in sculpture.

The Jews were, however, great historians and had a sacred history which was the equal of the best that the

Greeks had to offer. Moreover, Jewish history was of very great antiquity and, to its proponents, made Greek sacred history of the sort recounted by Hesiod in the *Theogony* seem at best a footnote to the Pentateuch and at worst a conscious plagiarism of events from the Hebrew past. Thus it is that from the appearance of the Septuagint in the third century down to Philo in the first century after Christ we find in the Jewish writers of Alexandria a constant effort to vindicate the Jews from the charge of a disreputable origin and to show the cultural superiority of the patriarchs over the great figures in Greek sacred history. The forms taken by their historical apologetic—or apologetic history —are many. Sometimes it is straight prose, as for example the work of Eupolemus (c. 150 B.C.), who wrote that "Moses was the first sage and the first to teach the Jews the alphabet, which the Phoenicians took from the Jews and the Greeks from the Phoenicians,"[8] or another such writer, Artapanus (c. 50 B.C.), who stated that Moses, "called by the Greeks Musaeus," invented ships, war machines, and philosophy.[9] Sometimes Hellenistic Jewish historians tried to rival the Greeks in their own forms. Philo the elder wrote an epic poem, *On Jerusalem*, of which a few fragments remain. Theodotus connected the founding of the city Shechem with Greek mythology in a poem in hexameters, and Ezechiel wrote a tragedy in Greek called *Exodus* which began with a monologue by Moses on his past life and ended with the destruction of the Egyptians and the escape of the Israelites through the Red Sea told by an Egyptian messenger in the best classical manner. The tragedy was in iambic trimeters.[10]

It is against such a historical and apologetic background that we must see the *Testament of Orpheus*, written in the language of Homer and modeled on his style, yet combining veiled allusions to Abraham and Moses with claims for the superiority of the one God. In its form the *Testament* draws upon yet another tradition of Hellenistic Jewish writing, that of the apocalyptic book, and it is this form which is perhaps the most effective element of the *Testament* in conferring new importance upon Orpheus. The apocalyptic book did not exist as a form until comparatively late—not until after Alexander's conquests and the establishment of the Jewish colony at Alexandria. At this time, according to the chronicle Seder 'Olam,[11] the Jews began to regard the canon of the Old Testament as permanently constituted for all time. Such an attitude, of course, made it impossible for the books of any new prophets to be added to the biblical canon. But the desire of men to speak what they felt to be God's will continued as before. Replacing the Hebrew prophets, a new class of men took up the burden of inspiration. These men were the "wise." They did not prophesy in their own names, but rather wrote in the names of famous men of history whose authority had been validated by time. So were produced the apocalyptic *Book of Enoch,* the *Testament of the Twelve Patriarchs*, the *Testament of Abraham*, the *Book of Jubilees,* and the *Assumption of Moses.*[12] While most of the names the wise adopted were biblical, not all were, and among their personae were the pagan Sibyl (who, it was claimed, was the daughter-in-law of Moses) and Orpheus. The wise amplified the canon of such illustrious figures of the past with many predictions—some "foreseeing" the recent Maccabean wars and other historical events pertaining to the Jews, others prophesying a falling away from the Law by the Jews, but, after great tribulation, the eventual triumph of Israel.

Much of this apocalyptic literature seems to have been written in the hope, as one historian has phrased it, "of strengthening the self-esteem of the Jews themselves and perhaps heightening their esteem in the eyes of the dominant environment."[13] Certainly propagandistic concerns led to the attribution to Jewish figures of achievements which had hitherto been laid to the Greeks. The

Sibyl, for example, is recorded in the Jewish part of the *Sibylline Oracles* as having predicted that: "There shall be an aged wight [Homer] false in writing, and false in birth-place. . . . Yet he shall have much wit, and a verse fitted to his thoughts blended under two names [*Iliad* and *Odyssey*]. Chian shall he call himself, and he shall write . . . with poetic skill; for he shall gain possession of my verses and measures."[14]

The form of a last will and testament, with its admonition to the children of the dying man, is common to many of the Jewish apocalypses. In the *Book of Enoch*, the patriarch urges his son Methuselah: "All these things I am recount-ing to thee and writing down for thee . . . preserve . . . and (see) that thou deliver them to the generations of the world."[15] There are similar accounts in the *Book of Jubilees* and the *Assumption of Moses*. The *locus classicus* for this form is apparently the account in II Esdras 14:3–8, 26, of God's twofold revelation to Moses. Here God tells Esdras that he revealed himself to Moses in a bush "and told him many wondrous things, and shewed him the secrets of the times, and the end of the seasons; and commanded him, saying, These words shalt thou publish openly, and these shalt thou hide . . . Some things shalt thou deliver in secret to the wise." Later we learn that the "things" to be delivered to the wise were seventy books of secret wisdom, presumably numbering among them many of the apoca-lyptic works which were to appear during Hellenistic times. Indeed, this passage in Esdras provides a kind of pedigree for all the secret wisdom dispersed by the various patriarchs to their sons.

Orpheus, though certainly not as old as Moses, was considered to be more or less contemporary with many of the men who gave their names to the Jewish apocalypses. Jews during the Hellenistic period, and Christians after it, had been fond of synchronizing pagan and biblical history, and we frequently find Orpheus' name associated with the earliest of the Hebrew seers. Artapanus tells us that Moses was the teacher of Orpheus. Firmicus Maternus, a Christian apologist of the fourth century, says that "Abraham, Orpheus and Critodemus" discovered astrology.[16] As late as the twelfth century, the Byzantine historian George Cedrenus gives several accounts of Orpheus which show him to have lived either a little after Abraham went to Egypt in his seventy-fifth year (Gen. 13:10) or during the period of Hebrew history covered by the Book of Judges: "Abdon . . . ruled the people of Israel for eight years. At this time Thracian Orpheus, the most celebrated lyric poet of all, became known among the Greeks."[17]

The *Testament* does not give Orpheus' age, but its writer is anxious to give monotheism a distinguished pedigree. He has Orpheus speak of "an ancient tradition" telling of the one God and the "word of the ancients" as to His powers, suggesting that these ancients are even older than he, Orpheus. Orpheus implies his familiarity with the Pentateuch by alluding to two specific ancients, Abraham[18] and Moses, the latter of whom was given the opinions of God "in the double-folded Law"—a dark statement which refers, perhaps, to the twofold revelation of the Law and the apocrypha described by Esdras or to God's delivery of the Law on two tablets of stone. It is interesting to note that while the recantation of Orpheus has the admonitory form which was common in Hebrew apocalyptic writing,[19] its content suggests quite a different purpose from the strengthening of Jewish community feeling described above. The *Testament* is not, as are most works of its genre, concerned with the destiny of Israel, but rather with the existence of one God. Most important, it seeks to dissuade the reader from polytheism. The technique of the *Testament* is particularly interesting because the author does *not* seek to establish Orpheus' credentials—which he would need to do if he were speaking to a Jewish audience—but

23

rather uses Orpheus' known antiquity along with the names of Abraham and Moses to help assert the antiquity of the Law. This approach suggests that the author is speaking as an apologist, not primarily to Jews, but to Greeks familiar with some of the names of the Hebrew patriarchs.[20]

The *Testament* of Orpheus names a double audience: "those fit to hear" and Musaeus, son of the light-bearing moon. Though Musaeus is addressed as "teknon emon" and later as "o teknon," it is doubtful that by this the author meant to refer to a direct line of descent. The "child" who is frequently addressed in Hebrew apocalyptic is not necessarily the child of the speaker's loins, but rather represents the house of Israel or tribal descendants of the speaker. Probably the author intended Musaeus merely as a disciple; there is no good biographical evidence for Orpheus as a father and he seems to have had many disciples.

Those intriguing "few fit to hear," on the other hand, suggest to us that Orpheus' apocalypse is addressed to an audience who had some familiarity with the conventions of the Greek mystery religions, much more perhaps than a Jewish audience could ordinarily be expected to have. Certainly the manner in which the Orpheus of the *Testament* introduces his wisdom implies that he learned it as a "mystery"—Hebrew though it may be in content—when he was in Egypt. Such a possibility is not far from the story of Orpheus' life as it was known in the time of Alexander, for Orpheus did, according to some writers of antiquity, bring back to Greece the mystery religions from Egypt.[21]

The opening of the *Testament* reminds us of the prorrhesis or proclamation of a Greek mystery, with the young Musaeus serving as the *mystes* and Orpheus as the seer who gives him secret wisdom not to be revealed to those "unhallowed." In its first lines, "I speak to all those fit to hear. All you unhallowed . . . close the gates," is an echo of similar warnings in Greek and Roman literature. Callimachus in his "Hymn to Apollo," placing the scene at the temple of the god, tells his listeners, "hekas, hekas hostis alitros" (l. 2), and the situation is even more parallel in the sixth book of the *Aeneid* where the Sibyl, introducing Aeneas to the mysteries of the underworld, shrieks, "procul o, procul este, profani" (l. 258).

The author of the *Testament* seems to have been, if we can judge by the poem, a Hellenized Jew with a considerable knowledge of Hellenic literature and much missionary zeal. Wishing to demonstrate to the Greeks that they had unknowingly worshiped the god of the Hebrews all along,[22] he produced the *Testament* as evidence that Zeus and Jehovah were one. Perhaps the clearest expression of this aim is the poem's thorough but nonetheless studied syncretism. Take for example the name of Zeus which Aristobulus, apparently a far more conservative man than the author of the *Testament*, says he excised from the poem. By Aristobulus' lifetime Zeus, as a name, probably did not mean much more than chief god of a very broad range of pagan deities.[23] It was, nonetheless, a name traditionally linked with polytheism and therefore was unorthodox in a description of Jehovah. Its presence in the poem is most easily explained if we assume that the author of the *Testament* wished to introduce the God of Abraham and Isaac to the gentiles by reference to his nearest counterpart in pagan theology. Though Aristobulus hoped to cleanse the poem of Zeus' presence, a good bit remains. Orpheus in the *Testament* still refers to him as *theos*, a common noun traditionally used of any god, and *Dia*, the accusative form of the proper noun "Zeus." The writer enforces the similarity between the deities by describing the powers of his God in language often used of Zeus.[24] Orpheus explains to Musaeus that "all things are brought to pass" by the God of whom he speaks; the verb he uses, *teleitai*, is reminiscent of the idea of Zeus as Perfector. In the *Agamemnon*, for example, Clytemnestra addresses him as *Zeu teleie* (1. 973). Moreover, says Orpheus in the *Testament*, this God "controls the winds of the air," and Zeus was frequently Zeus ourios or God of Good Winds.[25] Needless to say, these epithets associated with Zeus came into use many centuries later than the ostensible date of the *Testament*.

Several features of the poem suggest that the author was consciously trying to make it more palatable to men familiar with heroic poetry. The author cast his poem in hexameters (those same hexameters which the Sibyl had taught to Homer) and uses archaic genitives—*theioio, kosmoio, astroio* —and personifications borrowed from Hesiod's *Theogony*. Sometimes his fusion of ancient Greek and ancient Hebrew images is quite striking. Orpheus says of his God that: "He dwells in the great heaven on a golden throne, and His feet stride the earth, and He stretches His right hand to the boundaries of Ocean. The base of the mountains trembles at His wrath." Compare this with Isaiah 66:1, "Thus saith the Lord, The heaven is my throne, and the earth is my footstool," and Hesiod's description of Styx, "eldest daughter of backflowing Ocean," who "lives apart from the gods in her glorious house vaulted over with great rocks and propped up to heaven all round with silver pillars."[26] The base of the mountains which trembles at His wrath suggests many poetic theophanies of the Old Testament which are accompanied by earthquakes, floods, and storms.

The *Testament of Orpheus* has several features in common with the only other surviving work of Hellenistic times[27] to put Hebrew wisdom into the mouth of a pagan seer, the *Sibylline Oracles*. The similarity of language and imagery in the two works suggests a very close textual dependence. Consider, for example, the Proem to the *Sibylline Oracles* which exists almost complete in the apologetic work of Theophilus of Antioch. This Proem makes several assertions about the nature of God:

> . . . One God there is
> Who reigns alone, supremely great, unborn,
> Almighty and invisible, himself
> Alone beholding all things, but unseen
> Is he himself by any mortal flesh.
> For who is able with the eyes of flesh
> To see the heavenly, true, immortal God,
> Whose dwelling is the sky?[28]

> εἷς θεός, ὃς μόνος ἄρχει, ὑπερμεγέθης ἀγένητος
> παντοκράτωρ ἀόρατος ὁρώμενος αὐτὸς ἅπαντα,
> αὐτὸς δ' οὐ βλέπεται θνητῆς ὑπὸ σαρκὸς ἀπάσης·
> τίς γὰρ σὰρξ δύναται τὸν ἐπουράνιον καὶ ἀληθῆ
> ὀφθαλμοῖσιν ἰδεῖν θεὸν ἄμβροτον, ὃς πόλον οἰκεῖ;

One cannot help but be struck by the similarities of thought[29] between this passage and the corresponding passage from the *Testament*: "He is one, self-begotten, and all things are brought to pass by Him. He is immanent, yet transcendent. No man can see Him, though He can be known by the intelligence." In another part of the Proem, the Sibyl describes the visitation of evils on men:

> [God] rewards the good
> With an abundant bounty, but fierce wrath
> He rouses for the wicked and unjust,
> And war, and pestilence, and tearful woes[30]

> τοῖς ἀγαθοῖς ἀγαθὸν προφέρων πολὺ πλείονα μισθόν,
> τοῖς δὲ κακοῖς ἀδίκοις τε χόλον καὶ θυμὸν ἐγείρων
> καὶ πόλεμον καὶ λοιμὸν ἰδ' ἄλγεα δακρυόεντα.

The *Testament*, though not ascribing these evils to God, lists them in the same order and in the same language, as "War, Plague and tearful Grief."[31] According to one critic, the *Oracles* were used "in a serious attempt to place Jewish intellectual achievements clearly before the world . . . to propagate . . . the rudiments of the Hebrew faith, especially her monotheism and moralism."[32] Clearly the *Testament* also seeks to propagate monotheism; it contains, however, little moralism beyond the attack on idolatory implicit in any proclamation of an invisible God. Rather, it tries to establish the universality of the Hebrew God by referring to Zeus as but an aspect of this supranational being. The poem's lack of emphasis on the idea that God favors the Israelites above other men distinguishes it from the *Sibylline Oracles*. But both works, in form and style, look back to the Hellenic rather than to the biblical past, and both could be used to convince Greek-speaking peoples of the logic and inevitability of Jewish theology.

The importance of the *Testament* for the study of antique and medieval views of Orpheus is that it transmuted a Hellenic hero into Moses' pupil, a figure of wide Hellenistic appeal whose interest in monotheism was to render him useful, first to the Jewish apologists of Alexandria and then to a widening range of Christian writers during the early centuries of the Church. It might seem at first glance that claims for the great antiquity of Hebrew philosophy, while understandable against the background of social and cultural relationships in Alexandria, would not be useful to the early Christians, for whom the advent of Jesus had in a moment replaced the old ways. But a New Law is not tenable, or indeed understandable, without reference to the Old Law from which it departs. The early Christian apologists were faced with the need of a history against which their religion might take on a fuller significance; moreover they had to deal with the same charges of new-fangledness and a lack of culture which had formerly been levied against the Jews.

It is not surprising, then, that among the earliest

writers on behalf of Christianity we find some borrowing
of the apologetic techniques of the Alexandrian Jews.[33]
For example, just as Jews like Aristobulus had wished to
prove that the Greeks derived their philosophical ideas
from Moses, Clement of Alexandria produced a lengthy
apologetic treatise about A.D. 200 called the *Stromata* or
Miscellanies, much of which—in the course of discussions
on Christian doctrine, allegory, Gnosticism, and other
subjects—was devoted to proving that the Greeks "plagiarized" from Moses. Clement wrote that "we shall not
only show that . . . [the Greeks] have imitated and copied
the marvels recorded in our books; but we shall prove,
besides, that they have plagiarized and falsified (our
writings being, as we have shown, older) the chief dogmas
they hold, both on faith and knowledge and science,
and hope and love, and also on repentance and temperance
and the fear of God—a whole swarm, verily, of the virtues
of truth."[34] Interestingly, in subsequent books, Clement
uses both Aristobulus and the *Testament of Orpheus* to
make his point. From Tatian and Clement in the second and
third centuries up until Eusebius—who might be called
the first Christian historian—in the fourth century, we can
see the development of increasingly sophisticated uses of
these techniques to relate real and fabled Christian history
with ideology, and this development is reflected in the
Christian apologists' approach to Orpheus.

The earliest extant Christian apologists to use Orpheus
were Tatian and Theophilus in the second century. Tatian
looks back in spirit to the most propagandistic writing of
Jewish Alexandria, and his attitude toward Orpheus is
one of hostility. To him, Orpheus was a barbarian who
taught the Greeks the mysteries and a poet of false reputation (false, since Tatian claimed that all his works were
written by Onomacritus). He refers to Orpheus only as a
late figure in a chronology of early writers to show that
Moses was more ancient and hence has greater authority:

"it is evident that Moses is older than the ancient heroes, wars, and demons. And we ought rather to believe him, who stands before them in point of age, than the Greeks, who, without being aware of it, drew his doctrines [as] from a fountain . . . Moses is not only older than Homer, but than all the writers that were before him—older than Linus, Philammon, Thamyris, Amphion, Musaeus, Orpheus."[35] In his implication that the Greek philosophers and poets drew their information directly or indirectly from the Pentateuch, Tatian is similar to the Jewish apologist Artapanus, more concerned to discredit pagan learning by showing its borrowed character than to reply to it with a Christian counterversion of intellectual history.

Theophilus used the idea of Greek indebtedness to Moses rather differently. He was aware that pagan history offered much of value, but failed to provide information about Christianity that would be helpful to new converts, and was perhaps the first of the Fathers to attempt to supply this lack. In him we see combined an effort to formulate Christian history and a desire to conserve the best of Greek learning. While he denies the Greeks seniority to Old Testament figures, he does not assume that this is a sufficient ground for wholesale rejection of their achievements, and, making some effort to relate Greek and Hebrew historical events chronologically, he often assigns to the Greek achievements a lesser but nonetheless real value on the basis of their inspiration.

In keeping with this approach, Theophilus' treatment of Orpheus reveals an interest on his part which goes beyond the somewhat negative zeal of Tatian's list of writers: "Jubal is he who made known the psaltery and the harp . . . others say that Orpheus discovered the art of music from the sweet voices of the birds. Their story is shown to be empty and vain, for these inventors [that is, Orpheus] lived many years after the flood."[36] Theophilus as a practical apologist may not have wished to discard pagan mythology and history entirely lest he antagonize his Greek readers. As a Greek convert, moreover, deeply conversant with the literature of his culture, he was probably reluctant to abandon it for its own sake. Instead he distinguishes between pagan revelation, the sort of story which told of Orpheus' invention of music, and Christian or Hebrew revelation, which explains that Jubal really invented the harp, but still feels that God was present though to a lesser degree in the revelations of the pagans. "Did not the poets Homer and Hesiod and Orpheus profess that they themselves had been instructed by Divine Providence? . . . How much more, then, shall *we* know the truth who are instructed by the holy prophets, who were possessed by the Holy Spirit of God!"[37] By Theophilus' day the ingenuity of Alexandrian exegesis had proven that Homer and Hesiod spoke allegorically of the Pentateuch in the cosmogonical sections of their poems,[38] but Orpheus would hardly have been made the third member of this triumvirate were it not for the *Testament* which, consciously modeled on the works of Homer and Hesiod, gave him a place beside them in the history of philosophy and stated, without any need for allegorizing, Orpheus' belief in the One God of Israel. Theophilus, in his statements about the great writers of pagan antiquity, seems confident that they had direct knowledge of Jehovah. Such a view could only have come out of his reading of allegorical commentaries on the works of Homer and Hesiod, out of Jewish apologies attempting to prove Greek indebtedness to Moses, and out of pseudononymous "pagan" works like the *Sibylline Oracles* and the *Testament of Orpheus*. Theophilus alludes directly to the *Testament* when he asks of what use it was that Orpheus wrote of the "three hundred and sixty-five gods, whom in the end of his life he rejects, maintaining in his precepts [*Diatheke*] that there is one God."[39]

In many ways the *Testament* gained for Orpheus the

recognition and interest of Christian writers, both Greek- and Latin-speaking, as could no fabulous deed he might have performed. The services of such a notable convert from the ranks of polytheism were of very great value to the Church, particularly among the Greek-speaking converts who had grown up familiar with Hellenic culture and who, as pagans, would have known Orpheus for his other deeds. For such men it must surely have been a satisfaction to discover upon reading the *Testament* that Orpheus, like themselves, had seen the truth and accepted the one true God. Nine Christian works between the second and the fifth centuries cite the *Testament*, bearing witness to its wide circulation. It can be said to have served, in the growing Christian community, not simply as *a* source of information about Orpheus the pagan philosopher, but as *the* most relevant and interesting information about him.

Of all the Christian apologists, Clement of Alexandria was perhaps most interested in Orpheus. In his work we find not only the crystallization of various Hellenistic attitudes toward the Orpheus of the *Testament*, but also a strikingly new view of Orpheus as a prefiguration of Christ, about which we shall say more in the next chapter. Clement preserves for us one of the three extant versions of the *Testament*. His apologetic works, written about the middle of the third century, are marked by frequent efforts—often lively and sophisticated—to relate traditional Hellenic learning to Christian concerns.

Clement of Alexandria was a learned man converted to Christianity after a broad education in Hellenic and Hellenistic literature. He did not wish to discard Greek philosophy when he became a Christian, indeed, quite the opposite, he sought to apply it to the service of the Church. For him, as for Theophilus, the *Testament of Orpheus* and the Jewish historians were of fundamental importance in providing a rationale for the use of Greek wisdom. Clement explains to his readers that the wisdom of the Greeks was not in reality of Greek but rather of non-Hellenic origin and that most of it was derived from the Egyptians who, of course, got it from the Jews during the captivity. In his *Stromata*, he argues "And that the most of them [the oldest Greek philosophers] were barbarians by extraction, and were trained among barbarians, what need is there to say? Pythagoras is shown to have been either a Tuscan or a Tyrian . . . And Orpheus was an Odrysian or a Thracian. The most, too, show Homer to have been an Egyptian . . . and Plato does not deny that he procured all that is most excellent in philosophy from the barbarians; and he admits that he came into Egypt."[40] In another part of the *Stromata* Clement discusses the way in which God is intelligible but not sensible. He finds this idea not merely in the Old Testament, but also in the writings of Plato and Orpheus, who, he conjectures, first learned it from Moses. "'For both is it a difficult task to discover the Father and Maker of this universe; and having found Him, it is impossible to declare Him to all . . .' says the truth-loving Plato. For he that had heard right well that the all-wise Moses, ascending the mount for holy contemplation, to the summit of intellectual objects, necessarily commands that the whole people do not accompany him . . . And again Orpheus, the theologian, aided from this quarter [that is, Moses] . . . adds: 'Him no one of mortals has seen, but He sees all.'"[41] But notice how Orpheus has become "Orpheus the theologian." Orpheus, of course, is much less important to Clement than Plato as a precursor of Christian theology, but even he is shown as being in the direct line of Moses, one of those "taught in theology by those prophets . . . I mean Orpheus, Linus, Musaeus, Homer, and Hesiod, and those in this fashion wise."[42] If Plato and Orpheus had learned by way of Moses something of the nature of God, their works were not without value for Christians. One feels that Clement wishes to justify his own fondness for the thought of Plato by enlisting him in the "philosophical family," as Dante called them, who lived before or in ignorance of Christ: "there I saw Socrates and Plato, who stood before all others . . . and I saw Orpheus."[43] Certainly Clement would agree with the Neoplatonist Numenius, whom he quotes as having asked, "For what is Plato, but Moses speaking in Attic Greek?"[44]

Thus pagan philosophy, with the sanction of a Mosaic origin and—perhaps more importantly—offering the only available systematic approach to knowledge, received its own apology in the work of one of the greatest Christian apologists. "If the Hellenic philosophy comprehends not the whole extent of the truth . . . yet it prepares the way for the truly royal teaching; training in some way or other, and moulding the character, and fitting him who believes in Providence for the reception of the truth."[45] Clement was an exception in believing so strongly in the value of pagan culture for Christians. Most of the early Fathers railed against it. "What has Athens," Tertullian asked, "to do with Jerusalem?"[46] Yet the fact remains that each apologetic writer provided elaborate accounts of the ancient myths, disparaging the gods and heroes for licentiousness, violence, impiety, intemperance, and the like, and then dismissing them. Only Orpheus was treated more favorably and used—because of his monotheistic *Testament*—as an instrument of controversy.

Eventually the time came when Orpheus was no longer useful in this capacity; his decline as an apologetic figure began with the Edict of Milan in A.D. 312. When Constantine made Christianity the state religion, Christians saw their changed position in the Empire as the result of God's direct intervention in human affairs. The growing self-assurance of the Church during the fourth and fifth centuries was, of course, reflected in its apologetic literature. Whereas early apologies had often taken the form of "embassies" to a ruler, explaining Christianity, protesting

that its followers represented no danger to civil govern-
ment, and requesting toleration by the local powers, they
now became more frankly aggressive, proclaiming the
evident truth of their religion and counseling the immediate
conversion of all pagans. At this time both Theodoret and
Augustine, writing from the secure standpoint of men
who know that their religion is for all practical purposes
the established one in the Empire, ask a new question
about Orpheus. They wonder why, if he knew there was
only one God and if he believed in this God to the extent
revealed by his *Testament*, he did not commit himself to
monotheism publically and at once.

Theodoret (b. A.D. 396) exhorts his readers to turn away
from pagan writers and accept the Christian scripture as
the best revelation of God: "Why then, do we draw water
from this troubled and muddy trickle [of Greek myth] in
place of the limpid fountain where the Platonic theology
has sprung and in which he [Plato] mixed slime and mud?
Do you not know that Moses the law-giver of the Jews is far
older than all your poets, historians and philosophers?"[47]
Supporting his argument with the conjectures of Jewish
historians like Artapanus and others whom he presumes to
have authoritative knowledge, Theodoret points out that
Moses lived thousands of years before the Trojan War,
while "Homer and Hesiod lived long after this war.
Orpheus, the first of the poets, lived only a generation
before it, since with Jason and his company he took part in
the voyage of the *Argo*." It was probably after that trip
that Orpheus journeyed to Egypt and learned the doctrines
Moses had left behind him—"Odrysian Orpheus when
he arrived in Egypt learned thus about the being of God"—
which he wrote in his *Testament*. Theodoret may have
been familiar with the unedited version of the *Testament*
which so disturbed Aristobulus, for he concludes that
Orpheus was a coward and a deceiver for refusing to reject
completely his old thought. "Though Orpheus had learned

the true theology from the Egyptians, who in turn had gotten some idea of this from the Jews, he mixes in his theology some elements of error and transmits the infamous orgies of Dionysus . . . After having, so to speak, coated with honey the rim of the cup, he brought the baneful drink to those deceived."[48]

Saint Augustine is even more severe with Orpheus for knowing the truth without acting upon it. He cautions his readers not to revere one who spoke the truth through no effort of his own and who made no attempt to live in accordance with it. "If any truth about God or the Son of God is taught or predicted in the Sibyl . . . or in Orpheus . . . it may be useful for the refutation of Pagan error, but cannot lead us to believe in these writers. For while they spoke, because they could not help it, of the God whom we worship, they either taught their fellow-countrymen to worship idols or demons, or allowed them to do so without daring to protest against it."[49] Augustine, with his usual emphasis on the will, finds the heathen writers, with the possible exception of Plato, unworthy of Christian consideration in that they were only passive instruments for the revelation of truth and did not themselves contribute to it. Augustine could dispense with Orpheus as a prophet of monotheism because there was no longer any need for Christianity to vie with the pagan religions for more venerable origins. The position of respectability which Christianity had won in the Empire made obsolete the sort of "proof" supplied by the *Testament of Orpheus*, and fifth-century apologetic began to look forward to the establishment of the City of God on earth, rather than back to its roots in pagan history.

Yet while Orpheus as a monotheist was losing his appeal for Christian authors, another aspect of his legend continued to be a rich fund of imagery for the funerary art of antiquity. As early as the second century painters, carvers, and mosaicists had found in Orpheus a valuable image for

Christ the Good Shepherd and psychopomp who bears the Christian soul to the stars. Their particular portrait of Orpheus enjoyed a long and vigorous life in the visual arts. It was to persist into the early Middle Ages when typological treatments of pagan myth generally began to capture the imaginations of Christian writers, and when the instructive similarities between Orpheus and Christ, transmitted by funerary art and adumbrated in literature by Clement of Alexandria, were to be developed into other moral and didactic views of his legend.

III
Orpheus-Christus
in the Art
of Late Antiquity

Two of the most important reasons for the victory of the Christian religion over its other oriental competitors were its doctrines of the soul's immortality and the body's resurrection at the Last Judgment. Though neither of these ideas was exclusively the property of the Christian sect, they were stated in the books of the New Testament with a particular clarity and power—ranging from the simple "if a man keep my saying, he shall never see death" (John 8:51) to the complex stories of the Good Shepherd and Lazarus. Hope of consciousness and purpose beyond the grave was offered by Jesus and his disciples to a great variety of men dissatisfied with the grim prospects for the soul presented by most forms of Judaism, the civic cult of the Empire, and to some degree by the mystery religions.[1] By the second century Christ had come to be clearly established among pagans and Christians alike as a psychopomp—a leader of souls to an immortal home. This aspect of Christ's character is of particular interest to us because of the forms it took in early Christian art—most

notably the funerary art of the catacomb fresco, sarcophagus carving, and mosaic pavement. The early Christian
artisan, wishing to express his faith in a personal savior he
had never seen, was faced with a serious problem. How did
one, as a new convert from paganism convinced that deity
could never reside in dead stones, draw a picture or make a
sculpture of Jesus the son of God? How could his gift to
men best be depicted? One could not, on the one hand,
identify Christ too closely with the pagan divinities, since
his advent had cast them down—according to Prudentius
"Apollo writhes when the name of Christ smites him."[2]
And on the other hand, the artist found no Hebrew artistic
tradition from which to borrow, owing to the Jewish
hostility toward figurative representation.[3] Thus he was
compelled to use purified pagan types. In search of an
iconography for Christ the psychopomp, early Christian
artisans turned to the pictorial vocabulary of paganism.
There they found one figure who seemed not too unlike
their new savior in attributes and who, moreover, had to
some degree been sanctified as a spokesman for monotheism
in literature. This person was Orpheus.

There were, to be sure, other gods and heroes who had
led souls up from the underworld—Heracles and Hermes
come immediately to mind as pagan figures adapted by the
early Christian artisans[4]—but Orpheus, because of his
peaceful nature, his power of composing discord through
music and eloquence, and his tragic death at the hands of
his followers, was perhaps the most appropriate and
certainly the most long-lived of the pagan figures for Christ
to be used in funerary art. Undoubtedly his association
with Jesus helped to keep Orpheus alive during the early
centuries of the Church.

At first Orpheus was merely borrowed by the Christians,
to represent Christ the Good Shepherd. He was depicted
much as he had been in the mosaics of the Roman Empire,
surrounded by animals.[5] Occasionally, it is true, some

attempt was made to introduce Christian elements into these compositions, as for example several sheep, not common in pagan Orpheus mosaics, who might crowd the other animals away from the central figure. On the whole, though, as we shall see, during the second and third centuries Orpheus simply stood for a Good Shepherd that the artisans could not or would not depict.

In the late third or early fourth century, Orpheus began to take on attributes specifically associated with Christ, and a new figure—a figure we may call for convenience Orpheus-Christus—began to take shape. What he looked like is easily established from surviving works of art of the third through the sixth centuries. How he developed, however, and what he represented to the men of late antiquity can only be pieced together after some study not only of the works themselves but also of the cultural climate in which they were created. The ideas behind a visual image—and such is the case with Orpheus-Christus —are often to be found more fully expressed outside the world of the visual arts, in literature, philosophy, history, in sources, that is, which can tell us something about the people and the circumstances that produced the art.

Orpheus-Christus is the product of at least three strains of late antique thought, though these are far from mutually exclusive. Christianity, of course, is the most directly responsible for the perpetuation of Orpheus in artwork at all; Neoplatonism gives to his lyre and his power over animals a new significance; and the syncretistic world of magic and theurgy contributes to his importance as a guide of the soul after death. These strains of thought reveal themselves in art not so much in the figure of the man, Orpheus-Christus, as in the attendant details of compositions depicting him, which represent, in many cases, the attributes of the central figure or at least associate him with theurgy, Neoplatonism, or Christianity. Thus the animals around Orpheus-Christus become less miscellaneous and

40

certain ones begin to recur—the sheep, already mentioned, the eagle, the peacock, the dove. Seven stars appear over Orpheus' head and as his position among these symbols becomes less that of a natural depiction and more that of an emblem, the lyre, too, held out to the side as if it were on display, takes on a new stature as a symbol of his power.

The Christian origins of Orpheus-Christus can be traced most directly to the wall paintings of the catacombs which show the Good Shepherd in Phrygian dress, holding a lyre and surrounded by animals. These frescoes represent only a small proportion—six out of the ninety or so extant paintings[6]—of the Good Shepherd in the catacombs, all the result of attempts to make concrete the following passages from the New Testament:

> I am the good shepherd: the good shepherd giveth his life for the sheep . . . I am the good shepherd, and know my sheep, and am known of mine . . . I lay down my life for the sheep. (John 10:11–15)

> My sheep hear my voice, and I know them, and they follow me: And I give unto them eternal life; and they shall never perish. (John 10:27–28)

> If a man have an hundred sheep, and one of them be gone astray, doth he not leave the ninety and nine, and goeth into the mountains, and seeketh that which is gone astray?
> And if so be that he find it, verily I say unto you, he rejoiceth more of that sheep, than of the ninety and nine which went not astray. (Matthew 18:12–13)

> And when he hath found it, he layeth it on his shoulders, rejoicing.
> And when he cometh home, he calleth together his friends and neighbours, saying unto them, Rejoice with me; for I have found my sheep which was lost. (Luke 15:5–6)

1. Orpheus fresco, Cemetery of Domitilla. Rome, c. second century.

These passages, especially the ones from John, are primary sources for the idea of Christ as a psychopomp. Their appropriateness for funerary art is borne out by the strikingly large number of Good Shepherd frescoes in the catacombs. Most of the illustrations follow Luke and depict a shepherd bearing a sheep on his shoulders and often carrying a milkpot or staff. Clearly it was easier for the painters to represent the concrete version of the parable, with its emphasis on the visual image of a sheep carried on a man's shoulders. The artisans had, moreover, good models close to hand, for there must have been available many Hellenistic and Greco-Roman copies of the ancient mosco-phorus or Hermes-kriophorus figures[7]—statues of animal-bearing deities—as well as representations of Mithras the bull thief carrying the cosmic animal on his back.[8] The idea of the Good Shepherd as, so to speak, a physical psycho-pomp is fully developed in an early prayer for the dead from the Gelasian Sacramentary. Redeemed from death, absolved of sin, reconciled with the Father, the dead man goes to eternal life "borne on the shoulders of the Good Shepherd."[9]

Somewhat rarer are the frescoes which follow John and Matthew. In these a shepherd stands among his sheep with staff or milkpot, or sits among them on a slight hillock. The six pictures of the Good Shepherd as Orpheus all show the figure seated. Of these, the simplest sort—for instance the one in the catacomb of Domitilla (Fig. 1)—merely presents a seated pagan Orpheus surrounded by a cluster of animals. Here the Good Shepherd of John and Matthew has borrowed the clothes and the lyre of Orpheus, as well as his seated pose; his sheep have been replaced by Orpheus' miscellaneous animals, though a peacock and a dove, about which we shall have more to say later, are placed closest to him. It is hard to determine whether at this time the unaltered pagan Orpheus added a symbolism of his own to the composition.

2. Good Shepherd in an animal paradise. Mosaic from the Villa of Jenah, Beirut, c. 475–500.

Possibly the depiction of the simple Orpheus–Good Shepherd with wild animals on the wall of a tomb was also intended as a kind of Christian version of the animal paradise scenes popular in the mosaics of late antiquity.[10] These scenes show a group of animals, sometimes at peace, sometimes in combat, in a beautiful park presided over by a hunter or later a shepherd. Every person who has marched his parasang a day through Xenophon's *Anabasis* will remember the description of Cyrus' *paradeisos*, "and there was a great park, full of wild animals, in which he used to hunt on horseback whenever he wished to exercise himself and his horses. And through the middle of this park flowed the river Maeander."[11] Christianity replaced Cyrus the hunter with a shepherd figure who demonstrated the power of the Logos over wild nature, and the transition from the older to the newer model resulted in some curious compositions. One interesting blend of old and new ideas is to be found in a mosaic pavement from the Villa of Jenah, Beirut, probably of the fifth century (Fig. 2), which shows the Good Shepherd's calming effect on the animals almost as though he had been substituted for Orpheus among them. Here the shepherd's charges are both wild and domestic.

The destination of the soul's journey after death was apparently a celestial paradise rather like the animal paradise depicted in late antique art. In the Liturgy of St. Basil of Alexandria, which echoes the Twenty-third Psalm, Christ is asked to lead Christian souls, like sheep, to a "grassy place by quiet waters, in a luxurious park from whence pain, sadness, and groaning have fled."[12]

While the painting in the cemetery of Domitilla seems to have been based pretty much on late antique mosaics of Orpheus among the animals, another fresco, this one from the cemetery of Peter and Marcellinus (Fig. 3) shows a much more thoroughgoing effort to adapt Orpheus to the motif of the Good Shepherd. Unfortunately the painting is damaged to the point where the central figure is barely recognizable. Orpheus is depicted on the apse of a crypt, seated and surrounded by six sheep. Despite his lyre and his Phrygian clothes, he is clearly intended to represent Christ. The literal treatment accorded to the sheep and shepherd idea here is quite in harmony with the face of the crypt on which are paintings of four New and Old Testament scenes.

Yet another fresco, this time from the cemetery of

3. Orpheus fresco, Cemetery of Peter and Marcellinus. Rome, c. third century.

Callixtus (Fig. 4), shows Orpheus playing his lyre to two lambs and two doves. Around him are peacocks and sea monsters. The sheep still tie the composition to the New Testament, but the peacocks, as images of immortality in both Greco-Roman and Christian funerary art, have a purely symbolic function.[13] The sea monsters probably suggest the legend of Jonah. The focus of this fresco is thus more clearly on the ideas of immortality and of triumph over death, though symbolic elements have not completely overshadowed its narrative concerns.

Of all the Orpheus frescoes in the Roman catacombs, the one most important for the development of Orpheus-Christus is the painting from the Cemetery of the Two Laurels (Fig. 5). This painting, discovered in 1957,[14] is in a much better state of preservation than the five Orpheus frescoes brought to light in nineteenth-century excavations and now almost or completely destroyed by damp and by smoke from visitors' candles. It is from an arcosolium and portrays Orpheus as a beautiful youth, fully and richly

4. Orpheus fresco, Cemetery of Callixtus. Rome, c. third century.

5. Orpheus fresco, Cemetery of the Two Laurels. Rome, c. fourth century.

dressed and wearing a Phrygian bonnet. He sits in the frontal or Imperial pose characteristic of the art of the fourth and later centuries,[15] holding the plectrum in his right hand and the lyre in his left, and does not seem to be playing his instrument so much as displaying it to the observer. A dove and an eagle perch on each side of Orpheus in trees—perhaps laurels—whose ever green boughs promise eternity to the person or persons buried in the crypt.

This fresco is of particular interest because it depicts Orpheus in the midst of a primarily symbolic rather than narrative composition. His customary troupe of animals has been reduced in kind and number to two birds. Birds, of course, had appeared in the more commonplace Orpheus scenes, but here their number, placement, and species help to develop the static symbolism of the central figure. There

48

is no sense that we are looking at a narrative in which the characters act out their story. Most important, almost nothing is left of the portrait of Orpheus as Good Shepherd, or of any specific passages from the New Testament. Rather the central figure and his two birds serve as an emblem for the Christian soul in this life and the next, giving us what is in effect our first portrait of Orpheus-Christus.

The dove and the eagle who flank this figure have a long history in pagan and Christian eschatology. The dove, more familiar in Christian imagery than the eagle, needs only brief treatment here.[16] When it appears in catacomb paintings or in other forms of early Christian art, it seems to have signified the peace of those in the Church and a life of contemplation, simplicity, and innocence,[17] if we can judge from the treatment of this bird by the early Fathers. St. Ambrose, for example, offers a typological view of the dove, bringing together in one interpretation the dove in Matthew 3:16 and the dove who bears the olive branch to Noah in Genesis 8:11. "The dove," Ambrose explains, "is the form in which the Holy Ghost descended . . . who inspires in you peace of soul and tranquility of mind." Elsewhere he says that the dove is the Holy Spirit who bears peace in the form of the olive branch to the Church, the ark of Noah, as it floats on the flood of tribulations in this world.[18] For Maximus of Turin, the dove symbolizes peace and, more specifically, those baptized into the Church of Christ.[19]

In the early Saints' lives, on the other hand, the dove commonly signifies divine election in this life. The motif comes, of course, from the story of the Holy Ghost's appearance to Christ in Matthew 3:16, and it seems mainly to have been used for rather august persons. St. Fabian was elected Pope when a crowd saw a dove descend from heaven and perch on his head,[20] and Paul the Deacon, in his life of St. Gregory the Great, said that a white dove sat on the Saint's head to inspire him when he wrote his commentary on Ezekiel.[21] In these cases, the bird enforces an identification between the Christian in this life and Christ himself.

While the dove in the picture from the Cemetery of the Two Laurels is at rest, the eagle, with wings outstretched, seems meant to represent movement. This bird was a psychopomp in pagan, Jewish, and Christian thought, especially in the eastern part of the Roman Empire.[22] In the ancient East, the eagle symbolized the astral realm and came to be associated by the Jews with Jehovah's home in the heavens: "they that wait upon the Lord shall renew their strength; they shall mount up with wings as eagles" (Isaiah 40:31). In midrashic lore and Jewish pseudepigrapha there are accounts of the eagle as a voyager to extraterrestrial realms. Such an eagle carried Solomon to

6. Apotheosis of the emperor, Arch of Titus. Rome, first century after Christ.

the realm of spirits, where he conquered them,[23] and in the *Assumption of Moses* an eagle bears Israel to the stars.[24]

The eagle on sarcophagi and in other forms of funerary art was often a psychopomp for individual souls. Franz Cumont in his *Etudes syriénnes* publishes a Roman stele depicting a young man in a toga, seated on an eagle which is rising into the sky. A winged torch-bearing child lights the way for the pair (pl. 39). Eagles like this one bore only the souls of the wealthy, among whom the young man's aristocratic costume and mien suggest he has a place. Artemidorus (c. A.D. 175) explains that to be borne by an eagle "was a prophecy of death to kings, magnates and rich men" because it was an "ancient custom to make painted and carved representations of those who had died being carried by eagles; through such works they were honored."[25] Herodian (c. A.D. 225) tells how at the burning of the emperor's body "from a certain parapet an eagle is released into the air with the fire and smoke, who bears the soul of the emperor from earth to heaven."[26] This process is recorded very literally in a relief from the Arch of Titus (Fig. 6).

It is not surprising, then, that in early Christian art the eagle should have come to symbolize Christ the psychopomp who bore the souls of all good men, rich and poor alike, to the stars. This more democratic eagle is to be found frequently in the rough and inelegant art of Christian Egypt. A representative Coptic tombstone in the British Museum (Fig. 7) depicts an eagle holding a cross in its mouth; Christ's power and the eagle's wings will bring the soul to heaven.[27] A fresco from a funeral chapel in the monastery of St. Apollo at Bawît depicts an eagle with a cross in its mouth and another around its neck, firmly connecting the power of Christ's triumph over death with his power to carry the souls of men to heaven.[28] So too, the eagle can represent Christ who supposedly brought John up to heaven for his visions—"Come up hither, and I will

51

7. Coptic stele, seventh century.

shew thee things which must be hereafter" (Rev. 4:1)—
and this is why the eagle is a symbol for John.[29] This view
of the eagle might well be summed up in a gloss by the
unknown author of a sermon associated with Gregory of
Elvira: "by the eagle in this passage," declares the preacher
in a comment on Proverbs 30:19, "we should understand
Christ our Lord, who after a resurrection worthy of rever-
ence and which taught that mankind can return to life
after death, flew back to the Father, just like the eagle."[30]

Apparently, the painter of the fresco in the Cemetery of
the Two Laurels has employed the eagle and the dove to

symbolize two different aspects of Orpheus-Christus. The quietly poised dove may represent Christ's assumption of humanity and his temporal role as a bringer of peace to those in the Church. On the other hand, the impatient eagle, brought together in peace with the dove by Christ's New Song of Love, seems eager to leave this world, suggesting Christ's power to bear aloft the souls of those Christians buried in the crypt.

Though the exact symbolism of the catacomb frescoes we have discussed is not easy to determine, these pictures reveal, if not a clear-cut chronological development in the conflation of Orpheus and Christ, at least a series of increasingly imaginative approaches by which different Christian artisans came to terms with Greco-Roman Orpheus. Some of their adaptations were timid and comparatively unimaginative; they were probably the earliest. Though it is difficult to say with any certainty when the Orpheus frescoes were painted, the earliest is most likely from about the middle of the second century and the latest from well into the fourth. The Cemetery of the Two Laurels fresco, from its frontal pose and Imperial style, can be placed with some certainty in the age of Constantine, about two centuries later than the Domitilla fresco, generally dated about A.D. 150. The Two Laurels picture is a telling example of movement away from naturalistic treatments based on Greco-Roman models to an increasingly rigid, frontal, and above all symbolic style, which prepared the path for future artistic conflations of Orpheus with Christ.

While the artists of the catacombs were painting the earliest Good Shepherds, Clement of Alexandria compared Orpheus with Christ at some length in the opening to his *Exhortation to the Greeks*:

A Thracian, a cunning master of his art (he also is the subject of a Hellenic legend), tamed the wild beasts by

the mere might of song; and transplanted trees—oaks—
by music . . .

How, let me ask, have you believed vain fables, and
supposed animals to be charmed by music; while
Truth's shining face alone, as would seem, appears to
you disguised, and is looked on with incredulous eyes?
And so Cithaeron, and Helicon, and the mountains of
the Odrysi, and the initiatory rites of the Thracians,
mysteries of deceit, are hallowed and celebrated in
hymns. For me, I am pained at such calamities . . .

But the dramas and the raving poets, now quite
intoxicated, let us crown with ivy; and distracted
outright as they are, in Bacchic fashion, with the satyrs,
and the frenzied rabble, and the rest of the demon crew,
let us confine to Cithaeron and Helicon, now antiquated.

But let us bring from above out of heaven, Truth,
with Wisdom in all its brightness, and the sacred
prophetic choir, down to the holy mount of God . . . And
raising their eyes, and looking above, let them abandon
Helicon and Cithaeron, and take up their abode in
Sion . . . What my Eunomos sings is not the measure of
Terpander, nor that of Capito, nor the Phrygian, nor
Lydian, nor Dorian, but the immortal measure of the
new harmony which bears God's name—the new, the
Levitical song . . .

To me, therefore, that Thracian Orpheus, that
Theban, and that Methymnaean,—men, and yet unworthy of the name,—seem to have been deceivers,
who, under the pretence of poetry corrupting human
life, possessed by a spirit of artful sorcery for purposes
of destruction, celebrating crimes in their orgies, and
making human woes the materials of religious worship,
were the first to entice men to idols . . . But not such is
my song, which has come to loose, and that speedily,
the bitter bondage of tyrannizing demons; and leading
us back to the mild and loving yoke of piety, recalls to

heaven those that had been cast prostrate to the earth. It alone has tamed men, the most intractable of animals; the frivolous among them answering to the fowls of the air, deceivers to reptiles, the irascible to lions, the voluptuous to swine, the rapacious to wolves. The silly are stocks and stones, and still more senseless than stones is a man who is steeped in ignorance . . .

Behold the might of the new song! It has made men out of stones, men out of beasts. Those, moreover, that were as dead, not being partakers of the true life, have come to life again, simply by becoming listeners to this song.[31]

Orpheus was associated with three mountains— "Cithaeron, Helicon and the mountains of the Odrysi." He was the son of Calliope, a Muse on Mount Helicon; he sang the hymns and codified the theology of the god Dionysus on Cithaeron; and he tamed savage beasts and men in the mountains of Thracian Odrysia. Clement marvels that the Greeks should have hallowed and celebrated these mountains and all that they stand for, while they look at "Truth's shining face . . . with incredulous eyes." His personified Truth has scriptural overtones which connect it with another mountain and another prophet. One is reminded here of the account in the Book of Exodus of Moses' receiving the Law from God on Mount Sinai. After he had come down from the mountain he knew "not that the skin of his face shone while he talked with him" (34:29), and "when . . . the children of Israel saw Moses, behold, the skin of his face shone; and they were afraid to come nigh him" (34:30). Clement entreats the Greeks to abandon their sacred mountains and "raving poets," now antiquated, for the holy mountain of God where they shall hear the new song of Love.

We recall that the Orpheus known to the Alexandrians was capable of great eloquence and played beautiful songs on his lyre. But for Clement, this power of speech and music was misused, for it persuaded men to worship idols and to tie themselves to temporal things. The song of Orpheus on Cithaeron, then, contrasts sharply with the New Song, which brings peace to men, and frees them from the bonds of the flesh. If Clement seems unduly harsh here in his condemnation of Orpheus, we must remember that by the particular comparison he wishes to develop, Orpheus is like Christ only in that he too has been the object of some wonder because of his "song." It is to Clement's purpose—wishing as he did to emphasize to the gentiles the rational, peaceful, and redemptive aspects of Christianity—to offer them a portrait of a frenzied Orpheus surrounded by the wild Bacchantes, singing a song which, like that of the Sirens, maliciously lures men to destruction.

In his analysis of the Orpheus myth, Clement shows the Greeks that the deeds of Orpheus, a mere man, are only fables magnified by credulous people whereas the deeds of Jesus in their historical truth had made actual what was before only imagined.[32] And yet, Clement's elaborate comparison of Orpheus and Christ, designed to show the complete opposition between them, might for a careless reader, or one not too familiar with Christian doctrine or Clement's highly metaphoric style, serve to identify the two rather than to separate them. To a newly converted Christian artisan, the effects of time and the quirks of memory might leave only a recollection that an authoritative Christian writer had spoken of Orpheus and Christ in the same breath.

A writer much influenced by Clement's association of Orpheus and Christ was the apologist and Church historian Eusebius, whose interest in a monotheistic Orpheus we have already discussed. Whereas in the *Praeparatio Evangelica* Eusebius had compiled his tale of Orpheus from the words of others, in his *Praise of Constantine* he speaks in his own voice:

The Grecian myth tells us that Orpheus had power to charm ferocious beasts, and tame their savage spirit, by striking the chords of his instrument with a master-hand: and this story is celebrated by the Greeks, and generally believed, that an unconscious instrument could subdue the untamed brute, and draw the trees from their places, in obedience to its melodious power. But he who is the author of perfect harmony, the all-wise Word of God, desiring to apply every remedy to the manifold diseases of the souls of men, employed that human nature which is the workmanship of his own wisdom, as an instrument by the melodious strains of which he soothed, not indeed the brute creation, but savages endued with reason; healing each furious temper, each fierce and angry passion of the soul, both in civilized and barbarous nations by the remedial power of his Divine doctrine.[33]

Eusebius' handling of the legend seems a direct echo of Clement, though his disapproval is rather more implicit than explicit. He does not believe in the historicity of Orpheus' deeds, but neither does he excoriate him. His comparison is aimed only at emphasizing the powers of the Word of God, "he who is the author of perfect harmony."

The accounts offered by Clement and Eusebius are the main sources for the idea in the writings of the early Fathers that the pagan legend of Orpheus in some way prefigures the story of Christ's ministry, and that just as the coming of Christ outdates the Old Law, so Christ the new Orpheus replaces the old Orpheus of Helicon and Cithaeron. In the fourth and fifth centuries this idea became more widespread, and even well into the Middle Ages[34] writers compared the actions of Orpheus and Christ in the underworld, showing that what Orpheus had begun, Christ had finished, fulfilling prophecies inherent in pagan myth. One of the Nisibene hymns of St. Ephraim of Syria

(b. A.D. 306), for example, apparently based on the apocryphal *Gospel of Nicodemus,* is a dialogue between Death and Satan concerning the power of Christ and the harrowing of Hell. Death speaks of himself as a great conqueror: "as for wise that are able to charm wild beasts, their charms enter not into my ears," says Death, apparently alluding to the fact that Orpheus was unable to liberate his wife from Hades. "Death ended his speech of derision: and the voice of our Lord sounded into Hell, and He cried aloud and burst the graves one by one. Tremblings took hold on Death . . . the dead came forth."[35] This text is of considerable interest because it connects the adventures of Orpheus among the beasts not only with the underworld but also with Christ's triumph over death. An artisan or patron who did not have too accurate a knowledge of the myth of Orpheus and all its ramifications might easily forget or overlook the invidious comparison and simply identify Orpheus among the animals with Christ the psychopomp.

8. Orpheus on a magic amulet. Hematite, c. third-fourth century.

Orpheus-Christus emerges with somewhat clearer outlines on a hematite gem (Fig. 8) formerly in the Pergamum
collection of the Berlin Museum, but now lost or destroyed
in the Second World War.[36] The stone appears to have been
an amulet by possession of which the owner hoped to
attain for his soul an immortal existence among the stars.
It shows a crucified figure, above whose head are seven
stars and the crescent of the moon, and is inscribed, in the
fashion of late antique magical amulets, in such a way as
to be read directly rather than from an impression : OPΦEOC
BAKKIKOC.

This gem reminds us that Christ and Orpheus were
attractive beings to a variety of men in late antiquity whose
interests were not religious but theurgic. Such men hoped
by the use of charms, incantations, and secret lore to modify
the destinies assigned to them. In the Hellenistic and
Roman periods, astrology and the concept of astral fate
were taken very seriously by all levels of society and re-
garded as next to inescapable forces governing human life.
"Fate has decreed," wrote the Roman author Vettius
Valens in the second century, "as a law for each person the
unalterable consequences of his horoscope, controlled by
many causes of good and evil ; and their results are watched
over by two self-begotten deities who are her ministers,
Hope and Chance ; these rule over life."[37] Whereas in the
Hellenic age man had enjoyed, in the words of A. D. Nock,
"dealings with Zeus and Athena and Artemis, accessible
and placable Greeks of a larger build,"[38] now he faced a
more implacable and complicated system of deities, many
of whom might be the same god under different regional
names and some of whom might be totally unknown to
men.

The concept, however, of astrology as a universal law
left room for optimism in its very intricacy. With so many
forces operating at once to affect one's horoscope, certainly
some forces could be prevailed upon to affect it for the

better. Upon this optimism were founded elaborate Hellenistic systems of theurgy. The theurgist or person who can influence the gods was described by Iamblichus as one who "invokes the powers of the universe as superior, since he who invokes them is a man; again, he commands them, since by secret formulas he has, so to speak, assumed the sacred form of the gods."[39] Secret formulas consisting of names, words, or pictures, sometimes of the gods themselves, were written or drawn on papyri or inscribed on stone or metal amulets to be worn on the body. A large number of these objects, which are "religious" only in a very limited sense,[40] survive from the second through the fifth centuries, attesting to a widespread belief in their efficacy. Frequently they combined the most arcane incantations with the use of mundane objects, as for example this love charm from a Greek magical papyrus. The unrequited lover is instructed to prepare some olive oil to be "sent against" the girl he favors, by means of the following spell. It will then become the "sweat of Agathos Daimon." "I adjure thee [the olive oil] by the great god on the roof of heaven Arbaiēth Mouth Nouth Phthōthō Phrēthōouth Breisonthoth; hear me, O mightiest god, in this very day, in this (?) night, that thou mayest inflame her heart and let her love me, for I am invested with the power of the great god, the name which none save me alone, who am master, may name [lacuna] Aeethi eōēē Phēouab Phthaache Anou Esienes [lacuna] Ethoul Phimoiou, hear me because of Necessity, for I have named thee on account of N. child of N. that she may love me."[41] The papyrus counsels the lover, moreover, when preparing the olive oil, "have with yourself an iron ring on which is engraved Harpocrates sitting on a lotus and his name is Abrasax." Theurgic objects, such as the iron ring mentioned, were for the most part products of Greco-Egyptian culture and were made in Alexandria; the gems set in such rings were frequently engraved by Alexandrian Jews, who had a great reputation for magical abilities in the Roman period.[42] Such seems to be the case with the Orpheus intaglio; the interest of Alexandrian Judaism in a syncretistic Orpheus has already been demonstrated. It is entirely possible that the Orpheus gem was produced by an Alexandrian engraver and dealer in

9. Christ and the saints on a magic amulet, late Empire.

charms, perhaps on order as a particularly efficacious amulet for a customer troubled by his possible fate after death.

One of the most interesting things about both the gems and the magical papyri is their internationalism. The amulets and scrolls contain: "invocations to non-Greek deities, often accompanied by words that are sometimes corrup-

10. Christ-Horus, back of amulet shown in Figure 9.

tions of Egyptian, Hebrew, and Aramaic . . . letters. Such inscriptions are usually, but not always, accompanied by incised figures of various deities, sometimes the well-known gods of Greece in slightly Egyptianized forms, sometimes Egyptian gods more or less Hellenized in appearance, sometimes unfamiliar divine or demonic forms."[43]

Such attitudes as this lay behind the often bizarre syncretism of Greco-Egyptian magical matter. For example, a recipe for the treatment of madness is supposed to be Egyptian, but alludes to Pharaoh's plague and to the crossing of the Red Sea, and invokes a daimon to help in the treatment, adjuring him by "Jesus the god of the Jews."[44] An amulet in the British Museum represents on one face (Fig. 9) a bust of Christ, the saints, the adoration of the Magi, and other New Testament scenes common in early Christian art. The reverse (Fig. 10), however, contains Jewish inscriptions, the six-pointed magical star of Solomon, the figure of Christ-Horus, symbols of the sun and the moon, and the letters of Christ's name, the whole being surrounded by the self-devouring serpent, the Uroboros. The Christ-Horus-Harpocrates syncretism was not uncommon in these objects. A Greco-Egyptian amulet (Fig. 11) at University College, London, shows the figure of the young Harpocrates seated on a lotus, with the inscription "Iao, Iesous." These instances of Christ's connection with other religions than Christianity and of his appearance on theurgic amulets should give some idea of the syncretistic climate of thought which produced the Berlin amulet.

Those who wore magical gems thought that a portrait of a deity or its name inscribed on an amulet gave the wearer power over that deity. To name a thing was to evoke it and control it, and in the event that a god should go by more than one name—Greek, Egyptian, or Hebrew as it might be—to summon him by as many names as possible would, of course, be most effective. We are all familiar with the famous relief of Apollo-Mithras-Helios-Hermes at Com-

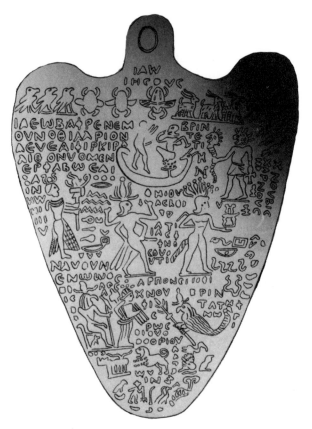

11. Greco-Egyptian magic amulet, c. third-fourth century after Christ.

magene.[45] The half-world of astrology, magic, and religion produced even stranger bedfellows among the gods—for example the Christ-Horus-Harpocrates[46] mentioned above —next to whom our crucified Orpheus-Bacchus seems almost pale by comparison.

All nations, including the Greeks, thought that foreign names were the most potent for magical purposes, and as a result of misunderstandings of these names some wholly new gods were created. Perhaps the best known of these was Sabaoth. In Hebrew, *sabaoth* means hosts or armies, and the Old Testament writers spoke of Jehovah as the lord of their hosts. As the phrase "Lord sabaoth" (I Sam. 1:3) was translated from Hebrew into the Greek of the Septuagint, a divine person *kyrios sabaoth* or Lord Sabaoth came into being from the Hebrew words. Probably as a consequence of the powerful deity Sabaoth, endings in "oth," the Hebrew feminine plural, were common in the inscriptions of magical gems and in the formulas of papyri. Apparently they were thought to be terminations of power.[47]

A phylactery of silver foil, found in Beirut and now in the Louvre, voices the appeals of one Alexandra, not only to Sabaoth, to protect her from demons, but also to the archons of the seven heavens, or presiding planetary deities, and to the God of Abraham, concluding, "the One God and his Christ, help Alexandra."[48] To this type of mind there would be nothing odd about conflating Christ, Orpheus, and Bacchus for magical purposes. Each combined a mortal and immortal nature, each had died a similar death, each had returned from the grave, and each possessed the ability to help men after death.

The Berlin gem contributes much to our portrait of Orpheus-Christus by means of the seven stars and crescent above the head of the crucified figure, for these symbols indicate the kind of power attributed to him. They represent the astral realm to which the owner of the gem hoped to travel after death, a realm through which the syncretistic deity pictured beneath was supposed to be able to lead him. The iconography of the astral symbols probably had its origins in ancient Syrian and North African religious thought and even earlier in Egyptian sun worship. Primitive examples of the motif in both pagan and Christian funerary art consist of simple ornamentation of tombs or stelae with solar discs and stars.[49] From these developed more narrative treatments of the dead person's relation to the heavens.

The sun often served as a synecdoche for the heavens in the funerary and religious art of the Hellenistic and Roman

12. Funerary relief from Albano, second century.

periods.[50] A Roman stele from Dura-Europos shows the dead man outstretched with the sun figured prominently above him.[51] On a stone found in Rome we learn that the occupant of the tomb was a *heliopais*, a child of the sun. Yet that this inscription was Christian in origin can be established by the presence on the stone of a lamb flanked by two fish.[52] Sometimes the sun was associated with immortality by a quirk of early Christian etymology—the prophet Elijah, *Elias*, who did not die, was linked with the sun, *helios*, as in the Cemetery of Peter and Marcellinus, where a nimbed sun, representing the prophet, guides a chariot to the heavens.[53]

The doctrine of the soul's home in the heavens is at least as old as Pythagoras, whom his biographer Iamblichus represents as having held that the sun and the moon were actually the Isles of the Blessed.[54] For Pliny, the soul, being a part of the heavens, wished to return there.[55] Plutarch tells us how the soul of Timarchus escaped the body and ascended through the spheres to the realm of fire. There he learned that some souls who have escaped the cycle of birth, decay, and death go to the moon, where the immutable realm begins. Other souls, however, are sent down to earth for reincarnation.[56] In a funerary relief found at Albano, carved about the end of the second century after Christ (Fig. 12), the bust of a child rests in the crescent of the moon and is surrounded by seven stars. Perhaps the parents who had this relief made were expressing the hope that their child's soul had escaped the round of generation and gone to the moon. The seven stars would then represent the seven planetary spheres through which he would have to ascend before reaching the immutable realm.

Christianity had borrowed from Hellenistic thought the idea of an afterlife among the stars, claiming for the devout Christian an exemption from Hades and the reward of translation to the heavens. Many Christian inscriptions dating from about the time the Berlin gem was carved explicitly reject the older, chthonic view of the afterlife and look forward to an ascent toward celestial light. "If excellence of mind," reads one of these epitaphs, "and a more tranquil enjoyment of the light come to one who dies in Christ, he does not suffer Tartarus and the Cimmerian lake. Through his merits he survives after death and defies the law of earth and tomb. After thus leaving the light of day, he holds a place among the stars and cannot die."[57] Similar hopes are implicit in the religious art of the period. A lamp in the Berlin Museum (Fig. 13) shows Christ the Good Shepherd bearing a sheep—symbolizing the soul of the dead man—on his shoulders. Above Christ's head are seven stars

13. Good Shepherd on a lamp, c. third-fourth century.

which represent the soul's new home. Patristic references to astral translation reflect these interests. According to St. Augustine, the souls of evil men must continue the round of reincarnation, but the souls of good men "go to the highest part of the heavens, to rest there in stars and be visible in their lights."[58] Gregory considers this idea for its metaphoric possibilities. "What is meant," he asks, "by the stars, if not the souls of those who have lived a singularly good life? Who in the company of depraved men stood out by their great virtue, just as stars shine in the gloom of night."[59]

The ascent of the soul was of particular interest to writers on white magic. Hermes Trismegistus presents this explanation of the ascent. At death the soul "mounts upward through the structure of the heavens. And to the first zone of heaven he gives up the force which works increase and that which works decrease; to the second zone, the machinations of evil cunning . . . and thereupon, having been stripped of all that was wrought upon him by the structure of the heavens, he ascends to the substance of the eighth sphere, being now possessed of his own proper power; and he sings, together with those who dwell there, hymning the Father . . . and thereafter, each in his turn, they mount upward to the Father; . . . [and] enter into God."[60]

Similar accounts could be found in eastern, and particularly Mithraic, religion as well.[61] In the mysteries of Mithras, Celsus was supposed to have said, the passage of the soul through the heavens was represented as follows: "There is a ladder with lofty gates, and on the top of it an eighth gate. The first gate consists of lead, the second of tin . . . the first gate they assign to Saturn . . . the second to Venus."[62]

In Judeo-Gnostic and magical lore, the seven stars stand for the archons or presiding deities of the planets. Elaborating on Celsus' system, Origen speaks of a diagram belonging to the Gnostic Ophites, which was a sort of map for the soul's progress after death. The soul must pass through the realm of each of the seven planetary archons; to avoid being trapped in any particular realm[63] it must offer the archon certain magical images and speak certain magical words. It says to Sabaoth, for example, whom we have met before, "O governor of the fifth realm, powerful Sabaoth . . . admit me . . . by the stamp of an image" (p. 587). A somewhat similar passage occurs in the *Gospel of Philip*. "The Lord revealed unto me what the soul must say as it goeth up into heaven, and how it must answer each of the Powers above."[64]

As we recall from the plan of the soul's ascent outlined by Hermes Trismegistus in the *Poimandres,* each of these archons—who were partly material, and so malignant, in the Gnostic and magical systems of antiquity—had power over a certain part of the soul. The chart of which Origen speaks sounds suspiciously like a magic papyrus, and the archons, Sabaoth, Iao, Ildabaoth, and so forth, are names of power found on magical amulets. The system of Origen's chart, of course, is nothing but apotropaic astrology. The archons are those planets and constellations thought to hold power over the various parts of man in apotropaic and medical astrology.

A version of Origen's chart exists on a gem from the Cabinet of Florence (Fig. 14). A. Delatte has interpreted the inscriptions around the seven stars as the names of the seven archons in a magical cosmology, and thinks that the gem may represent the soul descending into generation and arriving at the Lion[65]—that constellation representing a grade of initiation in the solar theology of the period. In Porphyry's *Cave of the Nymphs,* for example, bees are the souls of the *mystai* or initiated persons at the end of their voyage through the planetary spheres, an idea which may explain the bee in the mouth of the lion.[66]

The seven stars are not limited to pagan use, but recur

14. Magical gem, late Empire.

in many Christian contexts to indicate the all-inclusive power of God. In Revelation 1:4 John sends grace to the churches in Asia "from him which is, and which was, and which is to come; and from the seven Spirits who are before his throne." This description suggests that the seven spirits are the seven archons or angels of the planets. In the famous description of "one like unto the Son of man" we learn that he had "in his right hand seven stars . . . and his countenance was as the sun shineth in his strength." And he said to John "I am he that liveth, and was dead; and, behold, I am alive for evermore, Amen; and have the keys of hell and of death." We have already remarked on the Christian lamp of the third century which shows Christ the Good Shepherd bearing the sheep—that is the soul—to the seven stars just visible above his head.

Orpheus was, as we have seen, associated with a very similar function after death, and the seven stars pictured above him on the Berlin amulet allude directly to this function Certain "Orphic" gold plates from Southern Italy inscribed with descriptions of the topography of Hades

71

and instructions for traversing it were evidently intended as well to identify the dead man to the ruling deities.[67] Like these plates, the Orpheus gem must have been designed to propitiate malignant archons or otherwise aid the soul through the seven astral realms after death. Certainly the connection of Orpheus' name with that of Bacchus and with the crucifixion suggests that the original purpose of the gem was not to commemorate the passion of Christ, but rather to invoke the aid of as many gods as possible.

As Christianity grew stronger in the Roman Empire, as councils were held and creeds formulated and a distinctively Christian view of history evolved in which Old Testament figures replaced pagan heroes, we find a curious lag in the visual arts. The old pagan imagery continues to appear in Christian funerary monuments, often in conjunction with newer, wholly Christian motifs, but significantly not replaced by them. This phenomenon is not due simply to the conservatism of the artisans, but owes much to the vigor of the old motifs and the persistence of the ideas they represented. It also points up the fundamental difference between a verbal statement, made up of words which may be freely arranged and whose connotations shift mercurially from year to year, and a visual statement, which is less flexible and able to retain its symbolic appeal for a very long time. Owing to their concern with the image rather than with the word, artisans could remain relatively aloof from the doctrinal and Christological controversies of the period. Thus while the Councils of Ephesus and Chalcedon sought to define for all time the relation between human and divine in the person of Jesus, Christian artisans were still depicting Christ in the aspect of Orpheus. Truly it could be said that in the third, fourth, and fifth centuries, words and pictures ostensibly representing the same ideas were often straining in opposite directions.

Certainly one would expect that by the sixth century pagan Orpheus would have fallen out of favor as a guide to

15. Mosaic of Orpheus from Jerusalem, sixth century.

16. Detail of mosaic from Jerusalem, Theodosia and Georgia.

the Christian afterlife. One of the best known of Orpheus mosaics, however, belies this expectation. This mosaic (Fig. 15) was found northwest of the Damascus Gate of Jerusalem in 1901. It has been dated in the sixth century[68] and is presently in the Archaeological Museum of Istanbul. Its Orpheus among the animals—or, more properly, Orpheus-Christus—is the dominant scene of a larger pavement which includes compartmented pictures of hunters, wild animals rampant, and the two female figures labeled Theodosia and Georgia, separated by the sort of sacred pillar often erected in the groves of classical landscapes (Fig. 16).[69] Orpheus-Christus wearing Phrygian clothes sits in the frontal or Imperial pose of Byzantine art.[70] The birds and animals are of the sort commonly found in such compositions, except for the eagle who in this pavement wears a cross in a bulla around its neck. Below Orpheus, however, are two figures from hitherto separate myths, who by their size and placement seem to outrank the animals in importance. Pan stands under Orpheus' lyre at his left, clutching his syrinx and pointing to a centaur who lounges below the eagle at Orpheus' right.

The excavator of this mosaic believed—and his view has been generally accepted—that the pavement was the floor of what had originally been a tomb.[71] Two stone constructions rising from the pavement on either side of the two women seem to have been ossuaries or funeral caskets. They probably held the remains of the women pictured in the medallion. But the purpose of this room, unfortunately, is only a partial guide to the meaning of the pavement itself. Clearly, the very curious syncretism of the mosaic raises several questions. What is Orpheus-Christus doing in a Christian tomb of this late date? How are Pan and the centaur related to him? And finally what does this composition tell us about the occupants of the tomb?

Undoubtedly Orpheus-Christus appears in this funerary pavement because the artisans who made it and the people who commissioned it—perhaps Theodosia and Georgia themselves—in some way connected him with death and the afterlife. This, of course, is the primary association of Orpheus and is inherent in the myth of Orpheus and Eurydice in Hades. At the time this mosaic was made, however, Orpheus was, as we have already seen, associated with an afterlife among the stars perhaps even more than he was with the classical underworld. What might be called his secondary symbolism derived from the lyre of which he was master, as well as from parallels between the accounts of his deeds and those of Christ. The lyre connected Orpheus with a body of Neoplatonic ideas about the harmony of the universe and the return of the soul to its celestial home, while his power over wild beasts as well as over the gods of Hades caused him frequently to be compared with Christ and sometimes to be conflated with him. These two strands of thought, which are far from mutually exclusive in late antiquity, converge in the narrative of the Jerusalem mosaic, the Christian strand culminating in the only clearly Christian element in the picture, the eagle, and the Neoplatonic strand culminating in the lyre and the presence of Pan and the centaur.

Behind this combination of elements, we should bear in mind, lay a technical tradition of workshop-commissioned art, which fostered religious syncretism and made pagan imagery readily available to the artisans. We know, for example, that during the rise of the Church, the same artisans would often make pagan funerary monuments for pagans and Christian monuments for Christians. Goodenough quotes from a third-century saint's life a fine account of some of the difficulties faced by artisans in these shops. The Emperor Diocletian ordered "a large figure of Helios in the chariot, with accompanying symbols, and this the best cutters—of whom Claudius, a Christian, was chief—carved without objections, though they kept stopping to cross themselves as they worked."[72] Later, Claudius was martyred for refusing to make a statue of Asclepius. One wonders what sort of artisan was responsible for a Christian sarcophagus relief from Porto Torres, Sardinia,[73] which shows Christ in the pose of Mithras Tauroctonus but wearing the Phrygian costume of Orpheus (Fig. 17). The sheep or ram which replaces the bull of Mithras—compare Figure 18 for a typical representation of Mithras slaying the bull—may leave the figure posed a bit unsteadily, but otherwise the carver has admirably adapted his pagan material to a Christian context.

17. Sarcophagus relief of Orpheus-Christ-Mithras as the Good Shepherd. Porto Torres, Sardinia, c. fourth-fifth century.

18. Mithras tauroctonus, late Empire.

While such conflicts probably did not trouble the sixth-century artisans of the Jerusalem mosaic, a certain amount of pagan imagery must still have been part of their working repertoire, if we may judge from the contemporary art of the period. Not only classical motifs—for example, portraits of the winds or seasons—but also theurgic or magical symbols, especially the sun and planets, were still frequent in mosaic, sculpture, and fresco work of the early Byzantine era. Heracles and Roman personifications such as the Nile god appear in Christian settings; Enoch was depicted as Helios rising in his chariot; the grape vine and scallop shell had been absorbed into Christian art to become favorite decorative motifs, their pagan symbolism replaced with a more Christian one or simply forgotten. We might say that the visual image of the grape vine or shell survived its original meaning; in the cases of Heracles and Helios the death of the pagan ideas behind the picture is more questionable. Such instances of artistic fusion, where

78

pagan motifs have been used in Christian work with a clear consciousness of their source and implications, speak for the currency of ideas in the Christian community for which we do not always have written evidence in the works of contemporary apologists. The purposeful Orpheus-Christus in the Jerusalem mosaic is striking evidence for the blending at this time of Neoplatonic and Christian thought concerning death and the afterlife.

That Orpheus-Christus appears in this mosaic by virtue of his role as psychopomp should by now be evident. From the time of the earliest catacomb Good Shepherds, the Christian community's interest in Orpheus had been focused upon his ability to lead souls and on his similarity to Christ who led his flock to a better life after death. Strengthened by thaumaturgic ideas which took Orpheus to be a psychopomp in his own right, this connection alone could account for the use of Orpheus in a work of funerary art such as the Jerusalem mosaic. We need only recall the eagle's function as psychopomp—outlined earlier in connection with the Cemetery of the Two Laurels—to see the bird who perches at the right elbow of Orpheus as a confirmation of this role. The eagle wears a cross which identifies our psychopomp as a specifically Christian one. It is both an extension of the central figure and a reminder of Christ's power to raise souls to the stars. More important, in the context of the funeral chapel it seems intended as a symbol for the astral translation of the two women pictured in the compartment below it. We shall say more about this a little later.

The Neoplatonic strain in the Jerusalem Orpheus mosaic is represented in part by Orpheus' lyre, but more strikingly by Pan and the centaur, who, though they are not especially related to each other in mythology and are not at all related to the story of Orpheus, have been brought together by the religious syncretism of late antiquity.[74] Like the tradition that links Orpheus, Christ, and the eagle as psychopomps, the symbolism which connects lyre, centaur, and Pan also derives from a theory of the soul and its continuation after death.

According to some late antique authors influenced in one way or another by Platonic thought, the soul was merely on loan to the body on earth, and during its corporeal existence yearned to return to the stars where, after the death of the body, it would go to rejoin the One. The soul, attuned to the music of the spheres from which it had descended, was believed to respond instinctively to the harmonies of the lyre, for this instrument was constructed according to the pattern of the universe, its seven strings corresponding to the seven spheres. "When Hermes was a boy," according to Theon of Smyrna, "they say he invented the lyre, then first going up into the heavens and passing the planets, he marvelled aloud that from the swing of the planets through their orbits came forth a harmony similar to that of the lyre which he himself had constructed."[75] Macrobius, in his commentary on the *Somnium Scipionis*, itself an account of a man who went to the stars, wrote that: "Every soul in this world is allured by musical sounds . . . for the soul carries with it into the body a memory of the music which it knew in the sky, and is so captivated by its charm that there is no breast so cruel or savage as not to be gripped by the spell of such an appeal. This, I believe, was the origin of the [story] of Orpheus."[76] Some authors felt that the lyre was a help to the soul in its journey homeward and that a man wishing astral immortality could do no better than to associate himself with this instrument, for, as Cicero said, "learned men, by imitating this harmony on stringed instruments . . . have gained for themselves a return to this region" (heaven).[77] Others felt that the lyre was a necessity for the soul's journey. Orpheus—not un-naturally—was thought to be among these. In a gloss on *Aeneid* VI, 119, published from B.N. Lat. 7930 by J. J. Savage, there is a reference to a lost work ascribed to

Orpheus and called *Lyra,* in which "it is denied that the soul can ascend without a lyre," "negantur animae sine cithara ascendere."[78]

It should be added, moreover, that the lyre was associated with the ether and the empyrean itself. Aristides Quintilianus, a musical theorist of the fourth century, whose work was much influenced by Porphyry and Iamblichus, explained that "instruments made of tuned strings are somewhat similar to the etherial, dry, and simple part of the cosmos and to the soul itself"—τῶν ὀργάνων τοίνυν τὰ μὲν διὰ νευρῶν ἡρμοσμένα τῷ τε αἰθερίῳ καὶ ξηρῷ καὶ ἁπλῷ παρόμοια, κόσμου τε τύποι (*leg.* τόπῳ) καὶ φύσεως ψυχικῆς μέρη (*leg.* μέρει).[79] The lyre was, therefore, an enemy of the lower realms of earth and water, where humidity would cause its strings to lose their tension, just as material concerns would weight the soul and impede its journey to the One.

While such associations give an interesting symbolic resonance to Orpheus' lyre, they do not in themselves explain the presence of Pan and the centaur in the Jerusalem pavement. The lyre, however, was often contrasted with the flute, or with wind instruments in general, in an allegorical fashion. Whereas stringed instruments were thought to appeal to and have power over the rational part of the soul, wind instruments—like the martial trumpet or lascivious flute—were characterized by their power over the irascible and concupiscent passions, which held the soul to the earth when the lyre would draw it to the heavens.

Some writers believed that this was because the soul itself contained the properties of lyre and flute. According to Aristides Quintilianus, who was probably basing his view on a tradition which ran from Empedocles through Proclus,[80] the soul as it left the One on its descent into generation had a spherical shape. When it entered the mutable realms it absorbed some heavy elements and, filling up like a balloon with water, began to elongate. It stretched because its upper part yearned for its celestial home while its lower part strained toward earth, drawn by its incorporated matter. Aristides added the idea that by the time the soul reached the earth it had stretched into the shape of a man and filled with breath from the realm of air. The soul, he tells us, "takes out of the things in the lower realms a first sort of physical body for herself, welded together from certain membraneous surfaces, fibrous lines and breath" (ἐκ τῶν τῇδε προσλαμβάνει λοιπόν, ὡς εἶναι τοῦτο πρῶτον αὐτῇ σῶμά τι φυσικόν, ἔκ τινων ἐπιφανειῶν ὑμενοειδῶν τε καὶ γραμμῶν νευροειδῶν καὶ πνεύματος συγκεκροτη-μένον). [81] That is, the outer covering of the soul, a weblike membrane, was gradually formed into a mesh of coarser fibers rather like a cat's cradle, which then hardened in the fire of the empyrean during the soul's descent. This mesh of fibers contained the breath within.

Aristides explains that because the first form of the body was a combination of strings and breath—lyre and flute—man is most sympathetic to the music of these instruments. "Why should it seem strange," he asks, "if the soul, having taken a body similar in nature to the elements that put musical instruments into motion—that is, strings and breath—moves in unison with the movements of the instruments; and, when a wind instrument echoes with harmony and rhythm, she too moves in harmony because of the wind that is within her, and, when a string is struck harmoniously, vibrates through the tension of her own strings?" (Τί δὴ θαυμαστὸν εἰ τοῖς κινοῦσι τὰ ὄργανα, νευραῖς τε καὶ πνεύμασι, σῶμα ὅμοιον ἡ ψυχὴ φύσει λαβοῦσα συγκινεῖται κινουμένοις, καὶ πνεύματός τε ἐμμελῶς καὶ ἐρρύθμως ἠχοῦντος τῷ παρ' αὐτῇ πνεύματι συμπάσχει καὶ πληττομένης νευρᾶς ἐναρμονίως νευραῖς ταῖς ἰδίαις συνηχεῖ τε καὶ συντείνεται.)[82] Naturally, the music of wind instruments was to be avoided, since it appealed to the baser parts of the soul. And so teachers counseled men to seek the lyre and avoid the flute.[83] The sage Pythagoras, we learn from Aristides, "counseled his disciples, when they had heard the sound of the flute, to wash it away by purification, as if the breathing had defiled it, and to heed the good-omened notes of the lyre, which cleanses the soul of unreasonable passions" (ταῦτα καὶ Πυθαγόραν συμβουλεῦσαι τοῖς ὁμιληταῖς αὐλοῦ μὲν αἰσθομένοις ἀκοὴν ὡς πνεύματι μιανθεῖσαν ἀποκλύζεσθαι, πρὸς δὲ τὸ λύριον ἐναισίοις μέλεσι τὰς τῆς ψυχῆς ἀλόγους ὁρμὰς ἀποκαθαίρεσθαι).[84]

The myth of Apollo and the flute player Marsyas was sometimes interpreted as a victory for the rational part of the soul over the base appetites of the body, and by implication as a victory for the soul in its efforts to leave the mortal life and attain its celestial home. This moral version of the myth was depicted in at least one antique mosaic pavement.[85]

We should not be surprised, then, to find the irascible and concupiscent passions represented in the Jerusalem Orpheus mosaic by the figures of Pan and the centaur. Pan's syrinx was, we recall, a wind instrument created out of lust,[86] while he himself was part animal, always pictured with a goat's feet and horns. Pan does not play his syrinx in our mosaic, but merely holds it and seems to point to the effect of Orpheus-Christus' music on the centaur, who bemusedly lazes beside him. Both creatures seem caught by the power of Orpheus-Christus' lyre.

The centaur, of course, from his very birth was a creature of lust and violence and was commonly so described. Virgil stressed his irascible nature—"furentis / Centauros"—and put the whole tribe in hell.[87] St. Basil, following the Greek *Physiologus,* made the centaur a figure for the twofold nature of man, rational in his upper part and like a lustful horse in his lower.[88]

Our mosaic, then, portrays the power of the lyre—of stringed music and, by extension, the rational part of the soul—over wind music and the passions. This allegory seems all the more remarkable when one considers the late date at which its non-Christian elements were combined in a narrative fashion. Orpheus, his lyre, the eagle, Pan, and the centaur are not used as merely static emblems—like the Roman scallop shell—for the survival of the soul after death. Rather, they interact with one another on several levels, in such a way as to leave no question but that the designer of the mosaic was familiar with the resonances of each image: Orpheus is at once associated with the classical account of the beasts and gods tamed by music, with his partly Christianized deeds in the underworld, and with the Christian Good Shepherd in the catacombs; the lyre, with the power of stringed over wind music and Neoplatonic treatments of the soul's ascent to the stars; the eagle, almost completely Christianized by the sixth century but still retaining overtones of imperial majesty, with the psycho-pomp of Coptic funerary art; Pan, with the wild, generative powers of nature and with Neoplatonic and Christian views of wind music; the centaur, with a violent and malevolent classical race and with Neoplatonic and Christian views of man's twofold nature. Because our knowledge of the sixth century is so dependent on the writings of men unlikely to mention the continuity of Christian and pre-Christian culture except to inveigh against it, this mosaic provides valuable evidence as to the viability of antique motifs and ideas in early Byzantine Jerusalem and adds still another dimension to our portrait of Orpheus at this time.

The allegory of this pavement is an optimistic one, in both its Christian and its Neoplatonic senses, for the women whom it memorializes. The eagle who sits at Orpheus' right hand symbolizes the astral translation of the two women, while Orpheus himself reinforces the power of the eagle's cross by his own association with Christ the psychopomp. Once liberated by death, the souls of Theodosia and Georgia will ascend to the One. The impurities of wrath and concupiscence which might have held them to earth have been purged through the power of their Redeemer and His religion—a religion to which, perhaps, they had not fully acclimated themselves if we may judge by the syncretism of the mosaic. But the lyre of Orpheus, whether we take it as representing the New Song of Christ or the Neoplatonic music which recalls man to the harmony of the spheres, at once conquers the passions of their souls—visibly embodied in Pan and the centaur—and provides the music to accompany them on their astral voyage.

The symbolic uses made of the Orpheus myth in the works of art discussed above are instructive for our understanding of the syncretistic visual imagination in late antiquity. We have remarked on the relatively timid association of Orpheus and Christ through need for a figure type in the catacomb frescoes, as well as the more imaginative connection of the two figures in the Berlin amulet because of the similarity of their function as soul guides. From the fusion of Orpheus and Christ in the complex allegory of the Jerusalem mosaic, we can infer something, perhaps, of the religious uncertainty of its commissioners, as well as of the tolerance and sensitivity of the artisan who combined pagan and Christian imagery to express some of the mysteries of the Christian religion. Owing to their cultural and historical proximity to the pagan imagery they often employed, late antique artisans did not need to interpret this imagery as a fiction concealing a Christian truth. They simply used it as part of a rich arsenal of expression. The gods and their legends, however obsolete they were from the point of view of the Christian, were still provocative and interesting from the point of view of the artist. As we shall see, however, this pragmatic attitude did not last long beyond the time of the Jerusalem mosaic. Their growing cultural distance from the myths of Greece and Rome made the men of the early Middle Ages come increasingly to overlook the literal content of these stories and concentrate instead on the Christian allegories they saw there.

IV
Oraia-phonos and Eur-dike in Hell

Gilbert Highet speaks of "the detestable medieval habit of extracting a moral lesson from every fact or work of art."[1] Certainly, this habit of thought pervades European literature from about the sixth century until well into the Renaissance. To the men of the Middle Ages, however, the dividing line between the morally uplifting and the purely pleasurable was not so clearly drawn as it is to us. They believed that what God did not tell man explicitly in the Bible, he told him darkly in the Book of Nature. Like the Roman groves which vibrated with numen, the phenomenal world of the Middle Ages contained God's message to men, spelled out in countless ways, from his signature in the cross-section of a seed to a schema of creation in the pattern of a leaf. Sometimes the meanings of phenomena were to be found in their color or number, and sometimes the moral significance of an object or an event could be understood through the study of its name.[2] The conviction that everything in the created universe bore witness in some way to God's plan, when extended to include classical

literature, produced some remarkably ingenious explica-
tions. Nowhere is the allegorical bent of medieval man
exercised more thoroughly than when he is looking back-
wards to the literary products of Greece and Rome.

Allegorizers of pagan myth, of course, had existed in
antiquity. One of the most influential of them was the
author called the pseudo-Heraclitus, who flourished toward
the end of the first century after Christ. In his *Homeric
Allegories,* he had shown that the stories of the gods and
heroes concealed historical explanations of events, allegories of the conflicts between the elements and forces of
nature, and between moral qualities. His exegetical method
goes back at least as far as Chrysippus and other early Stoic
thinkers, who had explained the gods as symbolic representations of natural phenomena in their efforts to give a
philosophic base to the worship of the gods. For the pseudo-
Heraclitus, the myth of Ares and Aphrodite was an allegory
of the struggle between concord and discord; the story of
Ulysses' wanderings shows the vices and temptations to
which the sage is exposed and which he must reject. The
Homeric Allegories and the allegorizing treatise on Greek
theology by the Stoic writer Cornutus (c. A.D. 60) as well as
Sallustius' *On the Gods and the World* and Servius' commentary on the *Aeneid* in the fourth century were largely
responsible for the popularity of the allegorical approach
to the pagan gods in late antiquity.[3]

The utility of Stoic myth criticism in explaining the
licentious or incredible stories in the Old Testament had
been shown by Philo of Alexandria; and Origen, Clement
of Alexandria, and other Christian writers adapted the
allegorical exegesis of late antiquity to the study of all of
Scripture. In the Middle Ages, allegorical treatments of the
Old Testament provided a rationale for all kinds of exegetical methods to be applied to classical mythology.[4] It is,
for example, in discussing the levels of meaning usually
associated with Scripture that Dante offers the story of

Orpheus as an illustration of how pagan poetry can have an allegorical meaning. "The second [sense] is called allegorical, and this is disguised under the cloak of . . . stories, and is a truth hidden under a beautiful fiction. Thus Ovid says that Orpheus with his lyre made beasts tame, and trees and stones move towards himself; that is to say that the wise man by the instrument of his voice makes cruel hearts grow mild and humble, and those who have not the life of Science and of Art move to his will, while they who have no rational life are as it were like stones."[5] Dante, of course, did not make up this view of Orpheus, but could and did find it ready-made in the work of any one of a number of medieval commentators on Ovid's *Metamorphoses*.

The efforts of the commentators to find a moral allegory in the myth of Orpheus placed it in a new perspective and created a new portrait of him. Their view was not the only one to be held during the Middle Ages, for by the twelfth century a secular literature of entertainment was beginning to depict Orpheus as a model lover and courteous knight. The moral allegories the commentators found in the myth, however, were largely responsible for its vitality in medieval culture, and had a shaping influence even upon more romantic versions of the story. Perhaps the most striking effect of these allegories was to give new stature to Eurydice by making her represent a better or worse side of her husband. In some of the commentaries, Eurydice is the passional or concupiscent side of his nature, drawing him down to hell. In others, she is the Good which evades him. One account makes the love of Orpheus for Eurydice that of Christ for the Church, still another sees the lovers as symbolizing the art of oratory and its subject matter. In all cases, however, when Orpheus and Eurydice are made to represent something other than themselves, it is their relationship which becomes the *moralitas,* the central feature of the myth. No longer are the deeds of Orpheus among the Argonauts relevant. His sojourn in Egypt and his *Testament* appear not to have been well known to medieval writers. Even the power of his lyre over the animals is often reduced to a mere detail in religious allegory. How Orpheus will act with regard to Eurydice becomes the crux of the story. The qualities for which the two figures stand are manipulated with varying results, but the portrait which emerges is essentially that of husband and wife together.

The outlines of this portrait were laid down in the sixth century by Boethius and, to a lesser extent, Fulgentius. Fulgentius provided the first and most widely imitated etymological interpretation of the legend in his *Mitologiae,* a reference work which undertook to describe and explain the chief figures of Greco-Roman myth.[6] He derived the name Orpheus from *oraia phone,* "that is, best voice," and Eurydice from *eur dike,* or "profound judgment."[7] These two, in Fulgentius' opinion, represented two aspects of the art of music—the power of words to move the listener, and the more mystical harmony of tones. A third character, Aristaeus (from *aristos,* best), who appears in the Virgilian account which Fulgentius was following, was compared to the best sort of men who pursued the secrets of harmony. From this interpretation of the myth, concerned more with art than with morality, several notable descendants can be traced which make Orpheus a champion of eloquence or of music. The broadest appeal of Fulgentius' approach, however, lay not in his concern with the arts, but in his use of etymology, and it was this feature of his Orpheus interpretation that later commentators were to adapt freely to their own interests. By seeing in the names of his characters certain abstract qualities, Fulgentius was able to make Orpheus and Eurydice stand for these qualities—in effect, he transformed them into pawns whose possible moves were defined by their names. Subsequent commentators manipulated these pawns across a wide variety of symbolic landscapes.

Boethius was, with Virgil and Ovid, a primary source of the Orpheus legend for the Middle Ages. He was also, as Virgil and Ovid were not, an interpreter of it, and his interpretation was so influential that we could hardly consider medieval attitudes toward Orpheus without reference to it. Boethius used Orpheus as a key exemplum in his *Consolation of Philosophy*, seeing in him the man who, when he has almost gained spiritual enlightenment, looks back to material concerns and thereby "loses all the excellence he has gained." His didactic use of the legend appealed to the sensibilities of Christian readers in the sixth, seventh, and eighth centuries in a way that the secular accounts of Ovid and Virgil could not, at least not until they had been properly interpreted as moral allegories. The *Aeneid* and *Metamorphoses*, though known, were not widely studied until relatively late—the ninth century for the former and the twelfth century for the latter.[8] In the meantime the *Consolation* and the many glosses and commentaries written upon it had enjoyed remarkable popularity, especially in the schools, and exercised a formative influence upon medieval conceptions of Orpheus.[9]

Boethius and Fulgentius can be seen as representing two approaches to the myth—both allegorical—which were to remain more or less distinct throughout the Middle Ages. Boethius' was the more moralistic approach, concerned chiefly with spiritual progress. It was not only expanded upon in discussions of the *Consolation*, but also adopted by commentators on other works which contained the legend, most notably by commentators on Ovid's *Metamorphoses*. Fulgentius' approach, concerned with music or rhetoric, was somewhat less common in the early Middle Ages, but nonetheless important, for it contained many of the features which secular poetry was to give to the Orpheus myth in the twelfth and later centuries. By means of these features, Orpheus and Eurydice were eventually naturalized into the medieval world, finally to be seen not simply as allegorical figures or moral pawns, but as courtly lovers, the couple of high degree who inspired the anonymous *Sir Orfeo* and Henryson's *Orpheus and Eurydice*.

It would be hard to name a philosophical work which was more popular in the Middle Ages than the *Consolation of Philosophy*.[10] Over four hundred manuscripts of it still survive, some in crabbed hands, hastily copied and evidently intended for use in schools, others beautifully illuminated, the possessions of kings and noblemen. One reason for the great fondness of the Middle Ages for this book is that to medieval men Boethius seemed a classical author of the stature of Horace or Virgil. His familiarity with Hellenic and late antique thought, his use of Greek, his scientific and musical knowledge, and his philosophical views all inspired great respect. The conditions under which he wrote the *Consolation* also lent emotional power and credibility to the work, for his imprisonment under the Arian emperor Theodoric and his subsequent death stirred the sympathies of medieval Christian readers. It is hard to say whether the *Consolation of Philosophy* gave rise to certain of the literary and philosophical tastes of the Middle Ages or whether it only appealed strongly to those already in existence. Yet it does seem as though this work attracted commentators in such numbers and of so wide a range of interests that to describe the commentaries on it is, in effect, to outline the preoccupations of the Middle Ages.

Commentators on the *Consolation* found much to interest them in Book III, Meter 12, where the Lady Philosophy sings the story of Orpheus to her pupil Boethius. Her account combines details from both the Ovidian and Virgilian versions of the legend, and by the addition of philosophical remarks at the beginning and end makes of it a kind of parable:

Happy is he who can look into the shining spring of good; happy is he who can break the heavy chains of earth.

Long ago the Thracian poet, Orpheus, mourned for his dead wife. With his sorrowful music he made the woodland dance and the rivers stand still. He made the fearful deer lie down bravely with the fierce lions; the rabbit no longer feared the dog quieted by his song.

But as the sorrow within his breast burned more fiercely, that music which calmed all nature could not console its maker. Finding the gods unbending, he went to the regions of hell. There he sang sweet songs to the music of his harp, songs drawn from the noble fountains of his goddess mother, songs inspired by his powerful grief and the love which doubled his grief.

Hell is moved to pity when, with his melodious prayer, he begs the favor of those shades. The three-headed guardian of the gate is paralyzed by that new song; and the Furies, avengers of crimes who torture guilty souls with fear, are touched and weep in pity. Ixion's head is not tormented by the swift wheel, and Tantalus, long maddened by his thirst, ignores the waters he now might drink. The vulture is filled by the melody and ignores the liver of Tityus.

At last, the judge of souls, moved by pity, declares, "We are conquered. We return to this man his wife, his companion, purchased by his song. But our gift is bound by the condition that he must not look back until he has left hell." But who can give lovers a law? Love is a stronger law unto itself. As they approached the edge of night, Orpheus looked back at Eurydice, lost her, and died.

This fable applies to all of you who seek to raise your minds to sovereign day. For whoever is conquered and turns his eyes to the pit of hell, looking into the inferno, loses all the excellence he has gained.[11]

Boethius was the first Latin writer to develop an ethical allegory from the story of Orpheus and Eurydice in the underworld, and the effect of his version on subsequent conceptions of the legend cannot be overemphasized. He has just been discussing the importance of unity, both as the natural state of God and as the state toward which all creatures tend. The highest happiness, as Philosophy has shown Boethius, is to be attained only when the soul has purified itself enough to rise and reunite itself with God. While the mind, the higher part of the soul, naturally seeks to rejoin the intelligence from whence it came, it is hindered by the weight of the lower part or earthly desires.

The Lady Philosophy, singing this meter, makes a clear distinction between the shining source ("Fontem . . . lucidum") of good and the heavy bonds of earth ("gravis/ Terrae . . . vincula"). At the beginning of the meter we learn that heaven, light, and mind are opposed to earth, darkness, and weight. This theme is one in which Boethius takes considerable interest and one to which he returns several times in the *Consolation*. As early as the second meter of Book I he tells us how his mind was dulled, drowned in the overwhelming depths. It wanders in outer darkness, deprived of its natural light, whereas before his imprisonment and subsequent despondency, it used to course the heavens and understand the stars and seasons. Because of concern with his material losses, Boethius now "lies here, bound down by heavy chains, the light of his mind gone out; his head is bowed down and he is forced to stare at the dull earth." Philosophy urges him to reassess his values and turn to those of the intellect in order to free himself of despondency. "My wings are swift," says Philosophy, "able to soar beyond the heavens. The quick mind which wears them scorns the hateful earth and climbs above the globe of the immense sky, leaving the clouds below" (IV, m. 1). It is the mind or intellectual faculty by which "the human race alone lifts its head to heaven and stands erect, despising the earth. Man's figure teaches, unless folly has bound you to the earth, that you who look upward with your head held high should also raise your soul to sublime things, lest while your body is raised above the earth, your mind should sink to the ground under its burden" (V, m. 5).

In these passages, Boethius is developing a commonplace familiar in both pagan and Christian thought. Man was made so that he could behold the sky, or home of reason, while the irrational animal, whose nature is associated with the material rather than the spiritual world, faces the earth as he walks. Plato had made an early statement of the idea. "God invented and gave us sight to the end that we might behold the courses of intelligence in the heaven, and apply them to the courses of our own intelligence which are akin to them, the unperturbed to the perturbed; and that we, learning them and partaking of the natural truth of reason, might imitate the absolutely unerring courses of God and regulate our own vagaries."[12] Almost indistinguishable in thought is a passage on the creation of man from the *Homilies on the Hexaemeron* of St. Basil. "Cattle are terrestrial and bent towards the earth. Man, a celestial growth, rises superior to them as much by the mould of his bodily conformation as by the dignity of his soul. What is the form of quadrupeds? Their head is bent towards the earth and looks towards their belly, and only pursues their belly's good. Thy head, O man! is turned towards heaven; thy eyes look up. When therefore thou degradest thyself by the passions of the flesh, slave of thy belly, and thy lowest parts, thou approachest animals without reason and becomest one of them . . . Raise thy soul above the earth; draw from its natural conformation the rule of thy conduct; fix thy conversation in heaven."[13] It is the metaphors for conduct provided by passages like these that Boethius applies to the backward glance of Orpheus.

Boethius sees in the story of Orpheus and Eurydice a human soul, freed from the bonds of earth and *temporalia* by a special dispensation and at last moving toward union with the One, suddenly yielding to the power of an earthly concern, in this case love, and so failing of its goal. We recall that in the story, as Boethius and others tell it, Orpheus is just at the mouth of hell when he makes his mistake. Boethius renders it "the edge of night" (*noctis . . . terminos*), that is, Orpheus is on the brink of seeing the light of heaven after the darkness of the infernal regions. He is, then, leaving the material substance, dark earth, and moving toward the spiritual heaven.

For Boethius, the fable of Orpheus is monitory: it warns of the powers of the base passions over the upper part of the soul. Orpheus represents the human soul fleeing the body and the earth but dragged back by its inability to reject *temporalia*—love for Eurydice. By associating the wife of Orpheus with the spiritual darkness to which he returns, Boethius makes an implicit judgment against Eurydice. He does not, however, say more about her, and it lay with the medieval commentators who explained the *Consolation* to later generations of students to develop in detail her allegorical character as the passional faculty of man's soul.

Boethius was an *auctor*, that is, a man who was considered by the Middle Ages to be an authority in the kind of literature he wrote and a model worthy of imitation in style and substance.[14] A list compiled by Conrad of Hirsau names some of the *auctores* who were taught in the schools of the twelfth century, a sampling which would probably have been less extensive during the early Middle Ages. Conrad's list includes Donatus, Cato, Aesop, Avianus, Sedulius, Juvencus, Prosper, Theodulus, Arator, Prudentius, Cicero, Sallust, Lucan, Horace, Ovid, Juvenal, Homer in a Latin paraphrase, Persius, Statius, Virgil, and Boethius.[15] It is not surprising that Boethius' *Consolation*

95

had an important place in a list of school books of this sort; the educative appeal of a dialogue in which the Lady Philosophy instructs and encourages a despairing man to set his soul in order is self-evident.

Medieval commentaries on Boethius, as on other *auctores*, grew out of the special needs and conventions of education in the church schools. We can conjecture that most of these commentaries had their origin in lectures, carefully prepared by a teacher and taken down verbatim by students in the margins of their texts, between the lines, or at the end of their manuscripts. Because of the scarcity of books, it should be added, these manuscripts were often the students' own transcriptions, painstakingly written out from dictation, line by line.[16] Either at the same time as the student made his copy of the *auctor*, or at a later date, he would add explanatory glosses or a full-scale commentary dictated by the teacher. Simple glosses might eventually be expanded into a fully developed commentary when the student himself became a teacher.[17] Sometimes the owner of a text, not necessarily a person associated with the schools, would borrow or read another manuscript with marginal or interlinear comments and copy them into his own manuscript, expanding the borrowed material with his own views on the subject. When, through bequest, such texts became part of a monastic, cathedral, or (later) university library, the strata of commentaries they contained served as the yeast for additional exegeses to be produced by subsequent generations of teachers and students.

The commentaries which we have generally reflect the medieval *lectio* or teacher's discussion of the book.[18] The *lectio* was divided into three parts: the *expositio ad litteram* or explanation of the words; the *expositio ad sensum* or explanation of the evident or narrative meaning; and the *expositio ad sententiam* or explanation of the spiritual or philosophical meaning.[19] It is mainly in commentaries based upon the third type of *expositio* that details of the ethical allegory concerning Orpheus appear.

In the pages which follow, I have presented chronologically the main medieval commentators who deal with Orpheus, trying as much as possible to let them speak for themselves about the meaning of his legend. The earliest of these writers are commentators concerned to gloss all the difficult points of a specific text, whether they be mythological allusions, grammatical problems, or interesting rhetorical devices. A few later writers who deal with Orpheus are not commentators in quite this sense. Like Fulgentius, they are writing about classical mythology primarily and have little or nothing to say about grammatical and rhetorical matters. Some of these men wrote specifically on the fables in Ovid's *Metamorphoses*; others, like the three Vatican Mythographers, wrote on myth generally. Those writers who follow the method of Fulgentius also follow the general arrangement of the *Mitologiae*—chapters on various myths and on specific gods, introduced by some general statement on the nature and utility of the gods in the ancient world. Because this type of arrangement places emphasis on the myths, rather than on the more various topics of the school commentary, it has seemed useful to refer to the writers in this tradition as "mythographers."[20] Their work has, as might be expected, some special characteristics which set it apart from the school commentaries, and the difference in emphasis has a noticeable effect upon their treatment of Orpheus. Very probably there are some school commentaries and mythographic treatises which have not survived, and some of these may have treated Orpheus and Eurydice from different points of view than those presented in the following pages. Even a casual examination of the authors treated below, however, will indicate that they were a traditional and conservative lot, more comfortable in imitation of each other's works than in innovation, and that new details were added only very slowly. These authors, then, may be taken to represent the prevailing trends in the interpretation of the Orpheus myth in the Middle Ages.

The first extant medieval writer to comment directly on the Orpheus meter of Boethius, Remigius of Auxerre, wrote his commentary on the *Consolation* about A.D. 904.[21] Remigius taught at Reims for a time, went to Paris, where he was probably connected with the monastery of St. Germain-des-Prés, and probably died at Lorraine in the first decade of the tenth century. In addition to his work on Boethius he wrote glosses or commentaries on Sedulius, Martianus Capella, Juvenal, Horace, Virgil, Avianus, Cato, Persius, Arator, Terence, and Prudentius.[22] The Boethius commentary exists in a number of anonymous manuscripts as well as one in which it is specifically attributed to Remigius by the scribe, "Incipit expositio in libro Boetii de Consolatione Phylosophiae Remigii." Here begins Remigius' exposition of Boethius *Consolation of Philosophy*.[23]

Remigius opens his discussion of the Orpheus meter by telling the reader:

> This song is a fable and it praises above all others those who, having laid aside carnal desires, raise themselves to an understanding of the light of true blessedness. And this fable warns us that no one should look backward after he once finds the place where the true good is situated, and after finding the highest good. Now [God] esteems and commends as happy those who can come to His brightness. This song, on the other hand, speaks to those who, after they have recognized the way of truth and advanced on it, return to human desires and thus ruin the work

they have begun. Just so, Orpheus lost his wife from looking backward.

> Hoc carmen est fabulosum; et ex toto beatificat illos qui exuti carnalibus desideriis erigunt se ad cernendam uerae beatitudinis claritatem. Et admonet haec fabula, ut nemo aspiciat retro postquam inuenit locum ueri boni ubi est situm et post inuentum summum bonum. Iam magnificat et felices praedicat illos qui ad eius claritatem peruenire poterunt. Quod carmen inde respicit illos qui postquam uiam ueritatis agnouerint et in ea profecerint rursus ad saeculi desideria reuertantur sicque opus inceptum perdant, sicut Orpheus perdidit uxorem retro aspiciens. (p. 217)

Remigius has Christianized his original, changing Boethius' rather general "sovereign day" to "His brightness" (*eius claritatem*). His reference to those who have "laid aside carnal desires," while still general, gives a specifically Christian emphasis to Boethius' vision of the true good. Next Remigius supplies the background information that Orpheus was a harpist whose wife, beloved by Aristaeus, was killed in a wild place. This detail can only have come from the Virgilian account of the legend. While it is not developed further here, its inclusion in the commentary foreshadows later, more elaborate, treatments of Aristaeus as a part of the Boethian allegory. It is possible that Remigius, by this simple reference to Aristaeus, may have set the precedent which was ultimately responsible for the shepherd's becoming part of the allegory, for the fact that Aristaeus is not mentioned by Boethius appears not to have deterred later commentators from carefully working him into their interpretations of Meter 12.

One other feature of Remigius' approach to the legend which bespeaks things to come is a rather slighting reference to Eurydice. Remigius retells the story, both simplifying and elaborating upon his original. Explaining Boethius' use of the word *impotens* to describe Orpheus' grief, he says (p. 218), "it is a natural thing for those who are sad about insignificant things to give themselves up

99

entirely to grief and therefore add powerlessness to their exaggerated sorrows" (Naturale est, ut cum dolentes in nulla re fuerint alia occupati toto se luctui tradant et ideo ad exaggerandum dolorem addidit inpotens). Whether he views Eurydice as herself insignificant or whether he merely wishes to offer a common-sense parallel to his students, he stands at the beginning of a long line of clerical commentators who, in attempting to make the myth timely, do so at the expense of Eurydice.

Sometimes his explanations are euhemeristic. On the powers of Orpheus' music he explains that Orpheus "is reported to have made the woods run and the waters stand still because he was a theologian and led men from wild ways to a civilized life." (Qui ideo fertur siluas currere et aquas stare fecisse, quia theologus fuit et homines ab agresti conuersatione ad ciuilem uitam perduxit; p. 217).

Remigius' commentary is a straightforward, practical one, obviously intended for school use. It employs a variety of means to explain difficult points of the *Consolation* and whenever possible rephrases its original in specifically Christian terms. It does not show a very high level of philosophical sophistication—for example, it does not grasp the thought of Boethius' *moralitas* in Meter 12 very well—but it would have been eminently suitable for use in a cathedral school and would certainly have helped to disseminate the notion of Orpheus as an allegorical figure who needed to choose between material and spiritual concerns.

The view of Orpheus offered in Remigius' Boethius commentary was the dominant one for the next few centuries. Remigius also presented a less influential Fulgentian interpretation of Orpheus and Eurydice in the course of a commentary on the *De Nuptiis* of Martianus Capella, in which he develops the allegorical interpretation of Orpheus presented in Fulgentius' *Mitologiae*.

Eurydice is called profound thought. She is said to be the very art of music in its most profound principles, whose husband is said to be Orpheus, that is *orios phone* or beautiful voice. This husband, if he loses his singing power through any neglect of his art, thus descends into the lower world of deep study, from which he returns again, the notes of music being arranged according to the rules of art. But when [Eurydice] compares the corporeal and transitory notes to the profound theory of the art of music, she—that is, thought itself—flees again into her deep knowledge because she cannot appear in notes; and because of this Orpheus remains sad, having the mere sound of music without possessing the underlying principles.

> Euridice interpretatur profunda inventio. Ipsa ars musica in suis profundissimis rationibus Euridice dicitur, cuius quasi maritus Orpheus dicitur, id est orios phone id est pulchra vox. Qui maritus si aliqua neglegentia artis virtutem perdiderit velut in quendam infernum profundae disciplinae descendit, de qua iterum artis regulas iuxta quas musicae voces disponuntur reducit. Sed dum voces corporeas et transitorias profundae artis inventioni comparat, fugit iterum in profunditatem disciplinae ipsa inventio quoniam in vocibus apparere non potest, ac per hoc tristis remanet Orpheus, vocem musicam absque ratione retinens.[24]

Remigius' view of the legend here is a variant of one of the most important educational topoi in the Middle Ages, that of *sapientia et eloquentia*. We shall see this topos employed much more explicitly in the treatments of the Orpheus myth by William of Conches, Nicholas Trivet, and others. *Sapientia et eloquentia* is too familiar a concept to need much explanation here. Suffice it to say that Remigius' Wisdom, "profound thought," in its suspicion of Eloquence, "beautiful voice," follows the famous dictum of St. Augustine in the *De Doctrina Christiana*: "He should approach this work about which we are speaking who can dispute or speak wisely, even though he cannot do so eloquently, so that he may be of benefit to his hearers, even though he benefits them less than he would if he could also speak eloquently. But he who is foolish and abounds in eloquence is the more to be avoided the more he delights his auditor with those things to which it is useless to listen so that he thinks that because he hears a thing said eloquently it is true."[25] To combine these two qualities, of course, was the goal of the educated Christian, and Remigius' interpretation suggests the reconciliation of the two more than the permanent rejection of *eloquentia* by *sapientia*. Still there is the strong hint that Eurydice as musical theory or wisdom is superior to Orpheus as the practice of music. It is she who rejects her husband because of his corporeal and transitory nature, and not he her. In this, of course, Remigius is quite at odds with his interpretation of the myth of Orpheus and Eurydice in his Boethius commentary, where Eurydice had represented the world of *temporalia* which must be left behind. His Augustinian and Fulgentian view of their relationship, though not to become popular until the later Middle Ages, looks forward to the treatment of the couple by the writers of medieval romance. In Remigius' Martianus commentary, Eurydice, far from representing an undesirable side of man's nature over which he must attain *maistrye*, becomes an unattainable ideal whose relation to her husband is like that of the romance heroine to her lover.

The eleventh-century writer Notker Labeo (nicknamed Notker the Lip to distinguish him from Notker the Stammerer) is the first extant commentator to have translated Boethius into Old High German. He alternates the Latin of the *Consolation* with his own German prose, a few lines at a time, sometimes expanding upon his original by a Latin gloss, sometimes expanding his German text. The amplifications are of many kinds, including simple paraphrases, tags from the Latin poets, biblical references, and German proverbs by which he tries to make Boethius clear and relevant to the student. Frequently Notker follows the commentary of Remigius almost verbatim. In his discussion of Meter 12, for example, he supplies the same background information on the occupants of hell as did Remigius, adding this moral to the story of Tantalus: "a man can do no better than to taste God" (Tér gótes chórôt. témo nesól báz keskéhen).[26] He tells the student that when Boethius says "break the heavy chains of earth," he means "to conquer the burden of the flesh" (*sarcinam carnis vincere*, p. 222, 22), and in discussing the power of love cites Virgil's "omnia vincit Amor" as well as a German proverb.

The seriousness of Orpheus' fall is somewhat amplified by Notker's translation. Where Boethius had written, "finding the gods unbending [Inmites superos querens], he went to the regions of hell," Notker translates, "chiding the gods of heaven for being unmerciful" (*úngnâdige chédende die hímelgóta*, p. 223, 5–10). A reader of Notker's time would not have questioned the plurality of Orpheus' gods, knowing that this was a classical story, but he might well have sensed something wrong in Orpheus' chiding the celestial deities and turning to subterranean ones. Such an act could not help but have symbolic overtones for a Christian trained to associate the heavens with God and the bowels of the earth with death and evil, and certainly the implication is there that in turning toward hell for the object of his desires Orpheus was wrong from the beginning.

Notker does not elaborate upon this point, perhaps because of the obvious difficulty of explaining how a desirable object, Eurydice, could ever be found in hell. Further on, though, he implies that it was not her desirability, but rather Orpheus' error which caused him to journey to the underworld. Where Boethius writes, "whoever is conquered and turns his eyes to the pit of hell," Notker adds "because of the desires of the flesh" (*carnis desideris*), a Latin phrase which does not appear in his original. He then translates even more explicitly into German, *sînên gelústen fólgendo*, "following his lust" (p. 225, 10, 13–14). Eurydice is thus placed in the ambiguous position of seeming to be at once the object of carnal desire and the "excellence" Orpheus might have gained. Perhaps to resolve this contradiction, Notker glosses the closing *moralitas* of the meter with a passage from Luke (9:62): "No man, having put his hand to the plough, and looking back, is fit for the kingdom of God" (p. 225, 15–17). By this gloss "excellence" is clearly placed in heaven and Eurydice is dismissed as merely the object of a backward glance which cost Orpheus his entry into the kingdom of God.

Notker, like any intelligent, interested reader, brought to his reading whatever seemed applicable or parallel from his own background. For him to find in Boethius an echo of a biblical text seems entirely natural. But as his own background did not include a familiarity with Boethius' late classical environment, and certainly did not include a knowledge of the philosophic tradition in which his author was writing, his remarks, like those of Remigius before him, do not always explain very well the points Boethius was trying to make.

It is only in the twelfth century, with the Boethius commentary of William of Conches (1080–1145), that we find an expositor who has the necessary philosophical training to understand his original and who at the same time has sufficient imagination to make his text seem contemporary. William was associated with the famous school at Chartres, a center of proto-humanist thought and a place of great importance for the sudden upsurge of interest in Greek philosophy which was the most striking feature of the twelfth-century renaissance. At Chartres and elsewhere, of course, men had access to certain of Plato's ideas in the *Celestial Hierarchies* of the pseudo-

Dionysius, in Macrobius' *Commentary on the Dream of Scipio*, and in Chalcidius' Latin version of the *Timaeus*, as well as in Boethius' *Consolation*,[27] but during the eleventh and twelfth centuries there became available for study various new texts of Plato and Aristotle and their antique commentators.[28] William was particularly interested in Plato and the Neoplatonists; he wrote commentaries on the *Timaeus*[29] and Macrobius, as well as on Boethius' *Consolation*.

William's interpretation of Meter 12, while owing something to Remigius and Notker, drew on a wide variety of sources and was essentially a new work. Moreover, William's contribution, unlike that of his predecessors, was an extended commentary rather than a series of glosses on particular points of the meter. It focused directly on the moral or allegorical meaning from the very beginning. This is, said William, "the allegory of Orpheus. [Boethius] proves that as long as the attention is occupied with temporal things, one can neither know nor delight in the highest good, and this is revealed by the story of Orpheus" (Probat quod dum est intentio in temporalibus nec cognosci nec diligi possit summum bonum, et hoc per Orpheum).[30] William uses the word *integumentum*, which in the Middle Ages meant the surface history of a fable concealing a hidden truth. The *integumentum* was what the commentator might call the superficial part of the Orpheus fable—its plot. William, who is much more interested in the doctrinal or allegorical truth contained beneath the *integumentum* than were Remigius and Notker, sounds very like Philo or the pseudo-Heraclitus as he chides those people—straw men, perhaps, if we may judge from the literary evidence of the age—who do not look beneath the surface of the legend for its allegorical meaning.

At first, certain wise men, seeing the fable of Orpheus, wished to understand its allegory; nor was it believed of so perfect a philosopher, namely Boethius, that he would have placed anything superfluous or meaningless in such a perfect work. But our [modern] chattering magpies, knowing nothing of philosophy and therefore ignorant of the significance of allegory, being ashamed to say "I do not know" and seeking solace in their ignorance, said that trying to expound this fable were a vain deceit . . . We, however, are not like them, and it seems to us that we should explain this allegory.

> Qui apologus primum videndus est, deinde quid sapientes tali integumento voluerunt intelligere; nec credendum est a tam perfecto philosopho, scilicet Boecio, aliquid superfluum vel pro nichilo posuisse in tam perfecto opere. Sed nostri gartiones garrulitati intenti et nichil philosophie cognoscentes, et ideo significationes ignorantes integumentorum, erubescentes dicere "nescio," querentes solacium sue imperitie, aiunt hoc exponere trutannicum esse. Tamen, ne eis consentiendo similes simus, quod nobis videbitur inde exponemus integumentum.

From this beginning, William goes on to review the legend, filling in details from the Virgilian account which do not appear in Boethius, most notably the pursuit of Eurydice through a field by the shepherd Aristaeus. He then analyzes the story:

What does Orpheus represent? He stands for wisdom and eloquence and because of that he is called *Oreaphone*—that is, best voice. Eurydice is his wife; she is that natural concupiscence which is part of every one of us, and no one can be without her, not even a child on the first day of its life. The poets imagine this human desire to be a kind of god or attendant spirit [*genius*] which is born and dies with everyone . . . Genius is natural desire and Eurydice is rightly named. She is the judgment of good [*boni judicatio*], because what everyone thinks is good, whether it be so or not, he desires. This natural concupiscence or human desire, when it wandered through a field, was beloved by Aristaeus. Aristaeus stands for virtue, for *ares* is excellence. This excellence fell in love with Eurydice, that is, human desire, when she wandered through a meadow, that is, over the earth, which is sometimes green and sometimes dry. Aristaeus loved her, that is, he followed her, because excellence always tries to raise human desire aloft from earthly things. But Eurydice fled Aristaeus because desire struggles with virtue, wishing its own pleasure which is contrary to the way of excellence. But then she died and descended to the underworld, that is, to earthly delights. His wife having died, Orpheus mourned, because when a wise man sees his attention and pleasure controlled by *temporalia*, he is displeased. Though he conquered all by his music, he did not conquer his grief for his lost wife, because however much a wise man overcomes the vices of others by his wisdom and eloquence, he cannot withdraw his own desires from the grasp of *temporalia*, and for this reason Orpheus greatly mourned. Then Orpheus descended to the underworld in order to bring back his wife, just as the wise man must descend to a knowledge of earthly things in order to see that there is nothing of value in them before he can free himself from human desire. But one ought not return to those things which he has left behind, and he should not return nor look back for this reason: "No man, having put his hand to the plough, and looking back, is fit for the kingdom of God."

Quid sonet Orpheus. Orpheus ponitur pro quolibet sapiente et eloquente, et inde Orpheus dicitur quasi Oreaphone, id est optima vox. Huius est coniunx Euridice, id est naturalis concupiscentia que unicuique coniuncta est: nullus enim sine ea nec etiam puer unius diei in hac vita esse potest. Vnde iterum finxerunt poete quemdam deum esse, scilicet genium, qui nascitur cum unoquoque et moritur . . . Genius est naturalis concupiscentia. Sed hec naturalis concupiscentia merito dicitur Euridice, id est boni iudicatio, quia quod quisque iudicat bonum, sive ita sit sive non, concupiscit. Concupiscentia hec ab Aristeo, dum vagatur per pratum, adamatur. Aristeus ponitur pro virtute: *ares* enim est virtus. Sed hec virtus hanc Euridicem, id est hanc naturalem concupiscentiam, dum vagatur per pratum, id est per terrena que quemadmodum prata modo virent modo sunt arida, adamat id est sequitur quia semper virtus naturalem concupiscentiam a terrenis abstrahere nititur. Sed Euridice Aristeum fugit, quia naturalis concupiscentia contradicit virtuti quia appetit voluptatem propriam cui virtus contradicit. Sed tunc moritur et ad inferos descendit, id est ad terrenam delectationem. Sed, mortua uxore, Orpheus dolet quia cum sapiens videt intentionem suam et delectationem in temporalibus habitam displicet. Sed, cum cuncta modulationibus suis vincat, dolorem de amissa uxore non vincit quia, quamvis sapiens eloquentia et sapientia sua vicia aliorum superet, suam concupiscentiam non potest a temporalibus auferre: inde maxime dolet. Sed tunc Orpheus ad inferos descendit ut uxorem extrahat cum sapiens ad cognitionem terrenorum descendit ut, viso quod nichil boni in eis est, concupiscentiam inde extrahat. Sed redditur ei uxor dum concupiscentiam inde extrahit; sed redditur ei hac lege ne respiciat quia *nemo mittens manum suam ad aratrum et respiciens retro aptus est regno Dei.*

The first part of this interpretation derives from Fulgentius, to whom William acknowledges his indebtedness, and from Remigius on Martianus, to whom he does not. Seeing in *oraia phonos* and *eur dike* somewhat different qualities, however, from those they had been assigned by the African grammarian, he justifies his departure from the version given in the *Mitologiae* on the grounds that more than one explanation of a particular myth may have validity. "If certain people who have read Fulgentius see that he has explained the fable of Orpheus in another way, they should not condemn our interpretation on this account, because, though treating of the same book, various authors arrive at different interpretations" (si aliquis legens Fulgentium aliter hanc fabulam exponi videat, idcirco hanc nostram non vituperet, quia de eadem re secundum diversam considerationem diverse inveniuntur expositiones). William knew his author too well to believe that Boethius would have intended anything but a moral allegory in his use of Orpheus and Eurydice, and he wisely does not attempt to work in the Fulgentian allegory of the *artes*. His only concession to these treatments is his statement that Orpheus stands for wisdom *and* eloquence, the eloquence coming as much from traditional accounts of Orpheus as from Fulgentius' etymology and the commentaries on Martianus.

William perceives in the legend a Platonic drama of the soul—a conflict Plato described in the *Republic* (IV, 439–440) as occurring between *nous*, mind, and *thumos-epithumia*, passion and desire. William has simplified the conflict to that of Orpheus, representing mind, with Eurydice, representing the concupiscent part of man's soul.[31] The couple embodies the abstract components of the soul almost as allegorical characters stand for virtues and vices in a morality play, or as Orgoglio and Timias, both by their names and by their actions, stand for moral qualities in Spenser's *Faerie Queene*. In William's commentary, Eurydice errs; virtue, in the person of Aristaeus, tries to guide her; she, however, gives herself up to earthly pleasures and so dies; her husband, knowing the truth and recognizing that his destiny lies beyond her, lacks in the end the will to leave her behind. We have, then, the spectacle of intellect and passion acting in opposite directions, when only their united effort can bring the whole soul into unity with God. It is interesting to note that though the Platonism of Boethius is not antithetical to Christianity, William makes no attempt to place the legend of Orpheus in a Christian context. The idea of ending his allegory with the quotation from the Gospel of Luke he may have got from Notker.

Nicholas Trivet (d. 1334) commented on the *Consolation*

some time before 1307,[32] and his work, judging from the fact that there are thirty-eight manuscripts of it extant, became one of the most widely known of Boethius commentaries. Nicholas used much of William's work, though without giving credit to his source, referring to his predecessor merely as "Commentator." Moreover Nicholas tends everywhere to substitute his own Aristotelianism for the Platonism of William. Nicholas also relied on the commentary on Boethius by King Alfred, and for his interpretation of the Orpheus meter he used a twelfth-century commentator on Virgil, Bernard Silvestris, as well as Remigius, the Third Vatican Mythographer, and other familiar writers. Though it is not a highly original work, Nicholas' commentary is of great interest to us for its influence on Robert Henryson's poem *Orpheus and Eurydice*.

Not much is known about Trivet's life or education; Beryl Smalley tells us that he was the son of a knight, a student at Oxford, and a Dominican.[33] Apparently he was a very industrious man: he wrote commentaries on Virgil, St. Augustine's *City of God*, Livy, Cicero, Seneca's plays, and Boethius. Trivet's commentary on the Orpheus meter is quite long, but much of it is taken up with explanations of the topography of the underworld and other matters which do not directly concern Orpheus. His *expositio ad sententiam* gives evidence, however, that the legend of Orpheus was still undergoing changes at the hands of the commentators and that the resulting portrait was acquiring some distinctly medieval features.

> By Orpheus we should understand the part of the intellect which is instructed in wisdom and eloquence; whence he is said to be the son of Phoebus and Calliope, who is one of the nine muses, so called from *calo*, that is, beautiful . . . sound, because she represents eloquence . . . and Phoebus, the god of wisdom, because he

instructed [Orpheus] in wisdom. Orpheus, then, by his sweet lyre, that is, his eloquence, brought wicked, brutal, and savage men to right reason . . . Eurydice is his wife—that is, the affections. Aristaeus, that is, virtue, wished to join with her. But Eurydice, as she flees through the meadow, that is, the folly of present life, treads on a serpent, not crushing it but casting herself down, that is, joining herself to the sensuality by which she is bitten, and dies. Thus Orpheus descends to hell, that is, gives himself over to earthly cares. Orpheus, that is, the intellect, thought to carry her off by beautiful music which would appease the gods—for by sweet eloquence joined to wisdom one ascends to heaven. Such an ascent was difficult, however, for she must be drawn up through the many delights which impede virtue when it would ascend. Thus Virgil: "To recall thy steps and pass out to the upper air, this is the task, this is the toil! Some few, whom kindly Jupiter has loved, or shining worth uplifted to heaven, sons of the gods, have availed."

Orpheum intelligitur pars intellectiva instructa sapientia et eloquentia. Unde dicitur filius Phoebi et Calliopeae quae est una de IX Musiis qui dicitur a calo quod est bonus et phonos [*sic*] sonus quasi bonus sonus propter quod significat eloquentiam . . . et quia Phoebus est deus sapientiae ideo dicitur filius Phoebi quia instructus sapientia. Iste autem per suavitatem citharae id est eloquentiae impies brutales et silvestres reduxit ad normam rationis . . . cuius Euridice est uxor id est pars hominis affectiva. Quam sibi copulare cupit Aristaeus qui interpretur virtus. Sed illa dum fugit per prata id est amoena praesentis vitae calcat per serpentem non ipsum conterendo. Sed seipsam que superiorem inferiori scilicet sensualitati applicando a qua mordetur dum per sensualitatem ei occasio mortis datur. Sicque descendit ad inferos scilicet terrenorum curio se subiciendo Orpheus autem id est intellectus eam a talibus abstrahere modulationibus placat superos id est per suavem eloquentiam coniunctam sapientiae ratiocinatur commendando caelestia ut ab istis terrenis ipsam abstrahat sed quia ascensus ad caelestia difficultatem habet et ideo subtractionem multarum delectationum quae impediunt virtutem per quam sit ascensus. Unde de isto ascensu loquitur se Virgilius Eneidus VI de superasque evadere ad auras. "Hoc opus, hic labor est, pauci quos aequus amavit Jupiter aut ardens evexit ad aethera virtus diis geniti potuere."[34]

For Nicholas, Orpheus' eloquence has assumed a much greater importance than it had had in William's commentary. He has followed the Second Vatican Mythographer (Remigius) and the Third Vatican Mythographer (Albericus) in their remarks on the civilizing influence of Orpheus' eloquence, but he seems most specifically indebted to Bernard Silvestris' commentary on Virgil's *Aeneid*. Bernard said that "We must take Orpheus for wisdom and eloquence, whence Orpheus is called, so to speak, *orea phone*, that is, good voice. He was the son of Apollo and Calliope, that is, wisdom and eloquence . . . Calliope is called fine voice and is interpreted as eloquence because she makes the voice eloquent. Orpheus has a lyre, that is, the rhetoric of oratory, in which the various colors of rhetoric sound just as different quantities sound in music." (Per Orpheum ergo sapientem et eloquentem accipimus. Unde Orpheus quasi orea phone dicitur i.e. bona vox. Filius Apollinis et Calliopes i.e. sapientiae et eloquentiae . . . Calliope autem i.e. optima vox dicta est eloquentia quia vocem disertam efficit. Habet citharam, orationem rethoricam, in qua diversi colores quasi diversi numeri resonant.)[35] Nicholas has used this "lyre" in his own comment that Orpheus, the intellect, thought to bring up Eurydice from hell "by beautiful music which would appease the gods—for by sweet eloquence joined to wisdom one ascends to heaven." He would know Bernard's commentary from his own study of Virgil, and he may also have known the gloss on *Aeneid* VI, 119—mentioned above in connection with the Jerusalem Orpheus mosaic—which had attributed to Orpheus the belief that the soul cannot ascend without a lyre. There is a foreshadowing of the humanists' interest in the *artes* in Nicholas' treatment of the theme of eloquence in this part of the commentary, and his use of the tag from Virgil both to conclude and to gloss this part of his discussion of Meter 12 is especially interesting, since it makes Orpheus—already established as the prototype of the Christian humanist in his possession of both *sapientia* and *eloquentia*—into the poet-singer beloved of the gods and pre-eminent by his own achievements.

It is precisely this reconciliation of wisdom and eloquence in Orpheus which seems to have interested Nicholas the most about this part of the legend, for he treats other aspects perfunctorily. For example, Aristaeus, by whom we should understand virtue, appears without explanation, though he is not a part of Boethius' version and has not been referred to in any supplementary sense by Nicholas. Certainly Eurydice suffers at Trivet's hands. Dismissed by him in two sentences, she not only succumbs to "the folly of present life," but she also joins herself to the "sensuality by which she is bitten." His interest in Orpheus himself leads Nicholas, like William before him, to skirt the Fulgentian approach to the myth which makes Eurydice the equal of or the superior to Orpheus. He places both *sapientia* and *eloquentia* in the figure of Orpheus. Later in a gloss on the closing *moralitas* of Meter 12, Nicholas does not seem interested in developing Boethius' point beyond a simple paraphrase. "Then when he says this fable applies to you he means that whoever has acquired good by means of wisdom loses it when he sees hell, that is, when his attention is fixed on earth and on temporal things which are lowly" (Quando vos haec fabula . . . id est quicquid boni laborando acquisivit per sapientiam et eloquentiam perdit dum videt inferos. Id est dum est intentus istis terrenis et temporalibus quae sunt infima; fol. 102v).

It is, then, in his treatment of Orpheus' eloquence and of the serpent which bites Eurydice that Nicholas has the most to offer us. He is, as far as I know, the first Boethius commentator to bring in the serpent from the Ovidian and Virgilian accounts, though he is, of course, not to be the last. The combination of a concupiscent wife and a serpent is too fortunate a concurrence of symbols to be long ignored by allegorizers of the story, and it comes to be one of the most distinctive features of the medieval portrait of Orpheus and Eurydice.

One more Boethius commentator deserves mention here, though his contributions to the medieval portrait of Orpheus are somewhat peculiar and do not seem to have been adopted by other expositors of Meter 12. This is Peter of Paris, remarkable chiefly for what he did not know about his subject. His translation of Boethius into French, written about 1309, provides a medieval view of Orpheus uninformed by any knowledge of the classical myth. In its tone and general approach, if not in its details, it demonstrates the process by which the legend was ultimately transformed into a romance—a process which could not have taken place without a considerable distance between the commentators and their primary source material, nor without an effort on the part of various commentators to present very old material so as to appeal to medieval interests.

Peter's conception of the classical gods and goddesses was not only colored by medieval views of the supernatural, but also subject to his own instincts for what would make a good narrative. Thus his opening comments on Meter 12 refer to Calliope as an enchantress and present Orpheus' background in a style which might with little difficulty be transposed into romance: "He tells in the fable of a man who was called Orpheus, and he was the son of a goddess who was a great enchantress, and this goddess was called Calliope. This Calliope lived near a very beautiful fountain and she taught her son Orpheus to sing, and he became one of the best singers in the world. And thus, as it

is told in the Histories [*Metamorphoses*?] he sang so beautifully that the trees danced and moved to his music." (L'an
raconte en les Fablez que i. home fu qui estoit apeles
Orpheus, et estoit fis de une deesse qui estoit grant en-
chanteresse, et estoit apellee cele deesse Caliopes. Cele
Caliopes si habitoit apres de unes fontaynes molt delitables,
si enseingna celuy Orpheus, son fis, a soner; et devint. i.
des biaus soneors dou monde. Et, si come l'en raconte es
Estoyres, il sonoit si delitablement que les arbes à son
soner dansoyent et s'esmovoyent.)[36] It seems likely that
Peter got his information about Orpheus' mother from
another Boethius commentary, or from one on Ovid or
Virgil, especially since, later on, he supplies the standard
background material on the occupants of hell which appears
in so many of these. His knowledge of Ovid and Virgil,
however, could not have been extensive and was probably
only at second hand, or obscured by a faulty memory,
because no mention either of Aristaeus or of the snake
which bit Eurydice appears in Peter's work. Instead, we
find the following rather startling information: "And it
happened that Orpheus' wife nagged at him, and the
rancor between them grew so extreme that he struck her
and killed her. And when he had killed her a sadness grew
in his heart, so great that he could not rest." (Si avint que
sa feme se corrosa à luy, et tant murent les rancures de
l' .i. à l'autre que il la feri et l'ocist. Et, quant il l'ot tuee,
une doulor crut en son cuer si grant que il ne pooit reposer.)
Eurydice's fault—up until now merely assigned to her
symbolically—is here made concrete and the direct cause
of her death. Indeed, while it weakens the abstract balance
between earthly and spiritual tendencies so carefully
pointed out by other Boethius commentators, it makes a
better story, for shrewishness is more readily compre-
hensible as a reason for her death than the fact that she
represents carnal concupiscence. Peter is no less hard on
Eurydice than the Latin commentators, in his own way.

With perhaps a trace of misogynistic glee, he goes on to say that Orpheus decided to seek his wife in hell, "for he knew very well that she was there" (car illeuc savoit il fermement que elle y estoit).

Further additions to the story seem designed to make it more medieval in spirit. For example, the lyre of Orpheus is replaced by a more contemporary instrument: "thus he took his vielle," says Peter, "and tuned it very well, and went so far that he came to the door of Hell" (si prist sa vielle et la atempra molt bien, et tant fist que il vint à la porte d'Enfer). In his description of the torments of hell, Peter adds the interesting detail that Ixion's wheel was set with "rasours"—an innovation which reminds us of the vivid imagery of many medieval sermons on the last things.

Not the least of Peter's contributions to the story is a happy, or relatively happy, ending: "And the gods of the underworld gave his wife back to him with a covenant that he would never see the heavens and would be blind forever. And he took his wife by this covenant and she was called Urrices." (Si li rendirent par .i. tel covenant que jamais il ne verroyt des ziaus et seroit tous tens aveugle. Et il si prist sa femme par celuy covenant; et estoit apelee Urrices.) The spiritual blindness which earlier commentators had attributed to Orpheus thus becomes actual, and our hero, in spite of this misfortune, appears to have led his wife home successfully, for nothing is said about his backward glance and subsequent loss. One wonders what version of Boethius Peter made his translation from, for this detail is quite explicit in Meter 12. Peter is not, however, the only medieval writer to have granted Orpheus success. A number of contemporary poems, both in Latin and in various vernaculars, have survived which end happily. As they contribute directly to the tradition of Orpheus as a romance hero, we shall discuss them in the next chapter.

As one might expect, the *moralitas* at the end of Peter's

comment on this meter is neither long nor insightful. It is, in fact, simply a paraphrase of Boethius which sits a bit strangely with the version of the legend that has just preceded it. For once, that "detestable medieval habit" of extracting moral lessons appears not to have interested the commentator half so much as the narrative of his story.

Boethius and Ovid seem naturally to fall together in a consideration of Orpheus' medieval portrait, since Boethius was following, in the main, the account of Orpheus presented in Ovid's *Metamorphoses*. There the story appears in its entirety, differing from the Virgilian version only in that it does not mention Aristaeus and does not dwell upon the sad goodbyes of Orpheus and Eurydice. It does, however, contain certain elements which Boethius did not see fit to recount, and these understandably receive more attention in Ovid commentaries than they did in those on Boethius. One of these is the death of Orpheus at the hands of the Thracian women. Another is the famous snake whose bite sent Eurydice to hell. Yet another is the mention of Orpheus' love for "tender boys," which raised problems many medieval commentators preferred not to deal with.

Probably owing to the licentiousness of some of his tales, as well as to the difficulty and sophistication of his verse, Ovid seems to have inspired little clerical interest from late antiquity through the early Middle Ages.[37] His subsequent rise in popularity paralleled the growing interest of the times in a secular literature of amusement. Ovid had become an accepted *auctor* in the schools by the twelfth century,[38] and by the fourteenth century his influence on both Latin and vernacular literature had perhaps equaled that of Boethius.

Because the *Metamorphoses* was not a work with a clear didactic purpose like the *Consolation,* a great deal more explication was required to make it morally profitable for the Christian student. Indeed, many of the fables it contained were of sufficient indecorum to challenge the ingenuity of the most resourceful expositor. Students of Ovid, however, were able to find spiritual allegories in the most unlikely stories, and their treatment of the legend of Orpheus reflects some of this interpretive zeal.[39] It is perhaps ironic that Orpheus' appearance in Ovid—probably his most pagan presentation to the Middle Ages—should have produced the most elaborate Christian explanations, explanations in which Orpheus is identified directly with Christ.

Writers on Ovid's fables differed from those on Boethius' *Consolation* not only in their allegorical ingenuity, but also in their treatment of allusions to classical myth. By the twelfth century, when mythographic treatises began to appear, the characters of Greek and Roman mythology were more familiar to the general reader and did not usually require identification in a gloss. They were more familiar, in fact, *because* more people had read Ovid, a primary source who, we should remember, was known to writers such as Boethius but not necessarily to Boethius' readers during the early Middle Ages. A reader of Ovid would not need to be told who Ixion or Tantalus were, for their stories were told in the *Metamorphoses* and were self-explanatory. Consequently, expositors of the *Metamorphoses* concentrate rather more on the allegories contained in the myths than on the biographies of the mythological figures themselves.

Six treatises on the *Metamorphoses* will demonstrate the range of meanings which were found in the story of Orpheus. The earliest, written about 1125, already shows a greater concern with allegorizing every detail than had any of the Boethius commentaries; the latest, Thomas of Walsingham's *Archana deorum*, written about 1410, offers several ethical allegories of special interest to poets.

The earliest exposition of Ovid was the *Allegoriae super*

Ovidii Metamorphosin in fifteen books by Arnulf of Orléans. This work describes Orpheus as a "most wise and musical man,"[40] "quidam sapientissimus fuit et musicus," whence his name, and discusses briefly his lineage and the names of his parents. In this, as in some other details, Arnulf's treatment of the myth resembles those of the Second and Third Vatican Mythographers. Though Arnulf's avowed purpose in the *Allegoriae* was to interpret Ovid's fables sometimes in an allegorical way, sometimes in a historical, and sometimes in a moral way, "modo quasdam allegorice, quasdam historice . . . et quasdam moraliter," his interpretation of the Orpheus myth is concerned mainly with the opposition of virtue and vice. Eurydice is described as having fallen into vice, "poisoned by the serpent, that is, misled by the deceits of this life, when she judged the false and transitory things of this life to be durable and true," and her husband is shown as trying to save her: "But by singing, that is, disputing about vices and virtues in the very home of vice itself, he raised with himself his wife from hell and from vices which are inferior to virtues—his wife, that is to say, his judgment, which though it had held to vice before, now judged better. But because reason looked back to vice, he lost his wife, that is to say, his judgment fell back into vice." (Iste Euridicem . . . a serpente invenenata i. fallacia huius seculi decepta cum bona huius seculi transitoria et falsa, durabilia et vera esse diiudicat . . . Sed in cantando, i. etiam inter vicia de viciis et virtutibus disputando, secum uxorem suam i. diiudicationem qua prius vicia tenendo pocius diiudicaverat, ab inferis et a viciis que inferiora sunt virtutibus erigit ad virtutes. Sed quia ratio aspexit ad vicia, uxorem item suam i. adiudicationem ad vicia relapsam amisit.) After Orpheus has lost his wife, Arnulf has him try to join her again, but this time he makes no distinction between the wife and the vices which recall the singer to hell. Orpheus is saved from his moral regression only by the fearsomeness of Cerberus. "When he wished to go a second time to hell, impelled by vice, he was barred entrance by the porter of the underworld. Considering, however, how unhappy he would have been to have gone back to vice, he shuddered at returning, but going up onto the mountain, that is, ascending to the virtues, just as he had descended to the vices, he softened wild beasts, that is, savage men, by his song, that is, by his preaching." (Cum vellet iterum sequi ad inferos, viciose operando, prohibitus est a ianitore infernali. Considerato enim quam infelicissimus esset ad vicia introitus, introire abhorruit sed in montem ascendens i. ad virtutes ad quas est ascensus sicut ad vicia descensus, cantu suo i. sua predicatione feras i. efferos homines mitigavit.) Unlike the first attempt to regain Eurydice, which was sympathetically described, this attempt receives no approval from Arnulf, but is treated as an error from which Orpheus is fortunately turned away. The description of his song as "preaching" and of the mountain to which he ascended as "virtues" is an original contribution, later to be adopted by the anonymous author of the *Ovide Moralisé* and by the commentator Pierre Bersuire.

Arnulf is no more severe toward Eurydice than the earlier Boethius commentators had been, but perhaps because the Ovidian version of the story included an account of the death of Orpheus at the hands of the Bacchantes he felt it necessary to comment on the weakness of women in general. Arnulf's low opinion of the sex reflects back on Orpheus' wife as much as it does on the Thracian women. Here is his explanation of the death of Orpheus: "and he shunned women, that is, those acting in a womanlike manner, drunkards and vicious men, but transferred his love to men, that is, to those acting in a manly way. Whence, the women, because he shunned them, killed him by stoning him, that is, they killed him from lust. Women indeed are more prone to lust and vice than men." (mulieres i. muliebriter viventes et viciosos vilipendit, sed amorem suum ad mares i. viriliter agentes transtulit. Unde mulieres eum quia de suo non erant consortio lapidantes occiderunt s. luxuriose. Mulieres siquidem proniores sunt in libidinem et vicia quam viri.)

Another expositor, John of Garland, who wrote an *Integumenta Ovidii* about 1234, put his treatise into verse, reducing the Ovidian fables to brief allegorical outlines. He appears to have intended each verse as a memory tag rather than a full interpretation, and not surprisingly his verses are supplemented by more elaborate prose explanations in the manuscripts where they appear. His distich on Orpheus reads:

> Field is Pleasure, wife is Flesh, Viper is Poison,
> Man is Reason, Styx is Earth, Lyre is Speech.
> Pratum, delicie; coniunx, caro; vipera, virus
> vir, ratio; Stix est terra; loquela, lira.[41]

Essentially, this interpretation does not differ in approach from others we have seen, though its reference to the field and the viper makes it specifically Ovidian rather than Boethian. A reader or owner of an Ovid manuscript in which it appears has added the following explanation to the distich: "By Orpheus we are to understand the man who has discretion and who has a wife, that is, sensuality, who wanders through a field, that is, through the world which they quickly traverse. She was killed by a serpent, that is, by the fragility of her sex, and he gave her back to earth, that is, he gave her back again to hell. When Orpheus summons the trees with his song, we should understand foolish men, and by his lyre the speech which teaches them, and all of this is what these two verses mean." (Per Orpheum vir discretus habet intellegi, qui habet uxorem i. sensualitatem que per pratum vagatatur i. per mundana que cito transeunt. Morsa est vero a serpente i. a sexus fragilitate, et post redit ad terram i. iterum redit ad inferos. Per

Orpheum adducentum arbores cantu lire habemus homines stultos. Per liram loquelam qua illos docuit. Et hoc habetur illis duobus versibus.) Here again Orpheus is seen as a teacher or civilizer of men as well as a wise man himself.[42] His relinquishment of Eurydice is not fully explained, but the phrasing implies that it was voluntary, perhaps a sign of his reason or strength. Like most of the expositions of Ovid, this one features a series of allegorical equivalents— phrases beginning with "that is," attached to each detail of the story. Such assignments of meaning were to grow both more numerous and more elaborate in later treatments of the legend. Giovanni del Virgilio wrote an explanation of the *Metamorphoses* about 1325, of which one complete manuscript and seven fragments survive. His *Allegorie* are a series of Latin paraphrases of the fables, in both verse and prose, which do not so much allegorize the text as expand it, taking up the elaborations which had been growing increasingly common among the medieval exposi- tions of the Orpheus legend and incorporating them into a romancelike narrative.

> Orpheus was the wisest and most eloquent of men, and on this account was thought to be the son of Apollo, the god of wisdom, and of Calliope, the muse of eloquence. He took Eurydice to wife. Eurydice is to be interpreted as profound judgment, and Orpheus mar- ried her because she judged profoundly. But when profound judgment wandered through a field, that is, when she delighted in worldly things, Aristaeus—that is to say, the divine mind, from *aristos* and *theos,* that is, God—followed her [MS: *eum*]. Then the serpent, that is, the devil, bit her and killed her, because the devil drew her from the good path. Orpheus, seeing then that he had lost profound truth, began to praise God humbly, and his wife was returned to him on the condition that he not look back at her before they

reached the gates of Hell, that is, that he not succumb to temptation, but he broke this law and accordingly lost her. On this account Orpheus renounced Hell, that is, temptation, and reconciling himself to God began to spurn women, giving his soul instead to God, and began to love men, that is, to act in a manly way, on which account he was dead to the delights of the world; for such men are dead to the world; and thus he truly had Eurydice back, that is, profound judgment.

Orpheus sapientissimus et eloquentissimus fuit. Et ideo fingitur fuisse filius Apolinis dei sapientie et Caliopes muse eloquentie. Iste accepit Euridicem uxorem. Euridice autem interpretatur profunda diiudicatio quam sibi desponsavit Orpheus quia profunde diiudicabat. Sed dum profunda diiudicatio vagatur per prata i. dum delectatur in mundanis et Aristeus i. mens divina ab aristos et theos quod est deus insequeretur eum, tunc serpens i. diabolus momordit eam et occidit i. quod diabolus traxit eum de bona via. Sed Orpheus videns se amisisse veritatem profundam cepit laudare deum humiliter, et reddita sibi est uxor sub lege ne respiceret eam ante inferni exitum i. ne succumberet temptationi. Sed fracta lege iterum perdidit eam. Qua propter Orpheus dimittens inferos i. temptatores reversus est ad Deum et cepit spernere mulieres, dans animam suam Deo, et cepit amare viros i. viriliter agere unde mortuus est mundo. Nam tales moriuntur mundo. Et sic habuit Euridicem.[43]

Giovanni has extended earlier moral versions of the legend to their logical conclusion, the regaining of Orpheus' good judgment, and so provided a new version of the happy ending. By Christian renunciation Orpheus eventually gains that which he sought for himself earlier. The story has become a moral exemplum, presented in the form of one of those surprising conversions so popular in early saints' lives. As Giovanni tells it, Orpheus becomes a monk. Moreover, this interpretation derives from an imaginative handling of one of the thorniest points in Ovid's fable, the information that for three years after the death of his wife Orpheus had shunned women, giving his love to tender boys. Arnulf had circumvented this point by identifying women with the evils of the flesh; other authors refrained from discussing it; but Giovanni has explained Orpheus' rejection of women by his marriage to God, the source of the most profound judgment of all.

One other feature deserves mention in Giovanni's commentary, and that is the appearance of the devil, identified with the serpent—a popular identification among later commentators, since the devil was to assume an important role in the story.

The anonymous *Ovide Moralisé*, probably written by a Franciscan at the end of the thirteenth century or at the beginning of the fourteenth century, goes to the greatest lengths yet to Christianize every detail of its original. Paraphrasing Ovid's fables in French couplets, it appends to each a series of elaborate moral or allegorical explanations. In its section on the Orpheus legend—thirty-four pages in De Boer's edition—it takes the traditional view of Aristaeus as virtue, and has Eurydice fall when she treads barefoot on "le serpent de mortel vice":

> By Orpheus, then, rightly can be understood ruling reason, and by Eurydice, his wife, the sensuality of the soul. These two things through marriage are joined in the human race. The shepherd who beseeches the wife and requires her to be his love can be understood as the virtue of right-living, who knows how to enchant the soul and follow it in order to attract it to virtue. But sensuality, who madly separates herself too far from reasonable understanding, for she is such that virtue bores her and she refuses his love and flees him, goes running, unprotected and barefoot, through the green grass, that is to say, through the evils of those earthly delights which she abuses madly; she treads of her own consent on the serpent of mortal vice, who lurks beneath vain delights.[44]

Of the serpent the author has more to say, proposing that

it was Satan, "who had so grievously tempted our first mother formerly . . . to eat the fruit of damnation" (X, 466–476). This is, as far as I can establish, the first extant commentary to make such an identification between Eve and Eurydice. In conjunction with the author's minute attention to allegorical detail—even the grass over which Eurydice flees is explained—we find a certain worldliness of viewpoint in his description of Eurydice's relationship to her husband. The medieval concept of marriage, in which the husband properly exercises *maistrye* over the wife, underlies this version of the story, and Eurydice appears in a bad light not only in her allegorical role of Sensuality, but also in her role as a foolish and headstrong spouse. Orpheus' return to her receives strong condemnation. Sinners, says the *Ovide Moralisé*, "should fear to fall again. In this they do much evil, when they return to their dung as a dog returns to his vomit" (X, 532–535).

As the section on Orpheus progresses, condemnation is replaced by praise. Orpheus' ascent from Hades to a mountain, where he assembled "a great company of trees, birds, and wild beasts to the sound of his Apollonian harp" (X, 2507–2509), is compared with the works of prophets and early Christian preachers, even of Saint Peter, who sat "on the high mountain of holy Church" (X, 2556–2562). The seven strings of Orpheus' lyre are explained as seven virtues, and even the pegs to which the strings are attached undergo Christian interpretation. From this view of Orpheus it is but a short step to the ultimate comparison: "Thus . . . Orpheus clearly denotes Jesus Christ, Divine Word, the teacher of good doctrine, who by his preaching had converted many nations of men" (XI, 177–184). The same identification appears in slightly different form at another place in the *Ovide Moralisé*, where the whole legend is taken as a figure for Christ's harrowing of hell. A concise version of this passage appears in the prose abridgment of the *Ovide Moralisé* made about one century later: "By

Orpheus . . . we must understand the person of Our Lord
Jesus Christ . . . who played his harp so melodiously that
he drew from hell the sainted souls of the Holy Fathers who
had descended there through the sin of Adam and Eve."[45]
The cross traditionally carried by Christ in the harrowing
of hell has here been replaced by a harp, but its symbolic
significance is the same. Both Orpheus' lyre and the cross
had magical power over the king of the underworld, and
both had been interpreted as manifestations or symbols
of the Logos.

The identification of Christ and Orpheus as a single
figure is carried over in the popular and influential mythographic treatise known as the *Metamorphosis Ovidiana* by
the Benedictine Pierre Bersuire. Bersuire was born in the
last decade of the thirteenth century and died in 1362.
During his residence at the papal court in Avignon, and
later in Paris, he became friendly with Petrarch, Philippe
de Vitry, and other important writers of the period.
Bersuire was a voluminous author, his most well-known
books being the *Reductorium Morale* (c. 1325–1337), a
moralized encyclopedia, the *Repertorium Morale* (c. 1337–
1342), a moralized dictionary, and a French translation of
Livy. His *Reductorium* took its title from its intention to
lead (*reducere*) man to an understanding of the Book of
Nature and its relation to God and human salvation. To
this end he planned the work in sixteen books, though only
thirteen were completed at first. These books were a
moralization—designed to supply exempla for preachers—
of the encyclopedia *De Proprietatibus Rerum* by Bartholo-
maeus Anglicus. The fourteenth book was on marvels, and
the fifteenth, which underwent two revisions with the last
version dating from about 1350, was a moralization of the
fables of Ovid. It was designed to introduce the sixteenth
book, a moralization "Super Totam Bibliam."

Our concern is with Bersuire's allegories on Ovid's
Metamorphoses. This fifteenth book of the *Reductorium*

was early detached from the rest of the work and copied, and later printed, as a separate treatise on myth; it was long believed to be the work of Thomas Walleys. It follows the Fulgentian pattern mentioned earlier, though it is much more elaborate than the *Mitologiae*. There are a prologue and fifteen chapters treating the fifteen books of the *Metamorphoses*. The sources of the work are Fulgentius, Albericus, that is, the Third Vatican Mythographer, Remigius, indeed, most of the commentators and mythographers I have already mentioned, as well as the *Ovide Moralisé*, which Bersuire got through the good offices of Philippe de Vitry and used in the third version of his treatise.

Bersuire offers perhaps the most remarkable and inventive of the Christian interpretations of the Orpheus legend. Following his practice with regard to the other Ovidian fables, he presents several possible and even opposed explanations. He opens his discussion as follows:

> Let us speak allegorically and say that Orpheus, the child of the [sun], is Christ the son of God the Father, who from the beginning led Eurydice, that is, the human soul [to himself?]. And from the beginning Christ joined her to himself through his special prerogative. But the devil, a serpent, drew near the new bride, that is, created *de novo*, while she collected flowers, that is, while she seized the forbidden apple, and bit her by temptation and killed her by sin, and finally she went to the world below. Seeing this, Christ-Orpheus wished himself to descend to the lower world and thus he retook his wife, that is, human nature, ripping her from the hands of the ruler of Hell himself; and he led her with him to the upper world, saying this verse from Canticles 2:10, "Rise up, my love, my fair one, and come away."

Dic allegorice quod Orpheus, filius [s]olis, est Christus, filius dei

127

patris, qui a principio Euridicem .i. animam humanam per caritatem & amorem duxit ipsamque per specialem prerogativam a principio sibi coniunxit. Verumtamen serpens, diabolus, ipsam novam nuptam .i. de novo creatam, dum flores colligeret .i. de pomo vetito appeteret, per temptationem momordit, & per peccatum occidit, & finaliter ad infernum transmisit. Quod videns Orpheus Christus in infernum personaliter voluit descendere & sic uxorem suam .i. humanam naturam rehabuit, ipsamque de regno tenebrarum ereptam ad superos secum duxit, dicens illud Canticorum .ii. "Surge, propera amica mea & veni."[46]

Once again a happy ending has been provided for the legend; in this case Orpheus' descent becomes a version of the fortunate fall. Bersuire has seen the whole of Christian history summarized in the adventures of Orpheus and Eurydice, and must, therefore, end on an optimistic note with the redemption of human nature. His use of the verse from the Song of Songs is reminiscent of Clement, who compared Orpheus' song with the New Song of Christianity. Here, however, the two are not contrasted, but combined, and Orpheus singing his wife out of hell becomes Christ inviting the Church to join him in marriage.

Bersuire next presents a more Boethian view of Orpheus which contains echoes of the commentary of William of Conches.

> Or let us say that Orpheus is a sinner who, by the bite of the serpent, that is, by the temptation of the Devil, lost his wife, that is, his soul, when she was indiscreetly collecting flowers, that is, applying her mind to the flux of *temporalia*. But he recovered her spiritually when he descended to the lower world through thought and through the power of his sweet measured words. Fear alone of infernal punishment made him penitent for his sins and thus he regained his wife through grace . . . But many are there who look backward through a love of *temporalia* just as a dog returns to his vomit, and they love their wife too much, that is, the

recovered soul, and so they favor their concupiscence and return the eyes of their mind to it and so they put her by and Hell receives her again. So says John 12:25, "He that loveth his life shall lose it."

Vel dic quod Orpheus est peccator, qui scilicet morsu serpentis, .i. diaboli temptatione, uxorem suam .i. animam perdit dum indiscrete ad colligendum flores .i. ad congreganda fluxibilia temporalia intendit, sed tamen ipsam spiritualiter recuperat quando ad inferos per considerationem descendit & per orationem dulciter modulatur. Solus enim timor infernalis supplicii facit de vitiis poenitere & et sic facit uxorem per gratiam rehaberi . . . Verumtamen multi sunt qui quia retro per amorem temporalium respiciunt, & tanquam canis ad vomitum mentaliter revertuntur, & ipsam uxorem scilicet animam recuperatam nimis diligunt ita quod concupiscentiis eius favent & ad ipsam mentis oculos retrovertunt ipsam iterum amittunt & infernus eam recipit. Io. xii. "Qui amat animam suam perdet eam." (fol. LXXIIIr)

A misguided attention to *temporalia* is by now one of the standard reasons cited for Eurydice's or Orpheus' downfall, but Bersuire overlays this interpretation with a Christian emphasis heavier than usual—in some places, perhaps, heavier than the original story will bear. Orpheus is made guilty not merely of a philosophical error, but of sin, and because his guilt is assigned to him as the primary condition of this interpretation it becomes more the general guilt of fallen mankind than the result of any particular act. It should be clear that the commentator is not here concerned with his original text in the same way as were Remigius or Notker, for whom the author's intention (or at least their view of his intention) helped to shape the *expositio ad sententiam*. Bersuire is concerned far less to "explain" Ovid than he is to use his stories to the profit of the Christian reader. Thus, in the passage above, when he speaks of Orpheus' penitence for his sins and the regaining of his soul through grace, he is truly more interested in penitence and grace than he is in the integrity of the

129

Orpheus legend. The seeming arbitrariness of his assigned meanings stems from the Pauline dictum, stated in the introduction to both this work and the *Ovide Moralisé*, that "all things written are for our profit." Each detail which can suggest an improving idea is relevant to the Christian, be it a peg of Orpheus' lyre or a flower at Eurydice's feet. This approach to classical literature was later to elicit from Rabelais the scornful indictment of those who believe that Ovid in his *Metamorphoses* taught "the sacraments of the gospel as that parasitic brother [Bersuire] strives to demonstrate . . . to people as foolish as himself."[47] We should remember, though, that for Bersuire it was not a question of what Ovid thought, but of what would be useful for the reader, as a Christian, to think.

Between the extremes of Christ and sinner are other figures with whom the hero of this legend can be compared, and Bersuire does not neglect them. The psalmist David may be the subject of one such interpretation, though he is not named: "Orpheus signifies the preacher of the word of God and writer of songs who, coming from hell, that is, the world, must sit in the mountains of Scripture and religion and sing the songs and melodies of Sacred Scripture, and call to himself, that is, to the state of penitence or faith, trees and stones, that is, the insensible and hardened sinners, and from them, by the sweetness of the divine word, to bring together the people" (Orpheus significat predicatorem & divini verbi carminum dictatorem qui de inferis, .i. de mundo veniens debet in monte scripture vel religionis sedere, carmina & melodiam sacre scripture canere & ad se, .i. ad statum poenitentie vel fidei, saxa & arbores, .i. insensibiles & induratos peccatores trahere, & ex eis, verbi divini dulcedine, populum aggregere; fol. LXXIIIr). Like the author of the *Ovide Moralisé*, Bersuire finds Orpheus comparable to many early preachers of Christian doctrine. He continues, "Or let us say that Orpheus signifies the saints and doctors of the primitive church, and by the sweetness of his song, that is, preaching, called to the faith of the church stones, that is, hard hearts, and trees, that is, insensible and infidel men."[48] (Vel dic Orpheus significat sanctos & doctores primitive ecclesie, qui dulcedine cantus, .i. predicationis, saxa, .i. corda dura, arbores, .i. insensibiles, & infideles ad fidem ecclesie vocaverunt.) Further on in this commentary the Thracian women who killed Orpheus are described as cruel princes and tyrants who murdered the early martyrs (fol. LXXIIIIv).

This wide range of allegorical interpretations for one myth makes the *Metamorphosis Ovidiana* not really a commentary but an anthology of allegories. It demonstrates the process by which the mythographic treatise had evolved by the fourteenth century into a set of Christian and peculiarly medieval narratives in many cases little dependent on the original fables of Ovid. Several factors contribute to Bersuire's anthology technique. He had been in the habit of elaborating on particular items in the *Reductorium Morale*. His treatment of the bee and its moral significance, for example, is so lengthy as to be almost a separate treatise on this insect. More important, however, is the fact that he conceived of the *Reductorium* as a work of universal import, dealing with the moral implications of the phenomenal world. He had moved from concrete phenomena to marvels in the fourteenth book, and the fifteenth book—on the pagan gods and demigods, their deeds and legends—was to prepare the reader to advance to the moral implications of bible stories, which were to crown the whole work. His moral concerns then, made him treat more myths and treat them at much greater length and from many more points of view than the mythographers who had come before him. Further, since the purpose of the *Reductorium* was in part to serve as a treasure house of exempla for the use of preachers, he had to provide moralizations of Ovid's fables *in bono* and *in malo* as well as multiple interpretations of an allegorical and anagogical sort. All of these concerns gave his work on myth a very different emphasis than that of the conventional school commentary like that of Remigius on Boethius' *Consolation*.

The fifteenth book of Bersuire's *Reductorium* served as a model for another mythographic treatise, intended, however, not so much for the use of preachers as for the use of poets and those interested in reading classical poetry. Bersuire's work was utilized both for its form and its information by another Benedictine, the Englishman Thomas of Walsingham, who wrote an *Archana deorum* in fifteen books during the first decade of the fifteenth century. Thomas, however, did not, as Bersuire had done, support his interpretations of myth with scriptural quotations, and we look in vain in his treatment of Orpheus for specifically Christian allegories. Instead we find a series of ethical allegories, which—like those in Fulgentius, John the Scot, and Remigius on Martianus—are in the main concerned with wisdom and eloquence, and derive ultimately from the Fulgentian treatment of Orpheus and Eurydice.

In the tenth book of the *Archana deorum* we find the story of Orpheus and Eurydice treated at length. The head note deals with the fables in the tenth book of the *Metamorphoses* and tells very briefly the facts of Eurydice's death by the bite of the serpent, Orpheus' descent to the underworld in search of her, and her final loss through his backward glance. The first and second chapters then proceed to paraphrase the story in Ovid. Thomas quotes copiously from the poetry in order to give his account a dramatic quality. In his lengthy paraphrase, nothing is said about the meaning of the story. Finally, he comes to the "expositio" of the meaning of the Orpheus legend. What follows is an exposition of the myth drawn almost word for word from the works of Arnulf of Orléans and the Third Vatican Mythographer. The latter, who was probably

Master Alberic of London, wrote an enlarged version of the *Mitologiae* of Fulgentius in the twelfth century.[49] It is worth quoting this exposition in its entirety, because it was an important influence on the mythographic treatises of Boccaccio and Salutati.

Orpheus first discovered the tonal intervals [of the seven spheres] and their harmony, whence he was entitled to be called the son of Apollo and Calliope. Orpheus, moreover, was an outstanding man, shining not only by the splendor of his natural abilities but also by the sweetness of his eloquence. He was called a priest because he was a theologian and first instituted the orgia. And by the sweetness of his rhetoric, he brought wild, irrational, and uncouth men from their harsh and unrestrained state and led them to a mild and civilized way of life. For this reason he is fabled to have moved beasts, birds, rivers, stones, and trees . . .

Truly, Orpheus is interpreted as best voice. He loved Eurydice, and, wooing her by the sound of his lyre, made her his wife. And she, when pursued by an amorous shepherd, Aristaeus, stepped on a serpent as she fled, and died. Orpheus, as we have said before, should be interpreted as best voice, Eurydice as profound judgment. Orpheus—that is, anyone devoting himself to the practice of music—wished to join Eurydice to himself and make her his wife by means of his alluring lyre, because whoever studies music, unless he understands the most hidden profundities of the art itself, cannot be a musician. And he attained [her] at last by the frequent and skillful modulation of his voice. Truly this shows how much the loftiness of knowledge is loved by the best sort, just as [Eurydice was loved] by Aristaeus (for Aristaeus is called best in Greek). She declined the company of [all] men, however, and thus she died by the blow of the serpent, because when her exceedingly subtle secrets had been [discovered] she stole away, as it were, to the underworld. But he descended to hell to seek this art and bring it up again, and he was prohibited from looking back, and when he looked, he lost.

Remigius understood this fable in another sense. He said, indeed, that Eurydice is called Orpheus' wife because the companion of eloquence is said to be discretion. Truly, she descended to the underworld by the bite of the serpent, when, longing for the pleasures of this world, she was directed on the left-hand path by the poison of iniquity. But by the songs of Orpheus, she was recalled to the upper world when the desire for profit is corrected and restored to equity by splendid oratory. But if she looks back, she is drawn back to terrestrial things, nor can she be recalled by the supplications of Orpheus. For when the earthly spirit desires worldly pleasures exceedingly, oratory can scarcely raise it in any way to the state of rectitude, because of the charms of Proserpine, that is, the greatest of the vices.[50]

Orpheus primus deprehendit quot sunt discrimina vocum et illarum armoniam, unde Apollinis et Calliopes filius meruit appellari. Fuit autem vir maximus tam ingenii claritudine quam eloquentie suavitate prefulgens. Sacerdos dictus quia theologus fuit, et organa primus instituit. Et homines irrationabiliter viventes rethorica dulcedine ex feris et immanibus mites reddidit et mansuetos, et ex vagis durisque composuit, unde et bestias, volucres, fluvios, saxa, et arbores movisse dicitur . . .

Sane Orpheus optima vox interpretetur, qui Euridicen amavit et sono demulcens cithare duxit uxorem ; hanc dum quidam Euristeus pastor amans sequeretur, fugiens in serpentem incidit et mortua est taliter. Orpheus optima vox interpretatur ut prediximus ; Euridice profunda diiudicatio. Hanc Orpheus, id est quivis musice operam dans, ubi coniungi optat et cithara illectam ducit uxorem. Quia qui musice studet, nisi secretiorem artis ipsius profunditatem comprehenderit, musicus esse non potest, sed artem crebra et artificiosa vocis modulatione tandem assequitur. Hec vero scientie altitudo quamvis ab optimis ametur, sicut ab Euristeo (euristeon enim grece optimum dicitur), tamen communionem hominum renuit; sicque serpentis ictu moritur, quia nimie subtilitatis sue impercepto secreto, velut ad inferos transmigrat. Sed post hanc artem exquirendam atque elevandam descendit, et ne eam respiciat prohibetur, et dum videt amittit . . .

De hoc figmento Remigio videtur alius intellectus. Ait enim Erudicen ideo Orphei dictam esse coniugem, quia facundie comes dicitur esse discretio. Ipsa vero serpente lesa ad infernum descendit, cum terrenis inhiando commodis veneno iniquitatis ad sinistram partem flectitur. Sed Orphei carminibus ad superos revocatur, cum luculenta oratione lucri stimulis ad equitatem reformatur. Sed si respicit, retrahitur ad terrena, nec oranti Orpheo redditur. Nam cum terrenus animus secularia nimis concupiscit, vix eum aliqua oratio ad statum rectitudinis erigit, quia a Proserpina, id est maxima vitiorum, tenetur illecebra.

This passage looks forward in several ways to the portrait of Orpheus as eloquent lover in the late Middle Ages and Renaissance. The Third Vatican Mythographer combined a number of details to create an Orpheus who is the essence of the Renaissance gentleman, a man of natural abilities who by the eloquence of his oratory, one of the noblest of literary activities, civilized savage men and raised men's minds from the temporal to the ideal. It is, of course, particularly appropriate that such an exposition should be found in Thomas' book, a work designed for the use of orators, poets, and readers of poetry.

The mythographer's detail about Orpheus wooing his wife by the power of his music is not original with him but comes from the tenth-century musicologist Reginus of Prüm.[51] It is but a part of a long line of euhemeristic explanations for elements of the Orpheus fable, in the same vein as that about Orpheus moving trees, stones, and animals by his music given earlier in the passage. Such an explanation, however, fits well with medieval conceptions of courtly wooing, as we will see in the next chapter when we examine some of the miniaturists' treatments of the couple.

135

One particularly striking addition of the Third Vatican Mythographer to the story is the idea that Eurydice was directed on the left-hand path by the poison of iniquity. The writer employs here a famous interpretation of the letter Y or bivium, attributed to Pythagoras of Samos and popularized by Isidore of Seville.[52] Pythagoras had seen in the form of the letter the choice of life, with the straight stem standing for the period of childhood, and the branching ways standing for the time when choice must be made. The steep path to the right is the choice of virtue while the easier sloping path to the left is the choice of vice and pleasure.

Toward the end of the fourteenth century, we find a new kind of mythographic handbook. The *Genealogia deorum gentilium* of Giovanni Boccaccio (b. 1313) and the *De laboribus Herculis* of Colucio Salutati (b. 1330) differ from the expositions of Ovid's *Metamorphoses* we have been considering in a number of important ways.

First, the form of these two books is something of a departure from that of the earlier treatments of Ovid. His expositors had followed the Fulgentian pattern of a series of chapters or books on specific myths with a short preface on the gods, their origins and worship. The expositor's organizing principle was the fifteen-book structure of Ovid's *Metamorphoses*, and his presentation of mythographic information was geared more or less to the presentation of myths in Ovid. For this reason, expositions of Ovid's myths are usually called "commentaries" on the *Metamorphoses*; I have not called them that only for convenience in distinguishing them from the school commentaries on Boethius.

In contrast, the *Genealogia* and the *De laboribus* are works of quite a different format and principle of organization. The former, written between 1363 and 1373, is really a kind of encyclopedia in fifteen books. Only the first thirteen, however, deal with myth; the last two are a defense of poetry. As its title would suggest, the work's principle of organization is quite different from Thomas' *Archana deorum*. Boccaccio does not seek to cover only Ovid's fables; he takes as his province all of ancient mythology, and by the appropriately antique device of genealogy he collects and organizes the myths of the ancients and the later commentaries which had accumulated on them in *summa* form. While the *Genealogia* certainly conduces to Christian morality, that is not its main purpose, and he intended the work rather more as a help to students of pagan poetry and history and to future poets rather than for students of Ovid or preachers seeking exempla. Even in his interpretations of myth Boccaccio leans toward the moral rather than the tropological or anagogical senses of a given fable.

The Italian humanist Salutati's *De laboribus Herculis*, not completed at his death in 1406, is an allegorical interpretation of the myths associated with Hercules. In its present form, it is in four books. Though Ovid's account of that hero's labors is the source and impetus of the work, Salutati's book is in no sense a commentary on Ovid's *Metamorphoses*. Whereas the defense of poetry had come in the last two books of Boccaccio's *Genealogia*, this subject occupies the first book of the *De laboribus*. The second book deals with Hercules himself and the third with his labors. The fourth concerns hell and the famous descents made there, especially that of Orpheus. Salutati also considers the symbolism of hell and of its inhabitants.

Both treatises seek to defend poetry against certain detractors who seem often to have been puritanical friars more concerned with scholastic philosophy than with the *artes*. Such men appear to have been found in conventual schools rather than in the more liberalizing atmosphere of the universities. Another Renaissance humanist, Albertino Mussato, had written a defense of poetry in response to the attacks of a Dominican, Giovanni of Mantua; Salutati had engaged in a similar controversy, also with a Dominican. Boccaccio is more guarded, describing the enemies of poetry in language traditionally used by the secular party in attacks on the mendicants.[53] Little attention was paid to poetry by the six expositors of the *Metamorphoses* discussed earlier; it was merely the vehicle which conveyed the myths whose allegorical potentialities interested them.

While Salutati and Boccaccio and the expositors of Ovid all saw moral utility in pagan fables, the two humanists were more interested in the ethical possibilities in the myths. Vital to both writers' defense of poetry was the idea that it ennobled man and that the fables of the gods lead men to virtue by showing right and wrong courses of conduct. Boccaccio, for example, in explaining the polysemous qualities of myth, uses as an illustration the story of Perseus and the Gorgon. By the story, read morally, we see the triumph of the wise man over vice and his attainment of virtue. Salutati takes a similar position where he says in reply to those who believe poetry to be nothing but a fable: "Truly, our poets condemn vices and depraved men and celebrate with fitting praise the virtues of the worthy in order that they may deter the race of mortals from vice and allure and invite them to virtue by means of the splendor of their commendation." (Carpunt equidem nostri poete vitiosos et vitia, celebrant autem cum virtuosis honesta laudatione virtutes; ut ab illis deterreant genus omne mortalium, ad has autem splendore commendationis alliciant et invitent.)[54]

Both men range widely in their treatment of myth. They are eclectic, presenting many points of view. Coupled with their conscientious review of all that Christian scholarship has had to say about myths and their meanings, we find a great interest in Greek learning and in the history and religious practices of the Greeks and Romans. Boccaccio suggests that poetry first developed from the creation of Greek temples and the religious songs sung in them; he mentions especially how Orpheus devised songs to praise God (II, xiv, 8, pp. 702–703) and seems in general to know a good bit about Greek religion. Both men also demonstrate familiarity with all the mythographers we have met thus far and with many that we have not. Boccaccio, in the *Genealogia deorum gentilium*, cites as his sources on Orpheus alone Lactantius, Rhabanus Maurus, Virgil, Fulgentius, Pliny, Solinus, Statius, Eusebius, Leontius, and the mysterious Theodontius, a medieval Greek author now lost. Salutati's twenty-page excursus on Orpheus in the *De laboribus Herculis* alludes to even more authors: Fulgentius, Remigius, Boccaccio, Servius, Epicurus, Virgil, Thales, Aristoxenus, Cicero, Hyginus, Ovid, Lactantius, Claudian, Nicomachus of Gerasa, Germanicus Caesar, Plato, Hippocrates, Eratosthenes, and Alexander. It is rare to see one of the Ovid commentators mention more than one or two of his predecessors. Boccaccio and Salutati, however, see themselves as comparative mythographers, marshaling the information of a wide range of authors, both Christian and pagan.

Boccaccio brings together in his section on "Orpheus, the Son of Apollo" almost every detail which was part of Orpheus' history in antiquity, including the Virgilian and Ovidian accounts which he follows with standard medieval interpretations, both in the Fulgentian and in the Christian allegorical vein. Many parts of the legend which we have not seen discussed since late antiquity reappear here—the sailing with the Argonauts, for example, and the fate of Orpheus' severed head when it floated to Lesbos. Although Boccaccio does not appear to have known anything of the tradition which made Orpheus an early monotheist, he does mention the possibility of his having brought the Bacchic rites to Greece and the story that he was killed for his apostasy by the followers of the god Liber. Boccaccio's own contributions are interpretive and, understandably in the light of his predilection for the *artes*, deal with genius and eloquence. The most extended is his explanation of the story that Mercury invented the lyre and then gave it to Orpheus:

> Mercury gave Orpheus the lyre, because, as the lyre has notes of varying intervals, we should understand the faculty of oratory, which is not made of one voice—that is, the panegyric sort of oratory—but out of many, and is not suited to all men, but to the wise and eloquent and those endowed with a good voice. Since these qualities were found in Orpheus, they are said to have been given him in greater measure than other men by Mercury. By the lyre Orpheus alone moved the most fixed and firmly rooted trees, that is, men of obstinate opinions, who cannot be moved from their obstinacy except through men of eloquence.

> Lyra autem illi a Mercurio data est, quia per lyram diversa vocum habentem discrimina, debemus intelligere oratoriam facultatem, que non una voce, id est demonstratione, conficitur, sed ex multis, et confecta non omnibus convenit, sed sapienti atque eloquenti, et bona voce valenti; que cum omnia in Orpheum convenirent, a Mercurio mensuratore temporum eidem concessa dicuntur. Hac Orpheus movet silvas radices habentes firmissimas et infixas solo, id est obstinate opinionis homines, qui, nisi per eloquentie vires queunt a sua pertinacia removeri. (II, ii, 5, p. 245)

Boccaccio's description of the power of eloquence is in keeping with his humanistic interests—it ascribes to Orpheus not the conversion of hardened sinners, but the changing of obstinately held opinions, and sees him as gifted rather than as inspired by Christian doctrine. Later, however, when he was presented the allegory of Orpheus from the point of view of William of Conches, he adds to the Christian interpretation his own view concerning oratory. Speaking of Eurydice, he says, "when natural concupiscence has fallen completely into hell, that is, among *temporalia*, a prudent and eloquent man, that is, good oratory, tries to lead her back to higher things, that is, to virtue" (Cum naturalis concupiscentia ad Inferos, id est circa terrena, omnino lapsa est, vir prudens eloquentia, id est demonstrationibus veris, eam conatur ad superiora, id est ad virtuosa, reducere; II, ii, 5, p. 245).

Boccaccio also sees the account of the severed head as an allegory concerning the *artes*, insofar as it concerns the fame of the artist. According to Ovid, Orpheus' head, when it floated ashore at Lesbos, was almost eaten by a serpent, but Apollo turned the serpent to stone. Boccaccio writes: "I understand by the serpent who wished to devour the head of Orpheus and was turned into stone an allegory of time. The serpent, or time, as the rest of the legend demonstrates, tried to eat the head, that is, the name and fame of Orpheus or those works performed by his genius, since men of genius thrive by the head . . . Nothing stands in the way of time, and to be sure the serpent could not have gone hungry save to this extent, that a famous man lives [on] by his lyre, that is, his genius, as is reported by an older poet" (Quod autem serpens, qui caput Orphei devorare volebat, in lapidem versus sit, intelligo pro serpente annorum revolutiones, que caput, id est nomen Orphei, seu ea que ingenio Orphei composita sunt, cum in capite vigeant vires ingenii, consumere, ut reliqua faciunt, conate sint . . . nil illi posse tempus obsistere; quod quidem huc usque non potuit egisse, quin adhuc famosus existat cum cythara sua, cum ex poetis fere antiquior reputetur; II, ii, 5, p. 246). Whether Boccaccio was referring obliquely to the fact that Orpheus' lyre had been made a constellation and so was beyond the reach of time, or whether he meant simply that the works of a famous man can keep his name alive, the problem which concerns him is outside the tradition of previous Orpheus commentary. Only new knowledge of the legend (and the Lesbos episode was not newly uncovered, but part of the standard account in Ovid) or a different set of interests from those which had prompted men to comb the legend for Christian allegories could have produced this interpretation.

Salutati's treatment of Orpheus is much more elaborate than Boccaccio's in part because, concerned as he is with the implications of famous descents to hell, he finds the legend of Orpheus extraordinarily rich from this point of view. Thus Salutati spends almost twenty pages on Orpheus' descent. Well before the *De laboribus*, of course, the topos of the *descensus ad inferos* had interested medieval men. Virgil, Orpheus, and Dante were all poets who had made the voyage to hell and returned to tell of its mysteries. For the Christian, these stories were particularly instructive because they allowed him to make that journey vicariously rather than as a punishment for his sins in this world.

Servius[55] and Favonius Eulogius had treated hell from a moral and theological point of view in the early Middle Ages. The latter explains the "ninefold circles of Styx" of *Aeneid*, VI, 439, by the suggestion that these were the nine heavenly spheres and that the earth was the lowest or ninth region to which the river Styx flowed. Thus the souls Aeneas met in the underworld were those who had made the descent into matter, poured from heaven as far as the earth like a spring.[56] But it was really Bernard Silvestris in his commentary on the *Aeneid* who offered the most influential explanation of the descent to the under-world. His treatment influenced Dante and his commentators as well as Salutati. Bernard had said that there were four ways of descending to hell. "One is by the way of nature, another of virtue, a third of vice, a fourth by artifice" (Descensus autem ad inferos quadrifarius est: est autem unus naturae, alius virtutis, tertius vitii, quartus artificii).[57] The way of nature describes the descent of

the soul into generation, this "caduca regione." This process had been well detailed by Aristides Quintilianus, we
recall, though Bernard gives the Platonism of the idea a
Christian emphasis. The descent by way of virtue is the
way of the wise man who descends through his consideration of worldly things, not in order to cling to them
but rather by knowing them to reject them in favor of
"invisibilia." Orpheus, he says, is a wise man who descended this way. The way of vice is the descent through the
mind's subjection to temporalia; "we read that in such a
way Eurydice descended and this is irremediable."
(Taliter Euridicem legimus descendisse. Hic autem irremea-
bilis est.) The way through artifice involves black magic,
sacrifice to demons, and the like.

This scheme is borrowed by Salutati and developed
at much greater length, making use of the *Timaeus* by way
of Chalcidius and of Macrobius' discussion of the soul's
descent in his *Commentary on the Dream of Scipio*. Salutati
interests himself particularly in the distinction between
those who descend by way of vice and by way of virtue.
The Epicureans and the Stoics are examples of philosophers
who seek pleasure or virtue as the highest good. Here "the
poets have figured in Orpheus those Epicureans who
follow pleasure" while Hercules represents those Stoics
who follow virtue (II, iv, 5, pp. 488–489).

Salutati's approach to the legend of Orpheus is that of
the comparative critic. He reviews previous discussions of
the myth and compares his sources, rejecting those which
he feels to be false or unsatisfactory. His section on Orpheus
is divided into two chapters. The first, comprising about
one fifth of the whole, bears the rubric "Concerning the
descent of Orpheus, who wished to recall Eurydice from
hell," and contains an account of the myth derived from
various antique and medieval sources. This chapter ends
with the observation that "Fulgentius, Virgil, and Ovid
agree on few points." The remainder of his discussion

143

in the next chapter, which bears the rubric "the allegory of Orpheus and all matters which are related," is interpretive. It devotes eleven lines to the summary of earlier views: "I am not ignorant," says Salutati, "that Fulgentius has assigned this fable to the art of music . . ." (II, iv, 7, p. 493). He knows what Remigius and even "my father who can never be sufficiently praised by the studious for his poetry, Iohannes Boccatius," had to say on the subject of Orpheus. But, he says, it is more pleasing to go into every sense of a myth and find one's own interpretation. His interpretation develops the various ways in which the fable depicts those Epicureans who descend to hell by way of vice, since they seek pleasure.

The argument is a complex and lengthy one, proceeding mainly by means of etymology, breaking down all proper names connected with the fable into groups of words or even particles; Salutati takes evident pleasure in his knowledge of Greek. His interpretation is particularly interesting with regard to Orpheus' death. For him, Orpheus, by his descent, represents voluptuous man who, not directing himself toward the ends of reason and virtue, forgets the proper use of the powers of generation which are symbolized by the god Liber. Instead, Orpheus seeks the rites of Venus, indulging in pleasure for its own sake, and is torn apart by the Bacchantes, thus demonstrating that the work of Venus weakens a man and consumes the human body (II, iv, 7, p. 503). The place of his death is also significant in this allegory. Traditionally, Orpheus was a Thracian and was torn apart in Thrace by the furious women on Mount Pangaeus. Thrace, according to Salutati's source, Alexander, means Aphrodite, that is, Venus. Pangaeus comes from *"pan,"* or all, and *"geis,"* or earth. So Pangaeus is all earth. Now as Orpheus was a man of pleasure, what place could be so suitable for him to die in as Thrace, that is, the region of Venus, and on the mountain Pangaeus, that is, all of the earth (p. 505).

While this allegory is certainly not hostile to the Christianity of the mythographers we considered earlier, it requires very little of the God of the Hebrews, who is mentioned in it much less than the gods of the Greeks. By means of his ethical and philosophical allegory, Salutati has in effect placed a different frame around the medieval portrait of Orpheus and Eurydice, taking them out of the Christian allegorical hell in which we found them in the writers on Boethius and Ovid and making them once again citizens of the secular world.

V
King Orpheus
and His Queen
in Medieval Romance

The last portrait of Orpheus which we shall consider is of a knight whose comeliness is as famous as his skill on the lyre, and who is distinguished as much by love for his lady in this life as by feats on her behalf in the next. His relation to the gods has become more feudal, his abilities and accomplishments more magical, and his responses to his adventures more personal than they were in the commentators' portrait of Orpheus, which tended to show him a bit stiffly posed as an actor in an ethical drama.

Orpheus the hero of medieval courtly romance appears to have been a well known figure by the fourteenth century. Though only two full-scale Orpheus romances survive—the anonymous *Sir Orfeo* and Robert Henryson's *Orpheus and Eurydice*—sources, analogues, and antecedents for them are plentiful. Indeed, one of the chief difficulties in tracing the development of Orpheus as a romance hero is that the origins of this portrait seem to be more diffuse than the origins of the courtly romance itself.

A brief list of some of its sources should illustrate the breadth of background which must be taken into account. The commentators and mythographers who dealt with Orpheus and Eurydice as an allegorical couple were responsible to a large degree for bringing them to the attention of medieval readers and for giving to Eurydice a larger role than she played in classical versions of the story. Illustrators of the Orpheus legend, especially in the *Ovide Moralisé*, made their own contributions (for example, a dragon, a happy ending), often quite independently of their texts, and by the costumes and settings in which they depicted the main characters made them contemporary figures. School exercises to perfect the student in the techniques of rhetorical *amplificatio* and *descriptio* produced poems based on the story of Orpheus in which all the details that appealed to the sensibilities of the writers were expanded upon and all others omitted, telling us a good deal about medieval tastes and attitudes. Among these rhetorical poems were several with happy endings. More professional writers described Orpheus as the most loyal of lovers,[1] a courtly lover (amans fins),[2] and a vassal to the god of love; these views also found expression in works such as Henryson's. Perhaps the most telling changes wrought upon the legend reflect the demands of romance as a genre. The romance, typically filled with plaints and songs, made Orpheus a minstrel. Its frequent monologues and dialogues not only gave him something to say, but began to portray him with new psychological depth. Its penchant for the supernatural gave his deeds a more magical character, in keeping with the curious but very old tradition that he was a magician or wizard. All of these characteristics appear together comparatively late in the Middle Ages, but they have fairly definite and distinct origins. Among the earliest glimpses we have of the romance hero are the illustrations of certain Byzantine psalters where Orpheus is conflated with David. In these pictures, Orpheus-David sometimes has a nimbus, an elegant costume, and a female companion, the personification Melodia.

Clearly, the portrait of Orpheus which appears in *Sir Orfeo* and Henryson's *Orpheus and Eurydice* is the result not of any single line of development but of many. Before discussing these two romances, therefore, I should like to speak generally of the developments listed above, developments which brought about a gradual blurring of the legend's classical outlines and ultimately made possible the literary portrait of Orpheus as a romance hero.

The association of Orpheus with David came as naturally to medieval writers as the association of Orpheus with Christ, and was one of the earliest ideas to exert a modifying influence upon medieval conceptions of Orpheus. The resemblance between the psalmist and the classical musician would have been quickly apparent to persons accustomed to thinking typologically. Both figures were of noble or divine descent, David of the line of patriarchs and Orpheus the son of Apollo. David, sent to a remote countryside to pasture his flock, played upon his harp and later used it to drive the evil spirit from Saul. Orpheus played his lyre in the wilderness of Thrace, where he drew the animals around him, and later soothed and won to his cause the infernal gods. The power of both men's music was compared to that of Christ over death, hell, and the devil. In the account of David's surrounding himself with musicians and organizing them into classes (I Chron. 15:16–25) a medieval reader would have seen hints not only of Orpheus' pre-eminence among musicians, but also of his supposed discovery of the laws of harmony and arrangement of the tones of music. Moreover, both David and Orpheus were the authors of certain songs, the Psalms and the *Orphica*, for which they were said to be divinely inspired. Both their works treated of cosmology, that of Orpheus extensively enough to give him a reputation as a cosmologist which lasted well into the Middle Ages,[3] and that of David, in a different vein, enjoining sun, moon, and stars to praise God with him (Ps. 148:3), praising God's power in the starry sky (Ps. 147:4, 150:1), and affirming, "The heavens declare the glory of God; and the firmament sheweth his handiwork" (Ps. 19:1).

What expression did these similarities receive during the Middle Ages? The earliest written references to them, as might be expected, were in apologetic works or Christian tracts. Cassiodorus, writing in the sixth century, asked, "if we do not speak of Orpheus' lyre and the song of the Sirens on the ground that they are fabulous, what shall we say of David who delivered Saul from the unclean spirit by means of his redeeming melody?"[4] And the seventh-century poet George of Pisidia wrote, "For however much Orpheus smote his divinely tuned lyre [in cosmological song], so much the more David, seeing the glory of the heavens as they stretched from the height to the depths of creation, sang out about them."[5] Later comparisons of the two figures dwelt longer upon the Orpheus myth and began to take a particular interest in the medicinal and tranquilizing powers of the lyre. The Byzantine author John Tzetzes, for example, explained that Eurydice, in a swoon from her snake bite, was awakened by Orpheus' music, which drove out her suffering just as formerly David had banished the demon from Saul.[6] A similar comparison occurs in an anonymous commentary on the *Eclogue* of Theodulus, "Just as Orpheus played his lyre in hell, so David played before Saul; and just as Orpheus softened the gods of the underworld with his lyre, so David softened Saul's evil spirit."[7] The *Ovide Moralisé*, whose comparison of Orpheus with Christ we have already seen, identifies the "Apollonian lyre" which gathered beasts and trees around Orpheus with the harp of the psalmist: "Truly, it is the harp by which David, God's helper, gave aid and comfort to Saul" (X, 2925–2928). By the fifteenth century, the power of Orpheus' and David's

19. Initial of King David harping to the animals, Hebrew Bible (Psalms), Ambrosiana B. 32 inf., 3r, thirteenth century.

harps appears to have been a commonplace. The two
musicians, though often alluded to separately, are still
cited together as a means of reinforcing the associations
which each must have with soothing or curative music.
Thus John Lydgate, in his poem *Reson and Sensualyte*
refers to:

> The harpis most melodious
> Of David and of Orpheous.
> Ther melodye was in all
> So hevenly and celestiall
> That there nys hert, I dar expresse,
> Oppressed so with hevynesse,
> Nor in sorwe so y-bounde,
> That he sholde ther ha founde
> Comfort hys sorowe to apese . . .[8]

The two musicians partook of each other's fame not
only in literature, but also in art, though of course art did
not offer the occasion for them to be placed side by side
in one picture in the same way that literature could mention
them together in a single written passage. Instead of comparison we find conflation, which applied to illustrations
of David the attributes of Orpheus and vice versa. For
example, an initial from a thirteenth-century Hebrew
Bible (Fig. 19) shows King David—he wears a crown—
playing his harp in the frontal position of the Jerusalem
Orpheus mosaic. About him is a group of animals somewhat
different from those we might expect in a pastoral scene
from the psalmist's life. A lion and a bear are mentioned
in the story of David the shepherd (I Sam. 17:34–35), but
the camel, the leopard, and the rabbit in this initial seem
clearly to have come from Orpheus iconography. The man
who illustrated this manuscript apparently had before him
a picture of Orpheus among the animals, from which he
obviously borrowed heavily and there are other classicizing

touches throughout the miniatures, dragons battling with centaurs and the like.

The reverse of this process can, I think, be seen in two illustrations of Orpheus from separate copies of a homily of Gregory Nazianzen, *In sancta lumina* (Figs. 20 and 21). In these pictures the musician, who is mentioned in the text as the originator of depraved pagan customs, appears to have been taken by the illustrators from an early Byzantine psalter portrayal of David. Far from manifesting depravity, the Orpheus shown in the pictures is nimbed and dressed elegantly. A closer comparison of these homily illustrations with pictures of David in three early psalters reveals marked similarity in other respects.

The well-known Paris Psalter, whose miniatures have

20. Orpheus, from a homily, *In sancta lumina*, of Gregory Nazianzen, Mount Athos, Monastery of St. Panteleimon, cod. 6, 165r, eleventh century.

21. Orpheus, from a homily, *In sancta lumina*, of Gregory Nazianzen, B.N. Gr. Coislin 239, 122v, c. eleventh century.

been variously dated between the eighth and the eleventh century,[9] depicts a richly clad David (Fig. 22). He is surrounded by animals appropriate to his story—sheep, goats, and a dog—and by three allegorical figures, the personification Melodia, a mountain god of Bethlehem wearing a laurel fillet on his brow, and a nymph. These figures, it should be added, as well as the illustrator's attempts at naturalistic anatomy, suggest that the painting was done in imitation of what the illustrator thought to be a Hellenic style. He might even have copied his composition from an earlier Orpheus mosaic or from Roman wall-paintings of Orpheus such as the scene from the House of Orpheus in Pompeii which may have survived in late antique copies. Orpheus made animals, trees, and even rivers move to his song; David charms the mountain god of Bethlehem who reclines in the traditional attitude of the Nile god[10] and seems to serve, along with the listening animals and the nymph, as a symbol for the natural forces

22. David and Melodia, from a psalter. B.N. Gr. Coislin 139, 16, c. eighth century.

of the pastoral world. The muselike figure of Melodia who gives David his power of song could well be a replacement for Calliope, or perhaps Apollo, who inspired Orpheus. In the background of this portrait is a small mountain which frames the figure of David, and a sacred pillar or column. Two other psalters which appear to have been influenced by the Paris Psalter illustrations show similar scenes of David. In one of them he wears simpler clothes, is nimbed,[11] and accompanied by Melodia, the mountain god, and the nymph.[12] The other is almost identical to the Paris codex.[13]

154

These works, too, have the mountain in back of the psalmist.

Returning to the manuscripts of Gregory's homilies we see more clearly the extent to which biblical and classical figure types were interchanged by medieval illustrators.[14] Although the allegorical figures have been removed, the small mountain remains, as does the nimbus about the musician's head. Orpheus' lyre now rests on a small altar, which looks like a section of one of the pillars in the aristocratic psalters, or like the altar on which the figure of Christ-Orpheus-Mithras from the Sardinian sarcophagus supported his instrument.

Such pictorial conflations, while not radically altering the portrait of Orpheus as he was known during the Middle Ages, did help to blur the classical outlines of the myth and suggest new associations which it might have for the medieval mind. Orpheus, as a result of his similarities with David, might be more readily thought of as a king, for example, and his singing in the mountains as the activity of an exile. The underworld figures associated with him might be replaced by curious personifications comparable to David's mountain god of Bethlehem, while Eurydice, previously connected only with his underworld adventure, might play a more active role as lover or wife above ground, taking a place at the side of her husband as had Melodia at the side of David.

In at least one instance, the comparison of Orpheus with David seems to have been the link joining Orpheus to another tradition which attributed to him magical powers. We have already seen how David's curing of Saul by music was equated with Orpheus' taming of beasts. Christine de Pisan writes of this curative power in her *Vision*, but without mentioning David or Saul: "Orpheus made such melodious sounds on the harp that by the perfectly ordered proportions of his harmonies he cured several maladies and made sad men happy."[15] John Tzetzes, the Byzantine writer who described Orpheus as having aroused

Eurydice from her swoon by music, also tells us that when Eurydice was on the verge of death from the snake bite, the singer brought her back to life by means of "spells which he knew, both from the Muse and by his native wit and wide learning." As early as Strabo, men had believed that Orpheus was a wizard, for the geographer explained that: "Here [in Pimpleia] lived Orpheus, the Ciconian, it is said —a wizard who at first collected money from his music, together with his soothsaying and his celebration of the orgies connected with the mystic initiatory rites, but soon afterwards thought himself worthy of still greater things and procured for himself a throng of followers and power. Some, of course, received him willingly, but others, since they suspected a plot and violence, combined against him and killed him."[16]

23. Orpheus, Eurydice, and the animals, from Albericus, *De deorum imaginibus libellus*, Vat. MS Reg. Lat. 1290, 5r, c. 1420.

The effects laid to Orpheus' music ranged from this
rabble-rousing to power over the seven archons en-
countered by the soul after death, as discussed in Chapter III.
Usually, however, it was the more familiar parts of the
legend—the taming of animals, the moving of trees, and •
the winning over of the gods of Hades—that were cited as
evidence of Orpheus' magical powers. These powers were
assigned to a certain Artephius by Ristoro d'Arezzo in his
Composizione del Mondo (1282): "The great Artephius—
miraculous philosopher, of whom it is stated that he understood the voices of birds and of the other animate creatures,
who being in the woods at times in the great mountains
playing for delight an instrument of his, to which sound
would gather the birds and the other creatures of the place,
according as it is stated and we have many times seen
depicted by the learned artists: which creatures would go
round him rejoicing and as if dancing and singing each one
according to its own song."[17] Ristoro's description of the
scenes depicted by the "learned artists" can only refer to
portraits of Orpheus such as that presented in the mythographic handbook *De deorum imaginibus libellus,* associated with the name of Albericus. This work, written in
the fourteenth century, is an abridgment of the first part
of Bersuire's *Metamorphosis Ovidiana* and contains a
number of interesting miniatures of mythological scenes
and figures. The text accompanying that of Orpheus
speaks of "mountains and trees bending their tops towards
him," and this has been faithfully rendered in the picture
(Fig. 23), though the mountains appear as tall rocks.
Orpheus is thoroughly medieval in costume; he plays a
rebec and is surrounded by a company of birds and animals
which includes a dragon and a unicorn. The underworld
part of the legend is represented by a figure of Eurydice
emerging with two devils from a hell mouth toward which
Orpheus looks.[18] Ristoro apparently derived the fusion of
Orpheus and Artephius from the fact that the original

wizard and magical master Artephius was supposed to have written a work on the voices of animals, and there is a detail in the *Lithica,* a late antique poem ascribed to Orpheus, which tells how a man may learn the voices of birds and animals by the use of a stone called *liparaios.*

The musical skill of Orpheus was given yet another interpretation in the Middle Ages, and that was that it served him in the art of minstrelsy. Orpheus as minstrel appears to have been a purely medieval contribution to the myth, unless we consider Strabo's reference to the wizard who took money for his music as an early instance of the idea. By Carolingian times it was becoming commonplace for professional singers and poets to refer to themselves as "another Orpheus," and perhaps this is where the tradition had its start. Their boastful allusions to his skill could easily have come to be understood as allusions to his profession. Sedulius Scottus, for example, in a request to his patron, Bishop Hartgar, for more funds, wrote: "I am a writer, I, a musican, Orpheus the second/ . . . Muse, tell my lord bishop and father his servant is dry."[19] Baudri of Bourgueil, writing in the latter part of the eleventh century, speaks of the custom of minstrels singing for their supper at the banquets of great men. His poem to Odo, Bishop of Ostia, describes such a banquet, at which "among the singers, I was another Orpheus."[20]

Constantine Africanus (1015–1087), Chaucer's "cursed monk," had alluded to the success of Orpheus as a combination magician-minstrel during a discussion of the medicinal effects of wine on the lover's malady, *hereos,*[21] and his story was popular among writers on music. John Aegidius of Zamora, a thirteenth-century writer, quotes it: "Orpheus said that emperors 'invite me to their banquets, in order that they may gain delight from me, and I enjoy them too, when I can bend their souls from anger to pity.'"[22] A slightly different version is given by the fifteenth-century musicologist Adam of Fulda, in which

"Orpheus by his music changed the hearts of princes from sadness to joy; he woke the sleepers, put to sleep the vigilant and cured melancholy."[23]

Orpheus as minstrel was a figure peculiarly well adapted to the requirements of medieval romance. His profession would give him access to the halls of almost any castle, as well as frequent opportunities to display his legendary musical skill. One of the two Orpheus romances which have survived does, in fact, use minstrelsy as a ruse to get Sir Orfeo back into his castle incognito, but neither story makes of its hero a professional itinerant singer—apparently preferring to treat the adventures of a person of high degree. The romance contributed indirectly, however, to Orpheus' reputation as a minstrel, not to mention several other aspects of his character, simply by imposing its conventions upon the classical story, for typically, its hero, impelled by love, sets out upon a quest during which he undergoes many trials, meets supernatural beings in supernatural landscapes, and has occasion to engage in lengthy monologues, dialogues, complaints, and songs, often on the subject of love.[24] Plainly, the legend of Orpheus is well suited to this genre. Aside from the narrative line which might almost be said to be an archetypal romance, the legend lends itself in a number of other ways to romance treatment.[25]

For one thing, its hero was a famous person of classical antiquity, thus coming from one of the favorite sources for knightly adventures in the Middle Ages. The Alexander romances, the romances on Thebes and Troy legends, the *Apollonius of Tyre* and *Ipomadon* romances, and the *Roman d'Eneas* illustrate the medieval fondness for tales involving classical characters, albeit characters transformed into knights and subscribing to medieval ideas of chivalric behavior.

Second, the story of Orpheus is about love which knows no law, and offers much latitude for a treatment of the psychology of lover and loved one, as well as the rules of "fin amor."

Third, the adventures of Orpheus are removed from the facts of daily existence, set not only in the past but in a distant country, and partaking of the marvelous; his deeds among the Thracians and in the underworld bring to a literature of entertainment wide-ranging possibilities for exotic costume, strange customs, supernatural landscapes, and fabulous beasts.

The writers of medieval romances accommodated the Orpheus legend to their genre even further. They medievalized Orpheus, as they did so many classical heroes, not only in his ideals and behavior, but also in his dress, his dwelling place, and his customary pursuits. That they did this was as much a side effect of efforts to idealize ordinary life as it was evidence of an interest in contemporary description. Life in the romance had to be finer, more colorful, or more exotic than the daily existence known to its readers, and as a result of medieval efforts to embellish the lives of classical characters about whom little was known, ancient figures became marvelously up-to-date. In *Sir Orfeo* even the fairies go hunting with falcons, in the manner of the nobility of the period.

The romance penchant for talk also had its effect on medieval conceptions of Orpheus. In a typical romance we might find stichomythic conversations, introspective monologues imitated from Ovid's *Amores* and *Heroides,* and dialogues and intercalated songs within monologues taken from the form of the encyclopedic or Menippean satire, originally made popular by Boethius and Martianus Capella. Such songs and speeches often reflected a new interest in the psychology of the hero and in subjective presentation of feeling, as opposed to simple objective description of action. When these speeches and songs were made to come from the mouth of Orpheus, therefore, they began to delineate an interior life for him, and the songs, especially, to add to his reputation as a minstrel.

The effects of romance conventions upon the legend, effects which would be interesting enough if they appeared only in the romances themselves, show up, in fact, in many places other than *Sir Orfeo* and Henryson's *Orpheus and Eurydice*. Lyric poetry, academic exercises in rhetoric, and manuscript illustrations for various kinds of works also bear witness to the influence of this genre upon the tastes and imaginations of medieval men concerned to describe the hero Orpheus. Perhaps the most obvious example would be the numerous manuscript illustrations in which the classical musician appears dressed in the styles of the thirteenth or fourteenth centuries, playing a rebec, medieval harp, or early form of the guitar, with a castle in the background, greyhounds at his feet, or other evidences of a medieval setting around him.

As early as King Alfred's translation of Boethius, what might be termed a romance approach to the Orpheus legend was beginning to take shape. Alfred renders the opening of the Orpheus meter in the *Consolation*: "Once on a time it came to pass that a harp player lived in the country called Thracia,"[26] thus setting the story in an indefinite fairy tale time. He idealizes the characters in what was later to become standard romance style, saying that the "harper was so good, it was quite unheard of . . . he had a wife without her equal, named Eurudice." Alfred also supplies us with the information, to reappear in *Sir Orfeo,* that after his wife's death Orpheus "was off to the forest, and sate upon the hills both day and night." When he descends to hell, Orpheus so charms Cerberus that the dog of hell wags his tail. The dwellers of hell meet Orpheus enthusiastically, bring him to their king, and help him in his plea because all men are vassals to the lord of love. In his emphasis of certain points and subtle addition of new details, Alfred has presented the whole story from the perspective of a medieval English nobleman.

Interest in contemporary or local detail, one of the features which distinguishes the romance treatment of the legend, also shows up in lyric poetry and academic rhetorical exercises on the story of Orpheus, often tied to a stylistic concern with description for its own sake. This concern was both a heritage of the classical epic and a development from the *amplificatio* and *descriptio* of clerical rhetoric. But where Homer gave a catalog of ships and the medieval preacher expanded upon the significance of the seven heads on the beast of Revelation—down to their very hair—the secular writer on Orpheus was likely to describe the dishes at the wedding feast, the costumes and personal charms of the lovers, or the steps by which the king of the underworld was overcome by Orpheus' music. Orpheus had been subject to such treatment as early as the *Imagines* of Philostratus (c. A.D. 300), where his charming of the animals was portrayed at great length in an *ekphrasis* or set piece of elegant description. The *ekphrasis,* a legacy of sophistic rhetoric, was the forerunner of the medieval *descriptio.* It took its authority from Homer's description of the shield of Achilles and was widely practiced in Hellenistic and Roman times. The Greek rhetorician Himerius (fl. A.D. 360) explained the technique as follows: "I will draw this for you in words and will make your ears serve for eyes."[27]

The fortunes of the *ekphrasis* in the Middle Ages followed the fortunes of rhetoric itself. In late antiquity men like Claudian and Sidonius Apollinaris still followed its techniques in their own poetic practice—Claudian's famous porcupine poem is an example of his use of *ekphrasis.*[28] But by the seventh century, when Isidore of Seville came to write his encyclopedia, educational and political conditions in Europe were such that the creation, arrangement, and delivery of formal oratory had ceased to have much practical meaning. For Isidore, the fivefold division of classical rhetoric into invention, disposition, memory, diction, and delivery, with its attendant schemes and tropes, was a topic so dry and confusing that it made his head swim.[29] During the eighth, ninth, and tenth centuries *Rhetorica* was eclipsed by *Grammatica,* and the concern of the schools was to teach men whose native language was not Latin to read and write it correctly. When rhetoric did reappear in the eleventh century, only one of its original five divisions remained—the one most relevant to the needs of its practitioners, *elocutio* or style.

In this period the demand for polished rhetorical style was associated chiefly with the *ars dictaminis,* or elegant writing of diplomatic letters, and the *ars poeticae.* Both tended to lay heavy stress on the techniques for developing and amplifying the speaker's, writer's, or poet's ideas. These appear in the medieval treatises on rhetoric under the rubrics of *amplificatio* and *descriptio*; the terms pertain both to the development of the matter and the style in which one clothes it. In the *Documentum de modo et arte dictandi et versificandi,* Geoffrey of Vinsauf's prose version of his *Poetria nova,* the author offers the student information on how "to handle things copiously." "Descriptions and circumlocutions," he says, "are used for the increase and adornment of the material; digressions, personifications, and apostrophes are interspersed."[30] Here is one of Geoffrey's model exercises in *descriptio,* elaborating on a dinner: "When the festal couch welcomes kings and powerful princes, the image of milk is first of the table's delights: Ceres is honoured. Aged Bacchus grows young in goblets of gold; alone there, or mingled with fragrant nectar, he condescends to depart from his elegance and be merry. A royal procession of dishes parades in on platters of gold; courses and gold marvel at themselves and each other. The guests note above all the paragon of the table: his countenance vies with Paris, his youth with Parthenopeus, with Croesus his wealth, his lineage with Caesar."[31] He concludes that one can amplify the brief matter proposed by this sort of long description.

From the eleventh through the fifteenth century it was common practice for teachers to have students write poems which elaborated some point of classical mythology in order to give them practice in the use of Latin meter as well as in the techniques of amplification and in the figures of *ornata facilitas,* especially *effictio, notatio, similitudo, energia, demonstratio,* and the like. Such techniques, of course, were widely used in the Middle Ages by educated persons with literary tastes, no matter what their age or position in life. Thus it came about that many ingenious poems amplifying some classical subject were produced in the Middle Ages.[32] One of the most popular sources of ideas for such exercises was Ovid, especially his *Heroides, Amores,* and individual fables in the *Metamorphoses.* The exercise poem naturally must enlarge on the scene or situation that inspired it, and such works seldom follow very closely the original version of the story, but substitute details and add elaborate descriptions of landscape and costume, dialogue, apostrophe, intercalated lyrics, and other features of the medieval romance.

Among these poems are several dealing with Orpheus. They include a five-hundred-line piece by Thierry of St. Trond, a shorter poem by a certain Gautier, a friend of Marbod the writer of the lapidary, and a section of a long debate poem by Godefroy of Reims called the "Dialogue with Calliope." All of these were probably written in the eleventh century. There is also a treatment of Orpheus and Eurydice in the eleventh-century lyric "Parce Continuis" found in a manuscript at Augsburg, which also exists in slightly different and longer form in a manuscript in the Laurentian Library at Florence.[33] The six-hundred-line continuation of Martianus' *De nuptiis* has a long passage on Orpheus and Eurydice and should be mentioned here as well. A love poem from a fourteenth-century manuscript at Auxerre, but probably written in the twelfth century, also contributes to the rhetorical elaborations on the myth.

All of these poems are of minor interest poetically, but they are very important as evidence for the portrait of Orpheus as a romance hero.

Thierry's poem shows a certain indebtedness to the line of commentaries, of which we spoke earlier, which saw the story as an allegory of the *artes*. Here are the lines dealing with Orpheus' actions after he has looked back:

> Unable to control his thoughts, lover turned his eyes to beloved. Who can oppose the Fates? Who can escape the Fates? Already approaching the light, already almost his, his Eurydice is seized back, and seized she becomes the shade she had been. The noble lutanist, relying on the Muse, soon returning again to the desolation of the lowest pit, would soften stony hearts with his peace-bringing lyre, would appease the Parcae, bend the Eumenides; weeping he would play, playing repeat his prayers—and his genius cannot but have its effect. But he flees from the Stygians, hateful even in their offering of gifts, disdaining to become a suppliant to evil. So, trusting with all the power of his spirit in the divinity of his art, bravely he took what he desired from Styx by force. Thus art, aided by firm purpose, vanquished nature, showing that all things yield to Lady Virtue.

Impos mentis amans in amantem lumina flexit.
    Quis Fatis obstet? Fata quis aufugiat?
Iam subiens luci, iam paene sui, sua retro
    Eurydice rapitur, rapta fit umbra prior.
Musae confisus rursum fidicen generosus
    Squalores imi mox repetens barathri
Conciliante lyra molliret saxea corda,
    Placaret Parcas, flecteret Eumenides;
Deflens pulsaret, pulsando preces iteraret,
    Sollers effectum nec negat ingenium.
Sed fugit exosos Stygios, et dona ferentes,
    Indignans supplex Nequitiae fieri.
Numine sic artis fidens industria mentis,

165

Fortiter extorsit a Styge quod voluit.
Sic ars naturam vicit, studio mediante,
Virtuti dominae cedere cuncta probans.[34]

Thierry has expanded Ovid's brief account of this event to almost thirty lines in his own poem, making use of various techniques of the *ornatus,* such as *repetitio, conversio,* and *complexio.* He is really more interested, one feels, in the rhetorical possibilities of the myth than in the myth itself. His curious ending for the story, with its suggestion that Eurydice is taken from Hades on the second try, is rather ambiguously presented. It appears that Thierry, relying on one of the commentaries which said that Orpheus' eventual victory over *temporalia* won him that which he had sought in hell, has tried to make the allegorical happy ending into a literal one.

The portrait of Orpheus as a triumphant lover, showing the power of Amor over death, is enhanced by the treatments of Gautier and Godefroy, who also give positive endings to the story, though without reference to allegorical values. Gautier tells us that "at the god's command his wife is given back to him."[35] Godefroy, whose interest in the legend lies as much with Calliope the mother of Orpheus as with her son, says that it was by inspiration with Calliope's sacred harmony that Orpheus convinced the gods to release his wife; once free, according to Godefroy, Eurydice fled the portals of hell and the Furies.[36] Although the changed ending is handled abruptly by Gautier and Godefroy, and weakly by Thierry, one can see that these poets desired a happy ending for the story enough to overlook the inconsistency of their nominal method, *amplificatio,* with their actual practice, which was to alter rather than to amplify. In this respect each shows the influence of changing literary fashions which were coming to place more importance on the satisfactions of love than in the sometimes unhappy resolutions of classical legends—fashions which lay behind the happy ending of *Sir Orfeo*.

The power of Amor is the unifying theme of a lyric from Augsburg, found in a manuscript of Gregory's *Moralia,* which cites as examples the stories of Pyramus and Thisbe and of Orpheus and Eurydice. Its version of the Orpheus legend predictably places more emphasis on Orpheus' capacity to arouse love than on his skill with music.

> For his looks and voice and eloquence, Orpheus alone among all Thracian men was loved uniquely by Eurydice. Overcome by his love, she longs to flee from all others, and while she flees from her pursuer, the harbinger of death seeks her with his bite: the serpent, crushed by her heel. Orpheus, inconsolable, strains after her with his songs.

> Forma, voce, lingua bona
> gratus erat unice
> solus Tracas inter omnes
> Orfeus Euridice,
> cuius capta federe
> gestit omnes fugere;
> dumque fugit procum, illam
> dente petit laetifer,
> calce pressus coluber.
> Orfeus illam modulis
> urget insolabilis.[37]

Orpheus' beauty has been made as important an attribute as his eloquence in this lyric. His attractive qualities, moreover, are no longer mere descriptive tags, but provide motivation for the narrative. Eurydice loves Orpheus *because* of his looks, voice, and eloquence, much in the same way that a lady of romance might come to love, from a distance, the fine qualities of her knight. Love by reputation was to be used in Robert Henryson's *Orpheus and Eurydice* when Eurydice, the rich queen of Thrace, is struck

by the good report of Orpheus and sends for him to come
and marry her.

A Latin continuation of Martianus Capella's *De nuptiis,*
probably of the twelfth century, adopts not only the
romance emphasis on love, but also its characteristic use
of songs and plaints. In it, Orpheus sings a long hymn to
the gods, in which he relates their deeds, and then a song
about his descent to the underworld and what he found
there when he sought his wife. Everything in his account
is described at great length, from the gods themselves to
the topography of the underworld. At last the sad Orpheus
raises a tomb for Eurydice: after four hundred lines of
mournful song and ten days of fasting, "weeping, he raised
a tomb covered with laurels, gems and gold . . . and inscribed on the door this sad epitaph, 'this stone contains the
blessed remains of virtuous Eurydice . . . her husband
killed her at the gate of hell and one urn holds the ashes
of their double flesh.' "[38] (Flens, tumulum lauro gemmis
depingit et auro/. . . Inscribensque foris notat hoc epi-
gramma doloris:/'Contegit Euridice lapis hic pia membra
pudice/. . . Mortua consortis fit eidem ianua mortis;/
Vrnaque carorum cineres tegat una duorum.')

Between the twelfth and the fourteenth centuries
Orpheus and Eurydice became firmly established as model
courtly lovers. Sometimes this aspect of their portrait was
presented to the exclusion of any other material from the
legend, as in a Latin love lyric from Auxerre:

> Eurydice's starry looks and innocent laughter ravish
> the eyes of singing Orpheus, captivate his mind.
> Orpheus, whose habit was to research into the spirits
> of the sun, the monthly orbit of the moon, the numeric-
> ally established courses of the stars in heaven,
> now led to a pursuit of another kind, his studies
> modified, speaks of kissing, of embracing, and follows
> his beloved.

The philosopher has quite gone up in flames—
Ismarus stood amazed at his love-lorn spirit, while his
lute lay still.

Eurydice will have none of her suppliant—he would
waste his prayers in vain, but then she opens the gates
of her womanliness, and devotes her body to the sallies
and sports of love.

Taking the first fruits of her maidenhead, at last the
lutanist possesses his Eurydice, and now, playing a
melody, he dispels all his cares.

Predantur oculos, captivant animum/vocalis Orphei/siderei/
vultus et simplices risus Euridices./Qui solis animos luneque
menstru os/rimari solitus/circuitus,/celo fugam siderum/per
numerum/notatam,/Iam nunc ad alteram traductus operam,/
mutato studio,/de basio,/de amplexu loquitur/et sequitur/
amatam./In flammam abiit totus philosophus,/amantis spiritum/
solicitum/tacente cithara stupebant Ismara./Non vult Euridice/
de suplice;/preces perdat vacuas—/sed ianuas/pudoris/et grem-
ium/dat pervium/discursibus/et lusibus/amoris./Sumpto liba-
mine/de virgine,/suam tandem fidicen/Euridicen/cognovit,/et
lirico/sub cantico/iam spiritum/sollicitum/removit.[39]

It is hard to imagine quite such a freely reworked portrait
of Orpheus and Eurydice being written much before the
twelfth century, even by Philostratus or Ovid, to name
two early elaborators on the lives and loves of mythological
characters. What is not mentioned here is as significant as
what is. The death of Eurydice, Orpheus' pact with the
gods of the underworld, the enchantment of trees, stones,
and animals by his music—all have been deemed less
important than the relation of the lovers.

A fifteenth-century treatise on the *ars poeticae* shows us
Orpheus as an archetype of the *fin aman*: "Calliope taught
Orpheus to sing and harp and he was a very virtuous man
in love; for he loved only one woman, and when she died
he began the mourning song which he sang all the rest of
his life for his beloved, until the constraining sighs of

death took him, and he was named by the gods the most loyal of lovers. Orpheus was a powerful man, a loyal and ardent lover, and was called the god of melody."[40] (Caliope aprint Orpheus a chanter et harper, et fut homme moult vertueux en amours, car, oncques n'ama q'une seulle femme, et quant elle mourut, ill commencha pour li le lay mortel que toute sa vie chanta pour s'amie, jusques es estrois souppirs de la mort, et pour ce fut des dieux nommez seul loyal amoureux. Orpheus fut un puissant homme et loyal ardant amoureux, et est dit dieu de melodie.)

This view of Orpheus appears in manuscript illustration as well as in the literature of the Middle Ages. A courting scene, for example, in Lydgate's *Fall of Princes* (Fig. 24)

24. Orpheus and Eurydice courting, from Lydgate, *Fall of Princes*, B.M. Harley 1766, 76r, c. 1450.

shows Orpheus playing a medieval harp for Eurydice, who seems to have been won over by his charms or by the power of his music. The illustrator must have conceived of the couple as people of high degree, for both are dressed in aristocratic medieval costume. There is no hint in this picture of the death of Eurydice or of Orpheus' failure to bring her up from the underworld, nor are these episodes illustrated anywhere else in this manuscript. The manuscript does, however, contain a miniature depicting the death of Orpheus (Fig. 25), in which the Bacchantes resemble bourgeois housewives.[41]

25. Death of Orpheus, from Lydgate, *Fall of Princes*, B.M. Harley 1766, 76v, c. 1450.

A manuscript illustration in the *Letter of Othea to Hector* by Christine de Pisan (Fig. 26) combines romance and traditional elements of the legend in a different way. This work, in discussing the proper courtly behavior of a knight, cites Orpheus as an example of the knight diverted from his way by *temporalia*. "Go not to the gates of hell" says the caption of the illustration, but the artist, far from depicting any dire or unhappy results of Orpheus' descent, shows him playing his harp in a pleasant landscape with a castle in the background. Behind him is a hole in a rock, the entrance to the underworld, in which we can see a devil, and before him are ranged not only the traditional animals and birds attentive to his song, but also Eurydice lying on the ground, Aristaeus standing over her, and a draconopede or four-legged serpent who has evidently just bitten her. This picture seems too all-inclusive to portray the moral of Christine de Pisan's text, but as an assemblage

26. Orpheus and Eurydice in the upper world, from Christine de Pisan, *Letter of Othea to Hector*. Erlangen University Library MS 2361, 89v, c. fifteenth century.

27. Orpheus and Eurydice leaving Hell, from Christine de Pisan, *Letter of Othea to Hector*. Brussels MS Bib. Royale 9392. 73v, 1461.

of elements of the myth which were familiar to the Middle Ages it is very informative. The clothing of the figures, the harp, and the castle in the background establish a medieval setting, while the devil and indeed the moralizing caption of the picture show that the underworld with which Orpheus was associated was the Christian hell and not the classical Hades. Aristaeus, holding his shepherd's crook, is the contribution of Ovid, perhaps by way of the allegorical commentators, and the attentive animals could have come from many sources, being among the most constant of Orpheus' attributes. Of the draconopede we will say more a little later, for he is another possible connection of the story with the Christian hell. The only suggestion of unhappiness in this portrayal of the legend is the figure of Eurydice upon the ground, and she appears to be sleeping

173

peacefully, quite composed. The illustrator may even have
had in mind some version of the legend like that of John
Tzetzes in which, "overcome by pain, she swooned from
mental distress or from her heart's fear, as is the case with
the worst kind of snake bite, and cheerful Orpheus drove
out her suffering by music . . . and brought her back to

28. Death and restoration of Eurydice, from the *Ovide Moralisé*.
Verard, Paris, 1493, 131r.

life." Certainly the Orpheus of this picture appears cheerful enough, and not, as in Lydgate's description, with "ful doolful face."

The happy endings which Thierry, Gautier, and Godefroy supplied for the legend appealed also to illustrators of medieval manuscripts, or so we must infer from their miniatures. Not only do they fail to depict Orpheus' loss of Eurydice when he looks back, they frequently show Eurydice returning with him to the upper world, or being handed out to him by devils at the mouth of hell. The scene at the mouth of hell was most popular. I have included three versions of it, one from a Flemish manuscript of Christine de Pisan (Fig. 27), one from an *Ovide Moralisé* (Fig. 28), and one from pseudo-Albericus' *De deorum imaginibus libellus* (Fig. 23). The Flemish one is unmistakable in its happy ending. At the left Eurydice is delivered by two devils from a hell mouth that looks very like a prop from a cycle play; at the right she follows her husband off into a beautiful upper-world landscape. Other illustrations show Orpheus leading Eurydice, as if she were enchanted, out of the black entrance to hell while playing his harp (Fig. 29), or playing before the king and queen of the underworld and then leading her away, still playing (Fig. 30), with no hint that she is to be snatched back.

In sum, then, these pictures, along with the increasingly secular literary treatments of the myth, speak for a conception of Orpheus heavily influenced by romance conventions. To see these conventions applied in their own proper sphere, we must now turn to the two Orpheus romances themselves, which represent the flowering of the legend in the Middle Ages.

Sir Orfeo, one of the finest non-cyclic medieval English romances,[42] was written about 1325. Its authorship is unknown, and the corruption of the texts suggests minstrel recitation.[43] Incorporating details from many sources to produce a new portrait of his hero, the author has wrought upon the traditional Orpheus material a remarkable transformation.

The poem tells of King Orfeo of Winchester (once upon a time called Thrace) and his wife Heurodis, their separation and eventual reunion. Heurodis, asleep at undern-tide or noonday under a fruit tree, is visited by a fairy king, who takes her to the other world of the fairies and then returns her to the orchard, telling her that the next day he will carry her off to the fairy land forever. She is brought back to Orfeo in shock, and the next day he comes to the orchard with a host of armed men to defend his wife from the fairy

29. Orpheus leading Eurydice out of Hell, from Christine de Pisan, *Letter of Othea to Hector*. B.M. Harley 4431, 126v, c. 1410–1415.

king. In spite of her guard she is taken off. Orfeo mourns
and resolves to give over his kingdom to his steward and
live in the woods. He becomes a hermit with long beard
and ragged clothes. Whereas he used to eat delicacies he
now eats roots. He still plays his harp, however, better
than any man, and charms the animals of the woods. One
day he sees sixty fairy ladies hunting and hawking by a
stream, with his wife among them. He follows them through
a rock into a flat green land like paradise, in the middle of
which is a castle ornamented with precious stones. There
he sees people whom men had thought dead, but who
were captives of the fairies, some of them mutilated,
burned, or mad. He also sees his wife asleep under a fruit
tree. Telling the porter of the castle that he is a minstrel,
he gains entrance and sings before the fairy king and queen,
so well that the king tells him to name his own reward, and
he asks for Heurodis. Orfeo and his wife leave the fairy
land to return to Winchester where they put up at the house

30. Orpheus and Eurydice with shades and the rulers of Hell,
from the *Ovide Moralisé*. B.N. Fr. 871, 196r, c. 1400.

177

of a beggar, and Orfeo, meeting his steward on the street, pretends to be a minstrel and asks for food. The steward is generous and brings him to the court where he performs on his harp. Although the steward recognizes the harp as the property of his lost king, he does not recognize the bearded and ragged Orfeo. Orfeo tests the steward's loyalty by telling the company that he got the harp from a man killed by lions, and the steward, thinking that the king is dead, begins to mourn. Then Orfeo reveals himself, and he and his wife return to the court with music and rejoicing.

It should be quickly evident that this account bears only a slight resemblance to the story of Orpheus and Eurydice as we see it in Ovid, Virgil, and Boethius or in the commentators' versions of their accounts. The author has made a romance out of a classical story, not by allegorizing it or by simply elaborating upon it, as had the authors discussed in connection with *amplificatio,* but by drawing details from the various portraits of Orpheus we have seen and creating a new story in which to assemble them. *Sir Orfeo* is a unified whole of a quality far superior to any of the postclassical treatments we have seen so far, mainly because it relies more upon the imagination of the author than upon any single literary source, however evident its sources may be.[44]

Celtic otherworld legend and romance, for example, have contributed much to the story of *Sir Orfeo*, in the form of the fairy abduction, the entry into the fairy land by a stream and through a rock, the jeweled castle and so forth, as indeed many authors have shown. Yet the transmuted classical, patristic, and iconographical portraits of Orpheus which we have examined in the preceding pages can help us to understand the meaning and the structure of the work at least as well as an approach by way of Celtic legend. For Celtic details take us only so far. Though the poem seems at first glance connected with the Celtic otherworld reached by crossing over water, the only water mentioned is a stream that the fairy women ride by and a moat around the fairy castle. And these, of course, are phenomena natural to woods and castles of the time. They do not seem to be significantly magical bodies of water.

Latin legend is no more helpful as a key to the poem. It supplies the names of the hero and heroine as well as the genealogy of Orfeo. But curiously, "His fader was comen of King Pluto, / & his moder of King Juno" (ll. 43–44), an ancestry which raises the question whether the author had any idea that Pluto was the king of hell, or that he even knew who these figures were. All he says of them is that they "sum-time were as godes y-hold" (l. 45). Though Pluto was "kyng of Fayerye" in Chaucer's *Merchant's Tale* (IV E, l. 2227) and was colorfully described as "Pluto, the elrich incubus, / In cloke of grene, his court usit no sable," in Dunbar's *Golden Targe*,[45] the author of *Sir Orfeo* seems not to know the name of his fairy king. He certainly does not connect Orpheus and Pluto as an author directly following a classical account might.

More consistent, however, is his use of the highly sophisticated tradition which produced the medieval allegories of Oraia-phonos and Eur-dike in hell. This will shed a good deal of light on the central issue of the story, Eurydice's abduction by the fairy king, which hitherto has been seen only as part and parcel of romance.

Eurydice, Ovid tells us, went out walking with a group of naiads after her marriage to Orpheus, was bitten by a snake, and died. In Virgil's account she was fleeing Aristaeus, a lovesick pastoral demigod, when she stepped on the snake. In *Sir Orfeo*, however, Heurodis falls asleep in an orchard and is carried off by the king of the fairies. This king, in causing Heurodis' loss to her husband and to the world of mortal men, serves well enough as a substitute for Ovid's and Virgil's snake. Yet, by most canons of realism, his presence in the story is less credible than that of a snake. Indeed, the poet's use of a fairy abductor raises some serious problems, for with the fairy king must be provided a motive for the abduction. How did the king know that Heurodis was asleep in the orchard? Why did he choose her at all? In a narrative so carefully plotted that early in the story we are told that Orfeo grew a long beard in order that we will gracefully accept the fact that at the end of the story his steward does not recognize him, the unexplained capture of Heurodis by the fairy king seems all the more curious.

As I suggested earlier, something must be allowed here for the conventions of Celtic romance, where mysterious and often malevolent beings confront the hero or heroine no less frequently than do human enemies. I think it can be shown, however, that Heurodis' fairy abductor is more than merely appropriate to the genre. His appearance in *Sir Orfeo* is intimately connected with the medieval portrait of Eurydice herself. Heurodis, we must remember, while a simple romance heroine in many respects, still bears a name which links her with her often-excoriated sister in the commentaries on Boethius' and Ovid's accounts of the myth. Thus it is to medieval transmissions—or more properly, transformations—of Eurydice's legend that we must look if we wish to understand the abduction of Heurodis.

We recall that in the *Consolation of Philosophy* Boethius had used the Orpheus myth as an exemplum to show the distinction between worldly and spiritual desires. Taken in the larger context of the *Consolation,* Orpheus represented *nous* or mind and Eurydice *epithumia* or desire, the passional part of man's soul. In turning his eyes back to Eurydice, Orpheus had turned them away from heaven, the only proper object for mind. As we saw, Eurydice emerged from this interpretation as inferior to Orpheus and became identified with hell and *temporalia*. In the lengthy interpretation of the Orpheus myth by William of Conches, Eurydice was "that natural concupiscence which is part of every one of us." Fleeing from the good (Aristaeus) "because desire struggles with virtue, wishing its own pleasure, which is contrary to the way of excellence," Eurydice, in William's portrait of her, was fair prey for Satan.

Other commentators went even further, actually bringing Satan into the story. A twelfth-century manuscript of Arnulf's commentary on the *Metamorphoses* contains an anonymous gloss which explains that "Orpheus is a type of Christ . . . who provided a wife for himself, but through the teeth of the serpent, *that is to say, by the counsel of Satan*" lost her (Orpheus gerit tipum Christi qui Euridicem i. animam que bona radix dicitur ab eu quod est bonum et radix, sibi uxorem providit, sed dente serpentis i. consilio dyaboli . . .).[46]

Satan again appears in the *Allegorie* of Giovanni del Virgilio discussed earlier. "Orpheus took Eurydice to wife," we recall, "and Eurydice is to be interpreted as profound judgment, and Orpheus married her because she judged profoundly. But when profound judgment wandered through a field, that is, when she delighted in worldly things, Aristaeus, that is to say, the divine mind, from *aristos* and *theos*, that is, God, followed her. Then the serpent, that is, the devil, bit her and killed her, because the devil drew her from the good path" (*Allegorie*, p. 89).

In his elaborate interpretation of Orpheus as a type of Christ, Pierre Bersuire makes Eurydice into the human soul. "But the devil, a serpent, drew near the new bride . . . while she collected flowers . . . and bit her by temptation and killed her by sin, and finally she went to the world below" (fol. LXXIIIv).

While commentators such as Arnulf, Giovanni, and Bersuire may have introduced Satan into the legend, medieval artists went further yet and actually showed Eurydice being attacked by him. Several manuscript illustrations depict her being bitten by a winged dragon or serpent at least half as big as she is, a popular medieval guise for the devil. Illustrators handled Eurydice's encounter with him in different ways. In an *Ovide Moralisé* woodcut (Fig. 28) we see Eurydice walking in a field as a winged serpent or dragon bites her heel. The painter of an *Ovide Moralisé* miniature (Fig. 31), who worked in the fifteenth century, combines the Ovidian and Virgilian accounts of Eurydice's death. In this miniature we see Eurydice either falling from the bite of the dragon or lying on the grass about to be bitten by it—the artist's handling of perspective making her intended position unclear— while Aristaeus looks on, holding a shepherd's crook. An *Ovide Moralisé* manuscript done about 1375 (Fig. 32) shows Eurydice being bitten by the dragon as she lies—this time unmistakably—asleep beneath a tree, just as Heurodis slept when she was visited by the king of the fairies. A

31. Death of Eurydice, from the *Ovide Moralisé*. B.N. Fr. 871, 196r, c. 1400.

shepherd's crook lies beside her and Aristaeus, dressed as a herder, looks on.

The winged serpents or dragons of these miniatures look more like slightly human dogs than anything else, but the artists, I think, were trying to paint Satan in his popular guise as the draconopede, a medieval man-headed dragon. This beast was a patchwork creature. His winged serpent body came from the being described by Saint John in Revelation as "that old serpent, called the Devil" (12:9) and as "the dragon, that old serpent, which is the Devil, and Satan" (20:2). The development of Saint John's diabolic creature was furthered by a popular hymn, the *Altus Prosator*, attributed to the sixth-century Irish saint Columban. This hymn combines John's references to the great dragon with the story of the serpent-Satan found in

32. Death of Eurydice, from the *Ovide Moralisé*. Lyon Bibl. de la Ville MS 742, 166r, c. 1375.

Genesis. The composite beast which results is: "A great dragon, most abominable, ancient and terrible, who was a slippery serpent, wiser than all of the beasts and the wilder animals of the earth. Falling . . . he drew the third part of the stars with him into the abyss of the infernal regions." (Draco magnus taeterrimus, / terribilis et antiquus, / qui fuit serpens lubricus, / . . . tertiam partem siderum / traxit secum in barathrum / locorum infernalium.)[47]

The manlike head of the draconopede was attached to the dragon's body to help explain away a physiological difficulty in Genesis, namely how the serpent was able to speak to Eve. Rabbinical commentators had surmised that the serpent must have looked like a man. "Before the fall of man," they said, the serpent "was the cleverest of all animals created, and in form it resembled man closely. It stood upright, and was of extraordinary size."[48] The Midrashic commentators explained that part of the serpent's punishment was the loss of its hands and feet, chopped off by the angels after the fall; another part was the loss of its voice. The thirteenth-century encyclopedist Vincent of Beauvais alluded to such explanations when he said that Satan must have appeared to Eve as a draconopede when he tempted her in Eden.[49] The illustrators of the moralized Ovids—who were, after all, illustrating Christian allegorizations of Ovid's fables—would not, I think, have hesitated to draw a draconopede when they wished to show Satan attacking Eurydice. For the author of *Sir Orfeo* it would not be a far step from the man-headed draconopede to the king of the fairies formed as a mortal man.

It seems most probable, then, on the basis of both commentaries on and illustrations of Eurydice, that the *Orfeo* poet had a conception of her which *required* her to be attacked by Satan. As we have seen, there are several similarities between commentary versions of Eurydice's death and the account of Heurodis' abduction in *Sir Orfeo*.

184

Yet there is one serious discrepancy. Eurydice was susceptible to Satan's approach because her nature drew her to *temporalia*. The conduct of Heurodis, however, is blameless, and the poet does not depict her as having an oversensuous nature.[50]

Satan, however, was noted for his lustful character. He and his demons were thought of not only as the tempters, but also as the assailants, of innocent women. Some of the Midrashic commentators held that evil came to man because of Satan's lust. They said that "after the fall of Eve, Satan, in the guise of the serpent, approached her, and the fruit of their union was Cain, the ancestor of all the impious generations that were rebellious towards God."[51] While it is hard to know how widespread this idea of Satan was in the Middle Ages, we do know that Satan's demons were usually thought of as lustful. This view of them originated, I think, with Genesis 6:2 and its commentaries. The passage says, "the sons of God saw the daughters of men that they were fair; and they took them wives of all which they chose." The Church Fathers provided various interpretations of these "sons of God." Some saw them as judges or other high officials, others as the sons of Seth. One of the most popular interpretations in the Middle Ages was that the "sons of God" were angels who came to earth for various reasons. In the apocryphal *Book of Enoch* these angels band together out of lust, take as wives the daughters of men, and teach them forbidden knowledge. The women give birth to giants who turn against mankind, and for their crimes the angels are driven from heaven and become devils.[52] Solomon of Basra, however, denies this: "If the devils were able to have intercourse with women, they would not leave one single virgin undefiled in the whole human race."[53]

According to the *Clementine Homilies*, the angels were sent down by God to help mortal men, but, "They also partook of human lust, and being brought under its subjection they fell into cohabitation with women; and being involved with them, and sunk in defilement and altogether emptied of their first power, were unable to turn back to the first purity of their proper nature."[54] Lactantius explained for the Latin west that these fallen angels became the satellites and attendants of Satan (*Div. Inst.* II, 15). For him, Genesis 6:2 provided an explanation for the pagan gods, or more particularly demigods, who were seen as the spawn of the angels and the "daughters of men." In time, all evil supernatural beings of the Middle Ages came to be thought of as descendants of the fallen angels; some were evil fairies who attacked women, especially those who were so unfortunate as to be caught near trees and bushes. Like their ancestors, the fairies appeared to their victims in human form, ate like human beings, and reproduced as they did.[55] That the fairies were lustful and hunted women around trees was already established by Chaucer's day, for he alludes to such a legend in the *Wife of Bath's Tale*. In King Arthur's time, he says, England was full of fairies, but when Christianity came, and with it the friars, the fairies were driven out. Chaucer hints at fairy attacks on women when he says that "Wommen may go now saufly up and doun./ In every bussh or under every tree/Ther is noon oother incubus but he" (III D 878–880), meaning that the friars have now replaced the fairies as hunters of women. *Incubus* suggested to Chaucer not merely fairy in a general sense, but a fiend taking the shape of a man to tempt or to assault a woman. It is with the full awareness of such a tradition that later the Summoner says: "freres and feendes been but lyte asonder" (III D 1674).

It should be clear by now that the author of *Sir Orfeo* had good precedent for putting Heurodis into the hands of a fairy abductor. The king of the otherworld, both in his satanic and in his fairy aspect, was traditionally a creature with a penchant for fair women. Granting that it may be overingenious to supply, on the basis of tradition alone, a lustful motive for Heurodis' capture, still, evidence for such a motive does appear in the poem. We learn in *Sir Orfeo* that the day was a very hot one when Dame Heurodis took her maidens and "went in an vndrentide/To play bi an orchard-side" (ll. 65–66). A little further on we learn that the Queen grew drowsy and slept under a tree till "after none,/ʒat vnder-tide was al y-done" (ll. 75–76). Heurodis recounts to her husband how she was visited by the fairy king, using the same words, "as ich lay þis vnder-tide" (l. 133), and Orfeo, planning to protect her, takes a large army to the orchard the next day, "Amorwe þe vnder-tide is come" (l. 181). His army is, of course, to no avail, and Heurodis is taken off anyway. The word "vndrentide," however, gives us a clue which, if we follow it a little further into the poem, points directly to the tradition of fairy sensuality which we have been discussing. When Orfeo is living in the woods, he frequently sees supernatural beings:

> He miʒt se him bisides
> (Oft in hot vnder-tides)
> Þe king o fairy wiþ his rout
> Com to hunt him al about
> Wiþ dim cri & bloweing (ll. 281–285).

And when he enters the fairy otherworld, he sees within the castle walls a number of people lying about, all of whom, we are told, had been taken from the land of mortal men "Riʒt as þai slepe her vnder-tides" (l. 402). Among them is Heurodis.

Romances are rarely specific about time and space, and it is odd that the Orfeo poet should repeat the word "vndrentide" so persistently. Even more notable is the fact that all of the fairy king's visits to the land of mortals take place at this time. But to what time of day does the word actually refer? A. J. Bliss, the poem's most recent editor, explains in his glossary that "vndrentide" can mean either morning or noon. The editors of the *OED* assign its use in *Sir Orfeo* to the morning. Yet the word has a shifting meaning in Middle English which can apply to any time of day from about nine o'clock in the morning to three o'clock in the afternoon. I should like to suggest that the abduction of Heurodis by the king of the fairies makes more sense if it takes place at noon, and that with this time we have, in fact, the whole point of her being stolen away at all.

The significance of noon for this poem is that it was a time of danger, traditionally, not only for the Middle Ages, but for antiquity as well. The Psalmist David had written, in Psalm 90: 3–6 (AV, 91), "deliver me from the snare of the hunters . . . from hostile attack and from the noon-day demon [*daemonio meridiano*]." Rabbinical commentators on this verse explain that demons were particularly powerful at noon because the heat of the sun directly overhead rendered man weaker than usual. Here is what the *Midrash* has to say about the noonday demon: "He has no power when it is cool in the shade and hot in the sun, but only when it is hot in both shade and sun."[56] Several Fathers of the Church elaborated on the dangers of noon, warning their audience that *accidia* or spiritual sloth threatens men, particularly cloistered and holy men, at noon.[57]

A popular interpretation of Psalm 90 for the Middle Ages was that of Saint Jerome who said that the noonday demon was Satan.[58] This identification provided grist for many an exegetical mill; for example, Richard of St. Victor explained that by the noonday demon the Psalmist meant not only Satan but all of his demons who "when the heat and light of the day are at their greatest . . . come to us,"[59] eager to carry us off to hell. The idea of Satan as the noonday demon was long-lived; even Milton has Satan tempt Eve at midday.

The utility of this tradition for the *Orfeo* poet must by this time be plain. Even if we take all mention of the time to be merely decorative or coincidental to the poem, still we will be faced with the problem of the fairy hunting parties. For Orfeo, we recall, sees the fairy king and his rout *hunting* during the "hot vnder-tides"; their prey is not specified. As any amateur sportsman would know, the likelihood of their seeing much large game—of the commonly hunted varieties—would be slight after about seven A.M. Deer, for instance, are best hunted in early morning or at twilight when they come out to feed, and not during the hot hours of the day when they retire to inaccessible places to sleep. If, however, the prey were to be men—or women—the hunting parties might expect more success. Carrying this line of argument a step further, we are bound to view the collection of people inside the walls of the fairy castle as the catch of just such hunting trips.

In a commentary on the noonday demon psalm, attributed to Remigius of Auxerre, the author tells us that when David fears the "snare of the hunters," the hunters are to be understood as "the devil and his angels, who always, as though hunting, follow man, to trap him . . . For he arouses his love for and desire of temporal things."[60]

A medieval author such as the *Orfeo* poet need not have been a student of theology to be interested in the idea that the devil appears at noon; he need only have heard of it in a sermon or seen it illustrated in a manuscript, stained glass window, or church carving.[61] It is quite likely, however, that a poet of average education would know the works of Ovid and Boethius with their appended glosses and commentaries describing the concupiscent Eurydice. So if we ask: Could the *Orfeo* poet have known or heard of the authors and traditions I have mentioned? I think the answer is yes. The truth of the matter is, however, that a probable explanation is better than none at all. If we assume that the author did *not* know an allegorical version of the story of Orpheus and Eurydice or the convention of

Satan's noonday appearance, the "vndrentide" abduction of Heurodis remains inexplicable.

While the connection of the fairy king with Satan is made quite pointedly by the author of *Sir Orfeo*, there is little in the poem to suggest that it should be read as a Christian allegory. A number of biblical echoes—for example, the similarities between Saint John the Baptist's and Orfeo's trips to the wilderness—embellish the story, but do not, in my opinion, serve to create any meaningful pattern. On the contrary, *Sir Orfeo* contains a variety of elements from both secular and religious sources, which are blended into an imaginative work of entertainment rather than a tightly woven symbolic scheme imbued with Christian didacticism. This holds true particularly for the otherworld description in the poem, which might appear at first glance to contain pointed allusions to both Virgil's underworld and to the Christian regions of heaven and hell, but which upon closer investigation proves to be quite conventional and to lack a coherent symbolic structure in either pagan or Christian eschatology.

We would, of course, expect that medieval representations of any otherworld would furnish it with a certain number of medieval trappings, as would an illustration of any place distant in time or unknown to the illustrator. In the same way, our contemporary science fiction writers have peopled the planets of distant stars with anthropomorphic creatures who live, eat, and make war in a manner only slightly different from that with which we are familiar. Medieval versions of Paradise, the Virgilian *locus amoenus*, and the Celtic otherworld are, in this respect, predictably similar. But beyond a simple superposition of medieval detail, it should be noted that the land of the fairies in *Sir Orfeo* is neither an afterworld nor an underworld. It is actually a counter world which exists side by side with the world of man. The description of Orfeo's entry into it is unequivocal on this point:

In at a roche þe leuedis rideþ,
& he after, & nouȝt abideþ.
When he was in þe roche y-go
Wele þre mile, oþer mo,
He com in-to a fair cuntray,
As briȝt so sonne on somers day,
Smoþe & plain & al grene
—Hille no dale nas þer non y-sene. (ll. 347–354)

Orfeo follows the ladies through a tunnel or cliff passageway. He does not go down into the bowels of the earth as
Orpheus had in search of Eurydice, but rather to another
land, joined to this one by a mysterious passageway. The
idea that the world of the fairies was another but somehow
parallel land is reinforced by the fact that Heurodis sleeps
under an "ympe-tre" in the fairy world just as she had in
the world of Winchester.

The land of the fairies in *Sir Orfeo*, with its secret
entrance, green plain, jeweled and radiant castle, and unfortunate captives, is based on a variety of conventions
from medieval art and literature. In its existence as a
counter world to that of men and in its method of access it
does remind us of the otherworld of Celtic legend, which
was also located upon the earth rather than deep inside of
it, and was entered by a number of ways, including through
a mist, over water, or—closest to the *Orfeo* story—through
a fairy barrow or mound.[62] There is a description of such
a world in *Yonec*, a lai of Marie de France, in which a lady
in search of her knight goes through a hole in a hill and
comes out on a beautiful plain wherein is a silver-walled
city.[63] The Virgilian underworld, on the other hand, was
entered by a *descensus* through a cave, as we recall from
Aeneas and his sibyl guide.

What Virgil does seem to have contributed to this place
is the conjunction of happy and unhappy elements, and
the presence of Orpheus in a beautiful, supernatural land-

191

scape. In Book VI of the *Aeneid*, after having observed the unhappier shades, Aeneas crosses a "mid-space" and enters the gates of "a land of joy, the green pleasaunces and happy seats of the Blissful Groves. Here an ampler ether clothes the meads with roseate light, and they know their own sun" (637f). Aeneas finds Orpheus playing his lyre to the inhabitants of the Blissful Groves. The shades dance and sing and "the long-robed Thracian priest matches their measures with the seven clear notes, striking them now with his fingers, now with his ivory quill."

The two-part underworld of Virgil was popularized and Christianized in the Middle Ages by works like the *Vision of Tundale,* the *Cento* of Proba, and *Barlaam and Ioasaph.* In the eighth-century account of the vision of Ioasaph by Saint John Damascene, Ioasaph falls asleep after a long prayer and sees himself carried off by certain "dread men"

> and passing through places which he had never heretofore beheld. He stood in a mighty plain, all a-bloom with fresh and fragrant flowers, where he descried all manner of plants of divers colours . . . The leaves of the trees rustled clearly in a gentle breeze, and, as they shook, sent forth a gracious perfume that cloyed not the sense . . . They brought him to a city that glistered with light unspeakable, whose walls were of dazzling gold . . . built of gems such as man hath never seen . . . they crossed that mighty plain, and bare him to regions of darkness and utter woe, where sorrow matched the brightness which he had seen above. There was darkness without a ray of light, and utter gloom, and the whole place was full of tribulation and trouble. There blazed a glowing furnace of fire, and there crept the worm of torment.[64]

This two-part landscape seems clearly to represent the

conjunction of the Virgilian or classical *locus amoenus* with the Christian hell. *Barlaam and Ioasaph* was popular in many languages and may well have been known to the author of *Sir Orfeo*. Certainly the *Orfeo* poet's description of the fairy world contains some interesting parallels to the *Barlaam* vision.

Perhaps the most striking aspect of the fairy landscape in *Sir Orfeo*, however, is what it is *not*—how little resemblance it bears to the classical underworlds in which we have been accustomed to find Orpheus, with the enchanted Cerberus, stalled wheel, and distracted Tantalus. There is only a slight suggestion of any punitive or purgatorial region in the poem. Within the castle wall, Orfeo does find

> . . . folk þat were þider y-brouȝt,
> & þouȝt dede, & nare nouȝt.
> Sum stode wiþ-outen hade,
> & sum non armes nade. (ll. 389–392)

Virgil's underworld has been suggested as a possible source for these people, but the parallels do not hold true in all respects. Aeneas sees a number of people who have died unhappily or in an untimely manner and a number of fierce personifications such as Age, Fear, and Famine. But Deiphobus is the only shade he sees who is mutilated as are the people in *Sir Orfeo*. The other shades appear as simulacra of the people they represent, complete and intact.

In my opinion, the fairy king's threats to Heurodis provide a completely adequate explanation for the mysteriously torn men and women within the walls of his castle. The king had told Heurodis when he returned her to the orchard where he found her that she should be under the same tree the next day and that she would be taken by the fairies to live with them "euer-mo." If she hindered this plan in any way,

193

> . . . to-tore þine limes al,
> þat noþing help þe no schal;
> & bei þou best so to-torn,
> ȝete þou worst wiþ ous y-born. (ll. 171–174)

Presumably Heurodis did not struggle against the fairy
king, perhaps in part because of her identification with a
Eurydice who, as natural prey for Satan, was destined for
a demon world, and in part because of the narrative
requirement that she be eventually restored to the world
of man by Sir Orfeo. But the fairy king may have used
violence on other captives and what he threatened could
actually have transpired in the case of the people Orfeo
finds within the castle walls.

Interestingly, it is with Orfeo's entrance to the counter
world of the fairies that the poem's romance elements come
to overshadow the traditional myth of Orpheus and Eurydice and the late classical and medieval treatments of it
which we have been considering. And once Orfeo frees his
wife and returns to test his steward in Winchester we have
quite left the world of classical antiquity and entered the
world of romance.

Among the many attitudes toward Orpheus we have
seen thus far, two have stood out as notably imaginative
adaptations of the legend to the concerns of medieval men:
the romance tradition, which makes Orpheus a "hero" of
secular literature, and the ethical tradition, which makes
him a moral exemplum for the commentators and mythographers. While these two strains are far from mutually
exclusive and often influence each other, generally one or
the other is predominant in any given work. Thus, in *Sir
Orfeo*, romance conventions were responsible for the
narrative line and numerous local details; a knowledge
of the ethical tradition which saw Eurydice as prey for
Satan helps to illuminate only one important aspect of

the narrative. A near balance of romance and ethical strains has been achieved, however, in one medieval work dealing with Orpheus, the *Orpheus and Eurydice* of Robert Henryson.

This author, perhaps best known for his sequel to Chaucer's *Troilus and Criseyde* called the *Testament of Cresseid*, was a Scotsman, in daily life a schoolmaster of Dunfermline grammar school, and perhaps also a notary public. By the standards of his day Henryson seems to have been well educated. He was referred to by his contemporaries as "Master Robert Henryson," indicating that he may have been the person of that name licentiate in arts and bachelor of canon law incorporated in the University of Glasgow in 1462. Books and the company of learned men would have been available to him in Dunfermline, which was almost a royal city in his time, as we learn from the ballad "Sir Patrick Spens": "The king sat in Dunfermline town,/Drinking his blood-red wine." The town had a large Benedictine Abbey, a royal palace, and a number of important churches, all of which meant scriptoria and other appurtenances of learning.[65] Otherwise, nothing much is known of Henryson's life or circumstances. It is thought that he was born about 1430 and that he died about 1500.[66]

Although his death date brings him well into the period of the English Renaissance, his literary technique, subject matter, and didactic bent mark him as a man with his face turned to the past. He was considerably influenced by Chaucer's poetry, but was of a much more stern and moralistic nature and would no doubt have liked the *Parson's Tale* best of all the stories told on the ride to Canterbury. In certain ways, Henryson is among the last of the truly medieval English writers, and perhaps it is fitting that this book should close with a consideration of his treatment of the Orpheus legend.

I have said that a near balance of romance and ethical

elements was achieved in *Orpheus and Eurydice,* but if the intention of the author were honored, the ethical strain would certainly be the favored one. From the form in which Henryson presents the story it is clear that he wished to use the romance Orpheus as a vehicle for moral lessons; it is to his credit that he did this so well as to produce one of the most charming and memorable portraits of Orpheus to come out of the romance tradition. Henryson begins his poem with a trope in praise of the Greeks for their emulation of their fathers. He then gives a genealogy and describes the birth of "king schir orpheouss,"[67] whose proper upbringing instills in him all of the virtues desirable for a king. Hearing of his "noble fame," the queen of Thrace sends for Orpheus and marries him amid great splendor. Their wedded bliss, however, is short-lived, for Eurydice, fleeing Aristaeus as in the Virgilian version of the story, is bitten by a snake and languishes in a "deidly swoun" until Proserpine, the queen of the fairies, takes her off. Orpheus goes to the woods for a period of mourning, and then up to the heavens in search of his wife. He descends through the spheres, asking in each after Eurydice. Though he does not find her there, he does learn the secrets of celestial harmony and have an opportunity to pay homage to Venus in her sphere. Then he goes to the underworld, overcoming a number of obstacles by his celestial music, and plays before Pluto and Proserpine and a company of historical personages including Hector, Julius Caesar, Croesus, Saul, and Jezebel. Orpheus wins his Eurydice, but there is no happy ending for, unlike his counterpart in *Sir Orfeo,* he loses her again by looking back. He realizes and ponders on the dangers of earthly love, and the poem ends with a *moralitas* of some two hundred lines which is a close paraphrase of Nicholas Trivet's commentary on the Orpheus meter in Boethius.

Even a cursory reading of the narrative reveals the author's indebtedness to romance conventions. Love by reputation, the cause of Queen Eurydice's invitation to Orpheus to be her king, is a common motif in medieval romance. We saw it earlier in the Augsburg lyric in which "for his looks and voice and eloquence, Orpheus alone among all Thracian men was loved uniquely by Eurydice." In Marie de France's lai *Milun,* a girl who has heard of Milun's good looks and chivalry in a like manner falls in love with him sight unseen and sends for him:

> . . . a baron . . . had a beautiful daughter, and she was a most courteous damsel. She had heard Milun mentioned, and she began to love him very much. She sent word to him by her messenger that if it pleased him, she would love him. (ll. 21–28)

> . . . un barun,
>
> . . .
>
> Il aveit une fille bele,
> [E] mut curteise dameisele.
> Ele ot oï Milun nomer;
> Mut le cumençat a amer.
> Par sun message li manda
> Que, si li plest, el l'amera.

When Eurydice meets Orpheus she gives him many "blenkis amorouss" and takes him for her master much as Dorigen took Arveragus for hers in that other tale of courtly yet wedded love, Chaucer's *Franklin's Tale*. Henryson does not elaborate upon their wedding, but devotes a stanza to the growth of their love in the language of *amour courtois*. (Medieval illustrators, however, did not pass up the opportunity to paint the marriage of Orpheus. Two *Ovide Moralisé* manuscripts of the fifteenth century show the wedding feast. In one, Fig. 33, Eurydice is surrounded by revelers, while Hymen, the god of marriage mentioned by Ovid, has become an angel and blesses the gathering from above. In the other, Fig. 34, Eurydice has the same positioning of the hands and the same ornament at her breast; curiously, Orpheus seems one of her attendants, as though

197

he were socially less important—which is, indeed, how Henryson presents him.)

Another romance element in the narrative is the part played by Proserpine. The idea that Proserpine is the queen of the fairies seems to have come directly from Chaucer's *Merchant's Tale,* while the intervention of fairies in the legend at all is of course pure romance— possibly coming to Henryson by way of *Sir Orfeo.* One of Eurydice's waiting women tells Orpheus that her mistress was "with the phary tane befoir my Ene" and that when Eurydice fell into a swoon from the snake bite "the quene of fary / clawcht hir upsone" and took her off. There are, to my knowledge, no other references to Proserpine as queen of the fairies except by Chaucer. The fairy king and queen in *Sir Orfeo* are unnamed.

33. Eurydice and revelers at her marriage feast, from the *Ovide Moralisé*. Lyon Bibl. de la Ville MS 742, 165v, c. 1375.

"The Complaint of Orpheus," which he sings in the wood, is an instance of another romance convention, the intercalated lyric. This *planh* reminds us of some of the complaints in Chaucer's poetry, such as that of the Black Knight in the *Book of the Duchess* or that of Troilus. It is fitted closely, however, to the story at hand, in which Orpheus contemplates becoming a hermit as did Sir Orfeo.

"Fair weill my place, fair weill plesandis and play,
and wylcum woddis wyld and wilsum way,
my wicket werd in wildirness to ware;
my rob ryell, and all my riche array,
changit salbe in rude russet and gray,

34. The marriage of Orpheus and Eurydice, from the *Ovide Moralisé*. B.N. Fr. 871, 196r, c. 1400.

199

my dyademe in till a hate of hair;
my bed salbe with bever, brok, and bair." (ll. 154–160)

Henryson has devoted some care to making the complaint
"poetic," using heavy alliteration and ending each stanza
with the refrain, "quhair art thow gone, my luve euri-
dicess?" The result is a piece which could stand alone as a
secular lyric of the day on the theme of Fortune's mutability.

Orpheus prays to his father, Phoebus, and to his grand-
father, Jupiter, for aid in retrieving his wife, the one god
to lend him light, the other strength for the search. His
petitions have the same ring as those of Palamon and Arcite
in the *Knight's Tale* or those of countless other romance
heroes who turned to a particular god or goddess at the
onset of a trial, making a formal declaration of fealty and
requesting a favor for their service. Arcite, for example,
had called upon Mars:

> "O stronge god, that in the regnes colde
> Of Trace honoured art and lord yholde,
> . . .
> If so be that my youthe may deserve,
> And that my myght be worthy for to serve
> Thy godhede, that I may been oon of thyne,
> Thanne preye I thee to rewe upon my pyne."
>   (I A 2373–2374, 2379–2382)

Orpheus' appeals to Phoebus and Jupiter are almost as
formal, although they are based on a familial and not a
feudal relationship. The appeal to Jupiter, for example,
opens with a similar apostrophe: "O Jupiter, thow god
celestiall,/and grant schir to my self, on the I call" (ll. 174–
175). Later, when Orpheus comes to the sphere of Venus
during his search for Eurydice, he pays homage to the
goddess of love in the traditional manner of the romance
hero and, citing his past service to her, asks for her aid:

Quhen he hir saw, he knelit and said thuss:
"wait ye nocht weill I am your awin trew knycht?
In luve none leler than schir orpheuss;
And ye of luve goddass, and most of micht,
of my lady help me to get a sicht." (ll. 205–209)

His "none truer than Sir Orpheus" refers, perhaps, to the
reputation which we have already seen him acquiring in the
secular literature of the thirteenth and fourteenth centuries.
Certainly his conduct thus far in Henryson's poem con-
forms to his own description. The quest which he under-
takes, through heaven, earth, and hell in search of his lady,
leaves no doubt as to the devotion of Venus' knight.

This quest is, of course, another feature traceable directly
to the romance tradition—perhaps the most important
feature, since it structures the whole poem. Orpheus'
travels to strange and distant places, in which he has
dealings with supernatural beings and must overcome
numerous obstacles before finding that which he seeks,
conform closely to the archetypal romance pattern. Even
his method of countering opposition—that is, with his
music—has been made to fit into the genre by the use of a
simple convention.

In many romances built around a quest, we will recall,
the hero acquires some secret knowledge or magic object
which subsequently aids him in overcoming obstacles
along his way. Lancelot, in search of Guinevere, gets a
magic ring which will protect him from hostile enchant-
ments. Gawain, in his search for the Green Knight, is aided
by a green girdle. Chrétien's Perceval receives a magic
sword from the Fisher King, and a knight in Marie de
France's lai *Les Deus Amanz* is given a vial of potion by
an old woman "who has studied in Salerno." Orpheus, too,
acquires something that will be of use to him in his travels,
namely a knowledge of the music of the spheres, which he
hears on his passage among the planets. This knowledge is

described as very arcane by Henryson, who does not claim to understand it himself[68] ("For in my lyfe I cowth nevir sing a noit"); it includes not only "tonis proportionat, / as duplare, triplare, and emetricus / . . . Epoddeus rycht hard and curius," but also "diatesserone," "dyapasone," and "dyapenty," whose celestial combinations, "Compleit and full of nummeris od and evin, / Is causit be the moving of the hevin" (ll. 233–239). When Orpheus descends to hell, his musical knowledge enables him to overcome in turn Cerberus, the three sisters who guard the bridge, the water in which Tantalus stands, the thorny moor, the vulture on Tityus' belly, and finally Pluto and Proserpine, who grant him his Eurydice. Henryson's description of the winning over of the king and queen of hell quite explicitly credits the feat to Orpheus' use of the celestial music and not merely to general skill on the harp. Orpheus, sitting before Pluto, plays "mony sueit proportioun, / With baiss tonis in Ipotdorica, / With gemilling in yporlerica" (ll. 368–370), until he moves the company to tears and Pluto asks him to name his reward.

The magic of his music, which wins him Eurydice, is not enough, however, to bring her back to the upper world. Orpheus, forgetting the conditions of her return, looks back before they reach the gate. The happy ending which would have rounded out the story's conformation to a romance pattern is thus forfeited; only one more feature from the literature of *fin amor* remains, and that is Orpheus' sorrowful apostrophe to love.

"Quhat art thow, luve, how sall I the defyne?
Bittir and sueit, crewall and merciable,
plesand to sum, to uthir plent and pyne,
Till sum constant, to uthir wariable;
hard is thy law, thy bandis unbrekable;
Quho sservis the, thocht thay be nevir so trew,
Perchance sum tyme thay sall haif causs to rew."

(ll. 401–407)

With this plaint, whose oxymorons force us to consider the dangers of secular love, Henryson ties his fable to the *moralitas*. The didactic side of the poem, till now partially submerged in narrative, here becomes explicit, and the next two hundred lines discuss the story from a purely clerical standpoint, attempting to relate the adventures of the romance hero to the traditional views of the medieval allegorists.

Though the relations between the story and the *moralitas* are uneasy, with the *moralitas* sometimes contradicting the fable itself (for example, the "busteouss hird," Aristaeus, becomes "gud vertew"),[69] it is plain that Henryson meant for them to be taken together and saw them as a unified work. Henryson has prepared for his *moralitas* by a number of didactic asides throughout the poem, as well as by certain details carefully placed in the narrative itself. Even the introduction of his hero is accompanied by a sober observation on the importance of emulating one's forebears as did the Greeks.

One of the first points at which we have a glimpse of the moral issues Henryson associates with his story is the greeting of Orpheus by Queen Eurydice: "Welcum, Lord and lufe, schir orpheuss,/In this provynce ye salbe king and lord!" (ll. 82–83). Given the names and previous literary history of the couple, the fact that Eurydice accepts Orpheus as her lord is of particular importance, for it not only points up Henryson's Christian emphasis on domesticity—celebrating a love within, rather than, as was common in courtly love literature, outside marriage— but also hints at the ethical allegory of the commentators in which the couple are symbols for reason and passion and in which it is proper that Eurydice defer to Orpheus. Later, in the *moralitas,* the author explains Eurydice as "our effectioun," who, though she may find Reason, that is, Orpheus, attractive at one time, will vacillate to other pleasures before long. A prediction of the unhappiness to come follows the description of the couple's wedded bliss:

> . . . allace, quhat sall I say?
> Lyk till a flour that plesandly will spring,
> quhilk fadis sone, and endis with murnyng. (ll. 89–91)

When Orpheus has, indeed, come to mourn the loss of his queen and with her all his pleasure, Henryson is careful to stress the completeness of his devotion and sense of loss. Orpheus' complaint is quite in keeping with the romance view of him as the most faithful of lovers, but, more important for Henryson's purpose, it also reveals a misplaced sense of values. When he sings to his harp, "now weip with me, thy lord and cairfull King,/quhilk lossit hes in erd all his lyking" (ll. 137–138), he is showing for Eurydice a concern which ought rightly, in Henryson's view, to be directed heavenward. In the *moralitas* it is described as

> The perfyte wit, and eik the fervent luve
> We suld haif allway to the hevin abuve;
> Bot seildin thair our appetyte is fundin,
> It is so fast within the body bundin. (ll. 449–452)

Orpheus' journey to the heavens only establishes more clearly what the poet has known all along—that the object of his affections is not there. This celestial journey is of particular interest because it does not, to my knowledge, appear in any other work of literature about Orpheus. The narrative tells us that Orpheus "passit to the hevin, as sayis the fable" (l. 186), but the fable in question seems not to be known to anyone but Henryson himself.

The sources from which Henryson might have taken the idea for such a journey, however, are not far to seek. Ascents of other medieval figures, like Scipio in Macrobius' *Somnium Scipionis* and the narrator in Chaucer's *House of Fame,* provided familiar examples of men who sought wisdom in the heavens.[70] There were, in addition, less familiar ascents in Hermetic literature and in the Old Testament apocrypha. Perhaps the most noteworthy in its similarities to *Orpheus and Eurydice* is James I's *The Kingis Quair,* in which James is carried up through the spheres to the house of Venus and there asks for another sight of the beautiful young lady whom he has fallen in love with but never met. The date of *The Kingis Quair,* 1423, makes it a possible literary influence for Henryson, and a few other similarities between the works of the two authors suggest indebtedness.[71]

Another clue as to the origins of the celestial journey is provided by Henryson's reliance upon the Boethius commentary of Nicholas Trivet in the *moralitas.* It is possible that the physical search undertaken by Orpheus in the narrative was intended as a correlative for the spiritual quest which was referred to earlier in Trivet's commentary. Henryson versifies his source on this subject as follows:

> . . . dounwart we cast our myndis E,
> Blindit with lust, and may nocht upwartis fle;
> Sould our desyre be socht up in the spheiris,
> Quhen it is tedderit in thir warldly breiris,
> Quhyle on the flesch, quhyle on this warldis wrak:
> And to the hevin full small intent we tak.
> Schir orpheus, thow seikis all in vane
> Thy wyfe so he; Thairfoir cum doun agane.
>
> (ll. 453–460)

To interpret the love of Venus' knight as lust, as Trivet has done, transforms the whole journey of Orpheus into one of moral education. The places he visits thus take on symbolic significance—a significance which is in any case not far beneath the surface of the narrative. The heavenly spheres or realms of spirit could not, of course, harbor the object of material desire, while hell would be a most fitting place for her to be found. Hell, moreover, provides telling examples in its unfortunate occupants of other people who have followed their own passions. The reader of the tale, if not Orpheus himself, could not help but be warned by them of the consequences of taking a similar course.

Throughout the narrative Henryson has elaborated on the *de casibus* theme inherent in the myth. We have seen it already in his comment, echoing Job, on the fast-fading pleasures of worldly love, and in the Complaint of Orpheus in which the hero bids farewell to his high position and rich array and looks forward to a rude existence in the woods. At the end of Orpheus' quest we see it again in the poet's description of hell, which is filled with people formerly of high degree. The *moralitas* provides background information on some of the more prominent figures there, including Ixion whose wheel is seen as the ubiquitous wheel of fortune.[72] Many of hell's occupants are former rulers who were, to their disgrace, ruled by their own passions. Included in this villainous company are Hector, Priam, Alexander, Antiochus, Julius Caesar, Herod, Pilate, Croesus, Pharoah, and several popes and cardinals.

Here at last Orpheus finds his Eurydice. She fares as well daily, he is told by Pluto, as Pluto himself or as "king herod for all his chevelry." Herod had been described earlier as "with his brudiris wyfe," and it is interesting that his kind of "chevelry" should thus be linked with Eurydice. As she was not adulterous in the narrative, only her allegorical connection with the concupiscent passions could make such a reference meaningful.

Henryson's handling of Eurydice's condition prepares for a morally effective denouement. After she was bitten by the snake, the venom, going to her heart, had caused her to fall "on a deidly swoun," but not, apparently, to die. When Orpheus sees her again in hell she is "Lene and deidlyk, and peteouss paill of hew," but Pluto explains that she is merely showing the effect of languor: "War scho at hame in hir cuntre of trace,/Scho wald rewert full sone in [fax] and face" (ll. 364–365). Thus, although Eurydice seems to live in hell as a shade, she is not irretrievably dead. Henryson has left the way clear for her return and for a possible happy ending, should her husband prove wise enough to lead her out. The possibility of success makes Orpheus' failure, like that of Adam and Eve who were granted free will, the more serious for being fully within his power to avert.

Trivet had suggested in his commentary that Orpheus' attempt to bring his wife out of Hades could be seen as an attempt to draw his soul through the dangers and temptations of this life up to heaven, and we recall Bernard Silvestris' interpretation of Orpheus' descent by the way of virtue. As Salutati's treatment of the legend showed so well, however, the descent by way of virtue must have as its goal self-knowledge and the ultimate rejection of *temporalia*. When the sage cannot reject pleasure, he has descended by the way of vice. Henryson hints at such a denouement in his gloss on the dark and difficult way through which Orpheus must pass in the underworld.

> This ugly way, this myrk and dully streit,
> Is nocht ellis bot blinding of the spreit,
> With myrk cluddis and myst of Ignorance,
> affetterrit in this warldis vane plesance,
> And bissines of temporalite. (ll. 600–604)

Here, continues Henryson, men stumble on after their affections without the benefit of self-knowledge—as, presumably, Orpheus had done in his eagerness to find Eurydice. The return to the light can only be achieved when "our desyre and fulich appetyte/Bidis leif this warldis full delyte" (ll. 612–613). Orpheus, whom the *moralitas* interprets as our reason, gained control over his

207

own appetites when he played before Pluto, but unfortunately it was only a temporary victory. The difficult return was his undoing. The poet seems to have followed Trivet in this quite literally, shaping his narrative to fit the commentator's text: "Orpheus, that is, the intellect, thought to carry her off by beautiful music which would appease the gods—for by sweet eloquence joined to wisdom one ascends to heaven. Such an ascent was difficult, however, for she must be drawn up through the many delights which impede virtue when it would ascend. Thus Virgil: 'To recall thy steps and pass out to the upper air, this is the task, this is the toil!'" (fol. 101v). Even before Orpheus looked back, the seeds of disaster were sown, for Henryson tells us that as Eurydice and her husband walked away they were "talkand of play and sport," and that Orpheus, "with inwart lufe repleit,/. . . blindit was with grit effectioun" (ll. 385, 387–388). In such a condition he was unlikely to bring his soul up out of the concupiscent realms. His backward glance only manifests more plainly the moral backsliding of which, in Henryson's view, he was already guilty.

Orpheus or "ressoun" returns from hell a widower, but a wiser man. His sorrowful apostrophe to love, though couched in the language of the secular love lyric, shows that he has come to see the danger of earthly affection, and so complements the advice offered in the *moralitas,* that we should turn our thoughts heavenward.

Henryson's poem is in many ways the historical and logically inevitable outcome of the various reshapings of the Orpheus myth which we have observed in the eighteen centuries which lay between it and the *Testament.* His story of "king schir orpheouss" employs almost all of the postclassical changes wrought upon the myth. We have noted that in the *Testament* and in the remarks about Orpheus made by the religious controversialists who employed it, Orpheus acquired his knowledge of philosophy and cosmology as a pupil of Moses and that he himself denied the power of the pagan gods and taught monotheism to his son Musaeus. It is perhaps coincidental that Henryson should begin his poem with an elaborate genealogical discussion of the exemplary powers fathers have for sons and teachers for pupils. But Orpheus' rejection of the pagan deities does appear as the poem develops, for the gods are shown as powerless to aid the hero. Orpheus questions each planetary deity in turn as to Eurydice's whereabouts, and "thair gat he knawlege none" (l. 214). Indeed, his understanding of cosmic harmony comes to him not by the agency of those deities but as a result of his own observations during his journey through the somewhat Boethian heaven.

In the age of Constantine the *Testament* and the conditions which created the need for such a work were no longer relevant, and late antiquity produced its own adaptations of the Orpheus legend. The thought of late antiquity, as we have noted, had shifted its interest from the classical Hades to a Neoplatonic and Christian home for the soul in the heavens, and it is in this period that Orpheus makes his first ascent to the stars. Especially in the syncretistic art of the era he came to be connected with Christ because both figures were believed to guide the souls of men to a celestial home. Henryson employs both the classical and the postclassical journey in his poem. His Orpheus goes first to the heavens and then down to hell to seek moral knowledge and find his queen.

Eurydice was, of course, superfluous for Orpheus the monotheist and psychopomp, and she only rejoins her lover in the Middle Ages, in the commentaries on Boethius and Ovid. From the Middle Ages to our own day, Orpheus' love for Eurydice has been one of the most familiar elements of the legend. We should not forget, however, that for nearly a thousand years previous, writers and artists treating the myth of Orpheus had tended to keep the two apart. Even in the commentaries where we at last encounter Orpheus and Eurydice together, it is more as the abstractions of reason and passion than as true and tragic lovers. Medieval miniaturists, however, found it too difficult—or less interesting—to represent them thus, and in depicting them as lovers contributed richly to their iconography. Henryson shows us Orpheus and Eurydice both as abstractions and as people by the device of following his narrative with an allegorical commentary. Thus are balanced the tender "blenkis amorouss" and a denunciation of Eurydice as our dangerous "effectioun."

The key to a myth's vigor is its adaptability. The greatest myths of Western culture have been able to express the intensely felt but not always articulate interests of many ages, gaining additional resonance with each new adaptation. That the story of Orpheus was of vital interest and great use to many men we have seen in our review of its progress from the Hellenic age down to the end of the Middle Ages. Indeed, its viability and power to fire the imaginations of men did not stop with Henryson, but continued into the Renaissance and on down to the present day. But that is a subject for another book.

Notes
Index

Abbreviations

AJA   *American Journal of Archaeology*
Anal. Hymn.   *Analecta Hymnica Medii Aevi*
ANF   *The Ante-Nicene Fathers*
CIG   *Corpus Inscriptionum Graecarum*
CIL   *Corpus Inscriptionum Latinarum*
CR   *Classical Review*
EETS: ES   Early English Text Society: Extra Series
EETS: OS   Early English Text Society: Original Series
FGrH   *Fragmente der griechischen Historiker*
HTR   *Harvard Theological Review*
JEGP   *Journal of English and Germanic Philology*
JRS   *Journal of Roman Studies*
JTS   *Journal of Theological Studies*
JWCI   *Journal of the Warburg and Courtauld Institutes*
MLQ   *Modern Language Quarterly*
PBA   *Proceedings of the British Academy*
PG   *Patrologiae Cursus Completus: Series Graeca*
PGM   *Papyri Graecae Magicae*
PL   *Patrologiae Cursus Completus: Series Latina*
PNF   *The Post-Nicene Fathers*
PQ   *Philological Quarterly*
RES   *Review of English Studies*
RHR   *Revue de l'histoire des religions*
TAPA   *Transactions of the American Philological Association*

Notes

Chapter I

1. See Jane Harrison, *Prolegomena to the Study of Greek Religion* (Cambridge, Engl., 1903); Erwin Rohde, *Psyche* (London, 1925); André Boulanger, *Orphée* (Paris, 1925); V. D. Macchioro, *From Orpheus to Paul* (New York, 1930); R. S. Conway, "From Orpheus to Cicero," *Bulletin of the John Rylands Library*, 17 (1933): 67–89; M. P. Nilsson, "Early Orphism and Kindred Religious Movements," *HTR*, 28 (1935): 181f; I. Linforth, *The Arts of Orpheus* (Berkeley, 1941); D. P. Walker, "Orpheus the Theologian and Renaissance Platonists," *JWCI*, 16 (1953): 100–120; Edgar Wind, *Pagan Mysteries in the Renaissance* (London, 1958), ch. IV; and K. Ziegler, "Orpheus" and "Orphische Dichtung" in A. Pauly and G. Wissowa, *Real-Encyclopädie der classischen Altertumswissenschaft* (Stuttgart, 1893–1962), XVIII, 1.

2. For example, I have not discussed here the well-known Orpheus-David fresco from the synagogue at Dura-Europos because it appears to be something of a sport in the Orpheus tradition and does not seem to have had appreciable influence on later developments of the myth in the west. Henri Stern, "The Orpheus in the Synagogue of Dura-Europos," *JWCI*, 21 (1958): 1–6, gives a summary of the various interpretations of the fresco's meaning, though the reader should consult E. R. Goodenough, *Jewish Symbols in the Greco-Roman Period* (New York, 1956), V, i, and André Grabar, *L'Art de la fin de l'antiquité et du Moyen Age* (Paris, 1968), II, 705–706, for a full discussion of the painting.

3. Jean Seznec, *The Survival of the Pagan Gods* (New York, 1953), pp. 46f.

4. Charles G. Osgood, *Boccaccio on Poetry* (New York, 1956), p. xxiii.

5. *Pindari Carmina*, ed. Otto Schroeder (Leipzig, 1914), Fr. 139, 1. 10, and *Pyth*. IV, 177–179. The latter reference is ambiguous. Asclepiades of Tragilus in his scholia on Pindar weighs the question of Orpheus' parents at some length. He is reported to have held that Orpheus was "the son of Apollo, Orpheus whom both Pindar himself and others say to be the son of Oeagrus." *FGrH*, IA-a, 12, 168, 6a.

6. Simonides, Victory Songs, 51, in J. M. Edmonds, ed. and tr. *Lyra Graeca* (Loeb Library ed., Cambridge, Mass., 1952), II, 311; Euripides, *Hypsipyle*, in *Greek Literary Papyri*, ed. and tr. D. L. Page (Loeb Library ed., Cambridge, Mass., 1952), I, 87; Apollonius Rhodius, *Argonautica*, ed. and tr. R. C. Seaton (Loeb Library ed., Cambridge, Mass., 1961), I, 494f, 540f, 915; II, 685; IV, 905.

7. *The Greek Anthology*, ed. and tr. W. R. Paton (Loeb Library ed., Cambridge, Mass., 1919), VII, 9, II, p. 9.

8. References and discussion may be found in H. Weir Smyth, ed. and tr., *Aeschylus* (Loeb Library ed., Cambridge, Mass., 1936), II, 386–387.

9. Herodotus, II, 81; Euripides, *Hippolytus* 952; Plato, *Laws* VI, 782.

10. The standard text is that of Otto Kern, ed., *Orphicorum Fragmenta* (Berlin, 1922, reprinted 1963).

11. *Alcestis*, in *Euripides*, ed. and tr. A. S. Way (Loeb Library ed., London and New York, 1920), IV, 966; *Protagoras* 316.

12. Alcidamas, 24, in F. Blass, ed., *Antiphontis Orationes et Fragmenta* (Leipzig, 1871), pp. 182–183. Damagetus, in *The Greek Anthology*, VII, 9, vol. II, p. 9.

13. *Met.* XI, 1–66; *G.* IV, 467–506.

14. *Alcestis*, tr. Way, IV, 357–359.

15. *Isocrates*, ed. and tr. G. Norlin and LaRue Van Hook (Loeb Library ed., Cambridge, Mass., 1961), vol. III, xi, 8, p. 107. Isocrates uses the imperfect verb and plural object to suggest that Orpheus was accustomed to bring the dead from Hades.

16. Moschus, "The Lament for Bion," in *Greek Bucolic Poets*, ed. and tr. J. M. Edmonds (Loeb Library ed., Cambridge, Mass., 1960), III, 124, p. 454.

17. See J. D. Beazley, *Attic Red-Figure Vase Painters* (Oxford, 1963).

18. Isocrates, *Or.* XI, 39, ed. Norlin and Van Hook, III, p. 125.

19. Hyginus, *Poet. Astr.* II, viii, in Mary Grant, tr., *The Myths of Hyginus* (Lawrence, Kansas, 1960), p. 192.

20. Phanocles in J. U. Powell, ed., *Collectanea Alexandrina* (Oxford, 1925), pp. 106–107, ll. 1–10.

21. Ovid, *Met.* X, 83–84.

22. Phanocles, *Collectanea*, p. 107, ll. 23–28.

23. *The Life of Apollonius of Tyana*, ed. and tr. F. C. Conybeare (Loeb Library ed., Cambridge, Mass., 1960), IV, 14, p. 375.

24. Pseudo-Eratosthenes, *Catasterismi*, in A. Olivieri, ed., *Mythographi Graeci* (Leipzig, 1897), III, 28–29.

Chapter II

1. The term was commonly used in the titles of pseudepigrapha, for example, *The Testament of the Twelve Patriarchs*, in the old lists of apocrypha. See R. H. Charles, ed., *The Apocrypha and Pseudepigrapha of the Old Testament* (Oxford, 1913), II, 407.

2. E. H. Gifford, ed., *Eusebii Pamphili Evangelicae Praeparationis Libri XV* (Oxford, 1903), vol. II, bk. XIII, 12, pp. 259–260. A similar but shorter and more Hellenized text is to be found in pseudo-Justin, *De Mon.* 2 and *Coh. ad Gent.* 15. See also Clement of Alexandria, *Stromata* V, xiv, 123.

3. On the editing of Aristobulus' text see the discussions of the *Testament* by E. R. Goodenough, *By Light, Light: the Mystic Gospel of Hellenistic Judaism* (New Haven, 1935), pp. 278–281, and L. Cerfaux, "Influence des mystères sur le Judaïsme Alexandrin avant Philon," *Muséon*, 37 (1924): 36–48.

4. For an admirable discussion of Alexandrian Judaism, see Victor Tcherikover, *Hellenistic Civilization and the Jews*, tr. S. Applebaum (Philadelphia, 1959), ch. II, especially pp. 346–350.

5. See Josephus, *Contra Apionem* I, 27.

6. Philo, *Conf.* 129 and *Abr.* 230.

7. Jewish historians are discussed by R. H. Pfeiffer, *History of New Testament Times* (New York, 1949), pp. 200–210.

8. Quoted by Eusebius, *Praep. Evang.* IX, 26, *PG* 21, 728. For information on the various Jewish authors associated with the name Eupolemus, see Ben Zion Wacholder, "Pseudo-Eupolemus' Two Greek Fragments on the Life of Abraham," *Hebrew Union College Annual*, 34 (1963): 83–113.

9. Quoted by Eusebius, *Praep. Evang.* IX, 27, *PG* 21, 729.

10. Fragments from Theodotus' work are preserved by Eusebius, *Praep. Evang.* IX, 22, *PG* 21, 721, 724–725. Parts of the tragedy are quoted by Eusebius, *Praep. Evang.* IX, 28, *PG* 21, 736–737.

11. Seder 'Olam Zuta, XXX, in A. Neubauer ed., *Mediaeval Jewish Chronicles* (Anecdota Oxoniensia: Semitic Series, Oxford, 1895), vol. II.

12. See D. S. Russell, *The Method and Message of Jewish Apocalyptic* (Philadelphia, 1964), pp. 73–103.

13. Moses Hadas, *Aristeas to Philocrates* (New York, 1951), p. 60.

14. Ed. Charles, *The Apocrypha*, III, 419–424. Greek text in J. Geffcken, ed., *Die Oracula Sibyllina* (Leipzig, 1902, reprinted, 1967), p. 70.

15. Tr. R. H. Charles (London, 1962), LXXXII.1, p. 109.

16. *Mathesis,* ed. Wilhelm Kroll (Leipzig, 1897), Proem to Book IV, 5, p. 196.

17. *Historiarum Compendium, PG* 121, 180.

18. Abraham's monotheism is related to his being the first astronomer, for he learned that there was one God from the heavenly bodies, according to Josephus, *Jewish Antiquities* I, 156. He also fits well into the *Testament* as an authority because like Moses he gave scientific learning, astronomy in particular, to the Egyptians. See *ibid.,* I, 167.

19. See *Enoch* 92 : 1–5, and the *Book of Jubilees* 31 : 4–22, for examples. The device is discussed by J. Munck, "Discours d'adieu dans le Nouveau Testament et dans la littérature biblique," in *Mélanges offerts à M. Maurice Goguel* (Paris, 1950), p. 157. The tradition of secret wisdom transmitted from father to son is discussed by A. J. Festugière, *La Révélation d'Hermès Trismégiste* (Paris, 1949–1954), I, 332–354, with a wealth of examples.

20. One possible source would be the work of Alexander Polyhistor (*FGrH,* III A, no. 273, fr. 19, pp. 100–102), which presented Jewish history and beliefs to the gentiles.

21. See Diodorus Siculus, I, 23, 96; IV, 25.

22. An interesting example of this technique may be found in the apologetic work *Aristeas to Philocrates,* where the Jewish author masquerades as a Greek and explains to Ptolemy Philadelphus that he should release his Jewish slaves on religious grounds. "Release those who are afflicted in wretchedness, for the same God who has given them their law guides your kingdom also, as I have learned in my researches. God, the overseer and creator of all things, whom they worship, is He whom all men worship, and we too, Your Majesty, though we address Him differently, as Zeus and Dis." Tr. Hadas, *Aristeas to Philocrates,* 18, pp. 101–103. On this curious work, see V. Tcherikover, "The Ideology of the Letter of Aristeas," *HTR,* 51 (1958): 59–85.

23. H. A. Wolfson, *Philo* (Cambridge, Mass., 1947), I, 15n.

24. Philo does the same thing when, speaking of the hardships the Jews endured in Egypt, he says that Pharoah "showed no shame or fear of the God of liberty and hospitality . . . to guests and suppliants" (*Mos.* I, 36). The epithets Philo applied to Jehovah, $\dot{\epsilon}\lambda\epsilon\upsilon\theta\acute{\epsilon}\rho\iota o\varsigma$ and $\xi\acute{\epsilon}\nu\iota o\varsigma$, were the traditional property of Zeus. W. W. Tarn, *Hellenistic Civilization* (Cleveland, 1963), p. 225, gives some other examples of Jehovah's assimilation of Zeus.

25. Zeus controls the wind in *Od.* V, 303–305, and in a magical papyrus he controls both winds and waters as he does in the *Testament.* See Karl Preisendanz, ed., *Papyri Graecae Magicae* (Leipzig, 1931), XII, 254f.

26. Hesiod, *Theogony* 776–779, in H. G. Evelyn-White, ed. and tr.,

Hesiod, the Homeric Hymns and Homerica (Loeb Library ed., Cambridge, Mass., 1950), p. 135.

27. The pseudo-Phocylides, an unknown Jew of the first century B.C. who took the name of Phocylides of Miletus, must be excluded here because he is not really an apologist or propagandist for Judaism to the gentiles but rather a moralist.

28. Milton S. Terry, tr., *The Sibylline Oracles* (New York, 1890), p. 25. Greek text from J. Geffcken, ed., *Die Oracula Sibyllina*, pp. 227–228. For an analysis of the verbal similarities between the Proem and the *Testament*, see Goodenough, *By Light, Light*, pp. 283–284.

29. Both Orpheus and the Sibyl seem indebted here to Plato, *Laws* IV, 715e, 716a.

30. Terry, p. 27, and Geffcken, p. 231.

31. These phrases are taken directly from Hesiod, *Theogony*, 225–227.

32. Bard Thompson, "Patristic Use of the Sibylline Oracles," *Review of Religion*, 16 (1952): 125.

33. See Arnaldo Momigliano, "Pagan and Christian Historiography in the Fourth Century A.D.," in A. Momigliano, ed., *The Conflict between Paganism and Christianity in the Fourth Century* (Oxford, 1963), pp. 79–99.

34. *Stromata* II, i, *ANF*, p. 347.

35. *Ad Gr.* XL, XLI, *ANF*, p. 81.

36. *Ad Autol.* II, 30, *ANF*, p. 106.

37. *Ad Autol.* III, 17, *ANF*, p. 116.

38. For the development of Alexandrian allegory generally, see Jean Pépin, *Mythe et Allégorie* (Paris, 1958), pp. 266f. For Jewish interpretations of Homer and Hesiod, see Aristobulus in Eusebius, *Praep. Evang.* XIII, 12, *PG* 21, 1104.

39. *Ad Autol.* III, 2, *ANF*, p. 111.

40. *Stromata* I, xv, *ANF*, p. 315.

41. *Stromata* V, xii, *ANF*, p. 463.

42. *Stromata* V, iv, *ANF*, pp. 449–450.

43. *Inferno*, IV, 132, 134–135, 140, in *Le Opere di Dante*, ed. M. Barbi (Florence, 1960), p. 458. Some of the early commentators on Dante elaborated on this aspect of Orpheus' character. Glossing the reference to Orpheus in *Inferno*, IV, 140, Benvenuto da Imola explains to the reader that Orpheus "fuit magnus poeta theologus, de quo facit mentionem Philosophus primo de anima." *Comentum super Dantis Aldigherij Comoediam*, eds. G. W. Vernon and J. P. Lacaita (Florence, 1887), I, 175.

44. *Stromata* I, xxii, *ANF*, pp. 334–335.

45. *Stromata* I, xvi, *ANF*, p. 318.

46. *De praescriptione haereticorum* vii, *PL* 2, 23.

47. *Gr. Cur Aff.* II, *PG* 83, 840.

48. *Gr. Cur Aff.* II, *PG* 83, 841, 836.

49. *Contra Faustum* XIII, 15, *PNF*, p. 205.

Chapter III

1. Mithraism, for example, discriminated against women and the poor. See A. D. Nock, *Conversion* (Oxford, 1965), pp. 61, 70, 75.

2. Prudentius, *Apotheosis,* in H. J. Thompson, ed. and tr., *Prudentius* (Loeb Library ed., London and Cambridge, Mass., 1949), I, 402–403.

3. On the question of the gradually relaxing strictures against animal and human images in Jewish art of the third and fourth centuries after Christ, see the excellent discussion by Marcel Simon, *Verus Israel* (Paris, 1948), pp. 34–44.

4. See Kurt Weitzmann, "The Survival of Mythological Representations in Early Christian and Byzantine Art," *Dumbarton Oaks Papers,* 14 (1960): 43–68, for a fine discussion of classical types and classical poses as they were used by Christian artists. The scallop shell of Roman funerary art reappears in a sixth-century limestone niche holding a cross of resurrection, surrounded by a garland. Cairo Museum, published by Murad Kamil, *Coptic Egypt* (Cairo, 1968), p. 98.

5. For a handlist of such mosaics, see Henri Stern, "La Mosaïque d'Orphée de Blanzy-les-Fismes," *Gallia,* 13 (1955): 41–77.

6. I have enlarged slightly upon the figure given by C. Hopkins and P. V. C. Baur, *The Christian Church at Dura-Europos* (New Haven, 1934), p. 12f.

7. There are over eighty of these figures extant, according to the study of the kriophorus type by A. Veyries, *Les Figures criophores dans l'art . . . gréco-romain et l'art chrétien* (Paris, 1884). It is even possible that the parable of the Good Shepherd may owe something to the legend of the kriophorus. Among the various legends of animal-bearing gods is the one cited by Pausanias (IX, 22) in which Hermes averted plague from the city by carrying a ram on his shoulders. Thus in at least one tradition the figure of Hermes-kriophorus was a savior figure. So too, the name of the Good Shepherd himself is not entirely free from pagan elements. In I Peter 5:4 Christ is called the ἀρχιποίμην or "chief shepherd." A somewhat similar epithet was used for priests in the worship of Bacchus at Rome, where the priest was called Archibucolus Dei Liberi or chief herdsman of the god Liber (*CIL* VI, 504, 510, and 1675).

8. See Fritz Saxl, *Mithras* (Berlin, 1931), pl. XXVIII, 143, XXXIV, 193.

9. Ludovico Antonio Muratori, *Liturgia Romana Vetus* (Venice, 1748), I, 751, and Origen, *Hom. in Gen.* IX, 3, *PG* 12, 214.

10. See Doro Levi, *Antioch Mosaic Pavements* (Princeton, 1947), I, 362.

11. Xenophon, *Anabasis,* ed. E. Marchant (Oxford, 1947), I, ii, 7.

12. *PG* 31, 1641.

13. There is no certain evidence as to why the peacock was taken as a symbol of immortality. The notion probably is related to the story in Pliny *HN* X, xxii, 44, of how the bird shed his plumage every winter

and renewed it in the spring, and to St. Augustine's observation, *Civ. Dei* XXI, 4, that the peacock's flesh did not decay. Tertullian, *De An.* 33, and *De carnis resurrectione* V follows the story of Homer's metamorphosis in the guise of a peacock given by the Latin poet Ennius. The bird "cauda sidera portat" in Ovid *Met.* XV, 385. In the Vatican Museum, a peacock on a bust of Pomponia Helpis symbolizes her apotheosis. See Franz Cumont, *Etudes syriénnes* (Paris, 1917), 84–87 and fig. 38.

14. Published and discussed by Antonio Ferrua, S.J., in "Lavori e scoperte nelle catacombe," *Triplice omaggio a SS Pio XII* (Vatican City, 1958), pp. 49–64, pl. xvib. The story of the fresco's discovery is given on p. 55.

15. See André Grabar, *L'Empereur dans l'art byzantin* (Paris, 1936), pp. 24, 197, for a discussion of frontality.

16. For the dove in pagan antiquity, see D'Arcy Wentworth Thompson, *A Glossary of Greek Birds* (Oxford, 1936), pp. 238–247, and in Christian antiquity, see J.-P. Kirsch, "Colombe" in F. Cabrol and H. Leclercq, *Dictionnaire d'archéologie chrétienne et de liturgie* (Paris, 1914), III, 2, 2198–2231.

17. Eventually the dove was to become a symbol for the contemplative as opposed to the active life. In the fourteenth-century bestiary B.N. Fr. MS 12483, published by G. Raynaud as "Poème moralisé sur les propriétés des choses," *Romania*, 14 (1885), XLIV "Coulon," the bird "De nature est meditative," p. 480. A thirteenth-century *Liber Avium* in Vienna, Wald. MS 18(226), fol. 129v, depicts the active and contemplative lives. A man labeled "clericus" reads a book, and above his head sits a dove, while "miles" rides a horse, and above his head is a hawk. The dove as a symbol of simplicity and innocence occurs in St. Ambrose, *Sermo Contra Auxentium* XXI, *PL* 16, 1013.

18. *De Mysteriis* III, xi, *PL* 16, 392. *Expositio Evangeli Secundum Lucam* II, 92, *PL* XV, 1587.

19. Maximus of Turin, Sermo XCIV [*Corpus Christianorum*, XLIX, 3], *PL* 57, 722, and Sermo XI [*Corpus Christianorum*, LXIV, 2], *PL* 57, 655–656.

20. This story is told by Eusebius, *The Ecclesiastical History* VI, 29.

21. *Vita S. Gregorii Magni, PL* 75, 58.

22. See Franz Cumont, *Recherches sur le symbolisme funéraire des Romains* (Paris, 1942) and E. R. Goodenough, *Jewish Symbols in the Greco-Roman Period* (New York, 1956), V, 121–142. See also M. Meurdrac and L. Albanèse, "A Travers les nécropoles gréco-romaines de Sidon," *Bulletin du Musée de Beyrouth*, 2 (1938): 79–81, and S. Ronzevalle, "L'Aigle funéraire en Syrie," *Mélanges de la faculté orientale de Beyrouth*, 5.2 (1912): 1–62. For the eagle in Christian art see J.-P. Kirsch, "L'Aigle sur les monuments figurés de l'antiquité chrétienne," *Bulletin d'ancienne littérature et d'archéologie chrétienne*, 3 (1913): 112–126, and, more generally, T. Schneider and E. Stemplinger,

"Adler," in Theodor Klauser, ed., *Reallexikon für Antike und Christentum* (Stuttgart, 1950–) I, 87–94.

23. Louis Ginzberg, *The Legends of the Jews* (Philadelphia, 1911–1967), IV, 149f.

24. Charles, *The Apocrypha,* II, 422.

25. Artemidorus, *Onirocriticon Libri V,* ed. R. A. Pack (Leipzig, 1963), II, xx.

26. *Herodiani Historiarum Libri Octo,* ed. K. Stavenhagen (Leipzig, 1922, reprinted 1967), IV, 2, xi. See also Dio Cassius, LVI, 42, and LXXV, 5. Synesius used the word πτέρωσις to describe the soul, *PG* 66, 1293.

27. Department of East Christian and Byzantine Antiquities accession no. 1790. For description, see O. M. Dalton, *Catalogue of Early Christian Antiquities in the British Museum* (London, 1901), p. 165.

28. Published by J. Clédat, *Le Monastère et la nécropole de Baouît* (Cairo, 1916), II, i, pl. ix.

29. See Hubert Schrade, "Zur Ikonographie der Himmelfahrt Christi," *Vorträge der Bibliothek Warburg,* 1928–1929, pp. 161–163.

30. *PL* 17, 695 [718]. On this sermon, see E. Dekkers, *Clavis Patrum Latinorum* (Sacris Erudiri 32; Steenbrugge, 1961), no. 555.

31. *Protrep.* I, *ANF,* pp. 171–172.

32. His suspicion of the historicity of Orpheus' fabulous deeds Clement shares with earlier pagan interpreters of the story such as Horace and Quintilian, who also could not believe that Orpheus had really made the stones respond to music or tamed savage beasts. Instead they rationalized the legend to mean that he was simply an extraordinary *man* who served as a civilizing force and peacemaker among the savage tribes of Odrysia. See Horace, *Ars P.* 391, and Quintilian, *Inst.* I, 10. 9.

33. 14, *PNF,* p. 603.

34. See, for example, the Easter hymn "Morte Christi Celebrata," a few verses of which deal with the way in which Christ saved the church from the underworld and so became "Noster Orpheus," *Anal. Hymn.* VIII, 33. See also I, 115, 91. For a list of pagan figures in medieval hymns, see Joseph Szövérffy, "Klassische Anspielungen und antike Elemente in mittelalterlichen Hymnen," *Archiv für Kulturgeschichte,* 46 (1962): 152, and the same author's *Die Annalen der lateinischen Hymnendichtung* (Berlin, 1964–65), II, 18, for a discussion of the "Morte Christi Celebrata" hymn.

35. *PNF,* Hymn XXXVI, stanzas 5, 11, pp. 196–197.

36. Photograph in O. Wulff, *Altchristliche Bildwerke* (Berlin, 1909), LVI, 1146. I am greatly indebted to Professor Klaus Heitmann of the University of Marburg for his kindness in obtaining for me information from the East Berlin Staatliche Museen about the fate of this gem.

37. F. C. Grant, *Hellenistic Religions* (New York, 1953), *Anth.* V, ix, 2, pp. 60–61.

38. *Conversion,* p. 101.

39. *De Myst.* IV, 2, tr. Grant, *Hellenistic Religions,* p. 177.

40. This point is discussed by A. A. Barb, "The Survival of Magic Arts," in Momigliano, ed., *Paganism and Christianity,* p. 101.

41. Tr. H. I. Bell et al., "Magical Texts from a Bilingual Papyrus," *PBA,* 17 (1931): 255.

42. Barb, "Survival," p. 102.

43. Campbell Bonner, *Studies in Magical Amulets* (Ann Arbor, 1950), p. 7.

44. *PGM* IV, 3007–3085. There are seven references to Christ by name and more by attribute in the index to this collection.

45. Saxl, *Mithras,* p. 3, pl. I, 5.

46. A. A. Barb, "Three Elusive Amulets," *JWCI,* 27 (1964): 1–22, discusses Horus as a type of Christ.

47. F. C. Burkitt, *Church and Gnosis* (Cambridge, Engl., 1932), pp. 36f., deals with Sabaoth in Gnostic cosmologies. A bronze nail in the British Museum bears an inscription almost evenly divided between magical and Hebrew names of power. It reads "Abaraxas Astra El Iao Sabao Solomono," and is accompanied by a drawing of the Uroboros or self-devouring serpent. See H. B. Walters, *Catalogue of the Bronzes in the British Museum* (London, 1899), 370, no. 3192. The name Sabaoth has survived into our own day as a synonym for God in Martin Luther's chorale, "A Mighty Fortress is our God" (Ein' feste Burg), written in 1529 and adapted as a kind of battle hymn of the Reformation. It has remained one of the most popular of Protestant hymns. Its English version (tr. F. H. Hedge, 1853) contains the lines "Lord Sabaoth His Name, / From age to age the same, / And He must win the battle."

48. Cited in Bonner, *Studies in Magical Amulets,* p. 102.

49. See the Christian sarcophagi reproduced in J. Toutain, "Les Symboles astraux sur les monuments funéraires de l'Afrique du Nord," *Revue des études anciennes,* 13 (1911): 165–175. One is from Altava in Caesarea, the other from Ain Beida, pp. 167, 169.

50. See G. Michaïlidès, to whose article "Vestiges du culte solaire parmi les Chrétiens d'Egypte," *Bulletin de la Société d'Archéologie Copte,* 13 (1948–49): 37–110, I am much indebted for information on solar religion in this period.

51. *The Excavations at Dura-Europos, Preliminary Report of the Sixth Season* (New Haven, 1936), pl. XXXII.

52. *CIG* IV, 9727.

53. See A. B. Cook, *Zeus* (Cambridge, Engl., 1914–40), I, 178f. So too, many early Christians took literally Clement's metaphoric statement about Christ, "Christ [is] the Sun of the Resurrection . . . [who] with His beams bestows life" (*Protr.* 9, *ANF,* p. 196), and worshiped the sun as an aspect of Christ. Such are the people of whom Eusebius of Alexandria speaks. "For I have known of many who adore and pray to the sun; I know that they implore the rising sun and that they say 'have pity

on us,' and not only the Heliognostics and heretics do this, but the Christians as well, who, abandoning their faith, mingle with the heretics" (*PG* 86, 453). In an anathema against heretics, the speaker says, "I curse those who say that Christ is the sun and those who pray to the sun" (ἀναθεματίζω τοὺς τὸν Χριστὸν λέγοντας εἶναι τὸν ἥλιον καὶ εὐχομένους τῷ ἡλίῳ). J. B. Cotelerius, *Patrum Qui Temporibus Apostolicis Floruerunt Opera* (Antwerp, 1698), I, 538. Festugière, *La Révélation*, I, 299, offers two examples of these prayers to the sun.

54. *De Vita Pythagorica* 18, 2.

55. *HN* II, 24, 95.

56. *De Gen.* 590–592, 22.

57. Ernst Diehl, ed., *Inscriptiones Latinae Christianae Veteres* (Berlin, 1961), p. 326, Milan, 524 A.D. The text is probably defective, especially in line four. Consequently, the English is an approximate paraphrase.

58. Sermo CCXL 4, *PL* 38, 1132.

59. *Moral. in Job* XVII, 16, *PL* 76, 21.

60. *Poimandres* I, 25–26a, in Walter Scott, ed., and tr., *Hermetica* (Oxford, 1924), I, p. 129.

61. See the interesting recipe for immortality printed by Festugière, *La Révélation*, I, 303, which invokes the power of Helios-Mithras.

62. *Contra Celsum* VI, 22, *ANF*, p. 583.

63. This idea exists in the modern Mandaean liturgy. The soul, by means of a sacred letter worn around its neck, escapes the seven astral purgatories (*mataraiia*) and flies to the Gate of Life. See E. S. Drower, ed. and tr., *The Canonical Prayer Book of the Mandaeans* (Leyden, 1959), pp. 62–63.

64. M. R. James, tr., *The Apocryphal New Testament* (Oxford, 1955), p. 12.

65. A. Delatte, "Etudes sur la magie grecque," *Musée Belge: Revue de philologie classique,* 18 (1914): 14.

66. *De Antr. Nymph.* 13.

67. One of them, from Petelia, begins: "In the house of Hades, at the left hand, you will find a spring/And, just a few steps beyond it, a single white cypress." Tr. Grant, *Hellenistic Religions*, p. 108.

68. For detailed description and early bibliography, see F. Cabrol and H. Leclercq, *Dictionnaire d'archéologie chrétienne et de liturgie* (Paris, 1936), XII, 2740–2746. I follow the dating of M. Avi-Yonah, "Mosaic Pavements in Palestine," *Quarterly of the Department of Antiquities in Palestine,* 2 (1932): 173n. See also P. Bagatti, "Il Mosaico dell' Orfeo a Gerusalemme," *Rivista d'archeologia cristiana,* 28 (1952): 145–160; H. Stern, "La Mosaïque d'Orphée," who discusses this pavement on pp. 74–75; and Grabar, *L'Art de la fin de l'antiquité,* II, p. 766.

69. It may be objected that these two figures were intended to represent not real women, but personifications related to the central scene of Orpheus among the animals. While it is true that personifica-

tions were often associated with Orpheus-David in the psalter illustrations of the middle Byzantine period (the well-known illustration in B.N. Gr. Coislin 139, for example, shows a sacred pillar rather like the one in our mosaic and the personification Melodia sitting next to Orpheus-David), actually such works have very little in common with the Jerusalem pavement. In them, personifications and nymphs are clearly classicizing figures, partially clothed in classicizing drapery and wearing fillets on their heads. In the Jerusalem mosaic, the figures are fully and modestly dressed in clothes of the sixth century. They bear the rather mundane names of Theodosia and Georgia in contrast to the names found in the psalters: Nux, Sophia, Prophetia, Melodia. Certainly there is no evidence in the Jerusalem pavement that these figures were not meant to represent real people except for the pillar which seems to me to be nothing more than a pastoral and classicizing touch quite in keeping with the characters of Orpheus, Pan, and the centaur. The placement of their medallion between the ossuaries further suggests that Theodosia and Georgia were buried in this tomb and that they either commissioned it before their deaths or were memorialized by relatives or friends after they died.

70. R. M. Harrison, "An Orpheus Mosaic at Ptolemais in Cyrenaica," *JRS*, 52 (1962): 16, has noted the increasing frontality and symmetry of the late Roman Orpheus mosaics.

71. H. Vincent, "Une Mosaïque byzantine à Jerusalem," *Revue biblique,* 10 (1901): 436–444 and 11 (1902): 100–103. E. R. Goodenough, *Jewish Symbols*, V, 82, calls the piece "a mosaic from a Christian Church," but does not say why he disputes the traditional interpretation. Vincent's second article mentions a cross on the floor of the tomb beneath an arch, but adds that it seems to have been of a later date than the mosaic (p. 102).

72. *Jewish Symbols*, IX, i, 22.

73. Another such relief, from Ostia, has been published by J. Wilpert, *I Sarcofagi Cristiani Antichi* (Rome, 1929–1936), II, pl. 256.

74. Orpheus is to be found with Pan and the centaur, to my knowledge, in only three other late antique works of art. These are: the ivory pyxis from the monastery of St. Columbano at Bobbio, published by Joseph Natanson, *Early Christian Ivories* (London, 1953), pl. 26; a similar pyxis from the Abbey of St. Julien à Brioude and now at the Bargello Museum, Florence, published by H. Graeven, "Pyxide en Os," *Monuments et mémoires Piot*, VI (1899), fig. 2; and a Coptic textile in the R. Tyler Collection. See Hayford Peirce and Royall Tyler, *L'Art byzantin* (Paris, 1932–1934), II, pl. 159a and pp. 120–122. All of these pieces have been dated in the fifth-sixth century and are probably of Alexandrian origin. They are dissimilar to the Jerusalem Orpheus in that Pan and the centaur are merely two among a host of mythological creatures, they show no signs of Christian symbolism, and they have no funerary associations.

75. Theon of Smyrna, *Expos. Rer. Mathem. ad Legendum Platonem Utilium,* ed. E. Hiller (Leipzig, 1878), p. 142.

76. W. H. Stahl, tr., Macrobius, *Commentary on the Dream of Scipio* (New York, 1952), p. 195.

77. Cicero, *Somnium Scipionis,* in C. W. Keyes, ed. and tr., *De re publica* (Loeb Library ed., London and Cambridge, Mass., 1959), 6. 18.

78. J. J. Savage, "Some Unpublished Scholia on Virgil," *TAPA*, 56 (1925): 235–236. A. D. Nock suggests that this *Lyra* may have been a Neopythagorean work for invoking the souls of the dead, *CR*, 41 (1927): 170.

79. Aristides Quintilianus, *De Musica,* ed. R. P. Winnington-Ingram (Leipzig, 1963), 11, 18. For my versions and adaptations, as well as my discussion of this dark author I am much indebted to the French translation of parts of the *De Musica* by A. J. Festugière in his "L'Ame et la musique, d'après Aristide Quintilien," *TAPA*, 85 (1954): 55–78.

80. E. Diels, ed., *Fragmente der Vorsokratiker* (Berlin, 1952–1956), frag. 27, and E. Diehl, ed., Proclus, *In Platonis Timaeum Commentarii* (Leipzig, 1965), 2, 72, 13 and 3, 234, 27.

81. *De Mus.* II, 17.

82. *De Mus.* II, 18.

83. St. Clement, in the *Paedogogus,* II, iv, counseled Christians to avoid the flute and pipes, which were instruments of idolators, appealing to animals and the irrational part of man. He said the instrument for the Christian was the lyre. *Paed.,* III, xi. Gregory of Nyssa, *De Hominis Opificio,* IX, iii, says that the music of man's soul is a compound of flute and lyre, just as the soul itself is a compound of reason and passion.

84. *De Mus.* II, 19.

85. The pavement was published and its symbolism discussed by G. Picard, "Une Mosaïque pythagoricienne à El Djem," *Hommages à Waldemar Deonna* (Brussels, 1957), pp. 390f. It is worth noting here that the "geometry" of the Jerusalem mosaic is that of the triangle, with its base made of θυμός, the centaur, and ἐπιθυμία, Pan. Orpheus, at the apex, is νοῦς. According to Lucian, *Vita Auct.* 4, the Pythagoreans held that the triangle was a perfect figure. Picard points to a similar geometrical symbolism of the triangle in the composition of the Apollo and Marsyas mosaic. Jacob Gronovius, *Thesaurus Graecarum Antiquitatum* (Leyden, 1697–1702), I, signature FFF, reproduces a coin from the reign of Antoninus Pius which shows Orpheus among the animals; above his lyre is a large triangle.

86. Ovid, *Met.* I, 699f.

87. *G.* II, 455–456; *Aen.* VI, 286.

88. St. Basil, *Liber de Virginitate* 7, *PG* 30, 681–684, followed by St. Augustine, *De Moribus Ecclesiae Catholicae* I, iv, *PL* 32, 1313. It may be only coincidence that in his attack on wind instruments, St. Clement

mentions that men play tunes on the flute while horses copulate, *Paed.* II, iv.

Chapter IV

1. Gilbert Highet, *The Classical Tradition* (New York, 1957), p. 21.

2. On this point, see Fritz Saxl, "Illustrated Mediaeval Encyclopaedias," in *Lectures* (London, 1957), I, 230.

3. On the pseudo-Heraclitus, see Pépin, *Mythe et allégorie*, pp. 266f, and F. Buffière, *Les Mythes d'Homère et la pensée grecque* (Paris, 1956), as well as the same author's introduction to his edition, *Héraclite, allégories d'Homère* (Paris, 1962), especially pp. xxi–xxxviii. For Cornutus, whom Renaissance mythographers called "Phornutus," see the edition by B. Schmidt, *De Cornuti Theologiae Graecae Compendio Capita Duo* (Halle, 1912). The best edition of Sallustius is that of A. D. Nock, *Concerning the Gods and the Universe* (Cambridge, Engl., 1926, reprinted, 1966). Many of the doctrines concerning the moral, historical, and physical interpretations of the gods held by the Early Stoa are conveniently gathered in Cicero, *Nat. D.,* II, 63–69. For a fuller treatment of the points I make here about the origins of moral allegory, see Seznec, *The Survival of the Pagan Gods,* pp. 84–95.

4. The author of the Copenhagen Commentary on Ovid's *Metamorphoses,* after telling the story of Atlas and the Gorgon, reminds us that "mesmes notre benoist sauveur et redempteur Jhesus voulut user de parabolles et de similitudes en ses predicacions et euvangiles en plusieurs et divers lieux. Et pour ce doncques que je voy que l'escripture saintte use de fables et de parabolles a l'ostencion et demonstrance d'aucune verité ou passeé ou presente, et que aussi les poetes faindirent icelles a la designacion et signifiance d'avoir la verité des choses tant naturelles comme historiennes, il me semble chose bonne et honneste d'escripre sur chacune fable de ce grant volume [the *Metamorphoses*] aucunes moralisations . . . C'est a entendre que l'omme doit de toutes choses tyrer sapience et mettre a proufit pour lui et pour autres, en incitant a bonnes meurs et fuyans vices." Printed in C. De Boer, ed., *Ovide Moralisé* (Amsterdam, 1915–1938), vol. V, Appendix II, p. 388.

5. William W. Jackson, tr. *Dante's Convivio* (Oxford, 1909), II, i, p. 73. On the subject of Dante's references to Orpheus, see Julius Wilhelm, "Orpheus bei Dante," *Medium Aevum Romanicum,* 32 (1963): 397–406. The early commentators on Dante's *Comedy* give various interpretations of what the poet meant when he placed Orpheus among the virtuous pagans in *Inferno,* IV, 140; Pietro di Dante explains him as "*Orpheus,* idest *sapiens musicus*" and offers the familiar allegory in which the musician seeks his wife "bona dijudicatio" who has been sent to hell through the bite of the serpent "idest a fallacia hujus

mundi," *Petri Allegherii super Dantis ipsius genitoris comoediam Commentarium*, eds. G. Vernon and V. Nannucci (Florence, 1845), p. 15. Andrea Lancia, in his gloss on the passage, uses Orpheus as the occasion for a brief technical discussion of medieval music; Andrea Lancia, *L'Ottimo commento della Divina Commedia*, ed. A. Torri (Pisa, 1827–1829), I, 63. For Benvenuto da Imola, the story of Orpheus has several meanings, and he cites the accounts of Fulgentius, Macrobius, and so on. He himself feels that "allegorice Orpheus est vir summe sapiens et eloquens. Euridice, sibi dilectissima, est anima eius rationalis." The most interesting feature of Benvenuto's gloss is his comparison of Dante and Orpheus: "Orpheus vadit ad Infernum pro recuperatione animae suae, sicut similiter Dantes ivit" (pp. 175–176). Dante, however, did not look back, whereas Orpheus disobeyed the law and so "perdidit omnino animam suam" (p. 176).

6. On Fulgentius see M. L. W. Laistner, *Thought and Letters in Western Europe* (Ithaca, 1957), p. 42. On his influence, see Seznec, *The Survival of the Pagan Gods*, pp. 89, 106, 172. The most recent discussion of his identity is offered by P. Langlois, "Les Oeuvres de Fulgence le Mythographe et le problème des deux Fulgence," *Jahrbuch für Antike und Christentum*, 7 (1964): 94–105.

7. Fabius Planciades Fulgentius, *Mitologiae*, ed. R. Helm (Leipzig, 1898), III, x, p. 77. Some authors interpreted the first part of Orpheus' name as *aurea* or golden; thus to the author of a gloss in Vienna MS 2642, 53v, he is "Orpheus dit autant comme voiz d'or," and to Arnulf Gréban he is "Orpheus quasi aurea phanes id est aureum lumen" (B. N. Lat. MS 9323, 95r).

8. On the "aetas Virgiliana" and "Ovidiana," see E. R. Curtius, *European Literature and the Latin Middle Ages* (New York 1953), p. 96, and G. Pansa, *Ovidio nel Medio Evo e nella Tradizione Popolare* (Sulmona, 1924).

9. On the question of such commentaries in general and on Orpheus and Eurydice in particular, see Pierre Courcelle, "Etude critique sur les commentaires de la 'Consolation' de Boèce," *Archives d'histoire doctrinale et littéraire du Moyen Age*, 12 (1939): 5–140, and Klaus Heitmann, "Orpheus im Mittelalter, "*Archiv für Kulturgeschichte*, 45 (1963): 253–294.

10. For discussions of Boethius and his influence, see E. K. Rand, *Founders of the Middle Ages* (Cambridge, Mass., 1928); R. Carton, "Le Christianisme et l'Augustinisme de Boèce," *Revue de philologie, d'histoire et de littérature anciennes*, 1 (1930): 573–659; Howard Rollin Patch, *The Tradition of Boethius* (New York, 1935); Helen Barrett, *Boethius: Some Aspects of His Times and Work* (Cambridge, Eng., 1940), and, most recently, Pierre Courcelle, *La Consolation de Philosophie dans la tradition littéraire* (Paris, 1967). Courcelle gives a complete handlist of the commentaries on the *Consolation*, pp. 403–418.

11. All quotations from the *Consolation* are drawn from the translation of *The Consolation of Philosophy* by Richard H. Green (Indianapolis, 1962).

12. *Timaeus* 47a, in B. Jowett, tr., *The Dialogues of Plato* (New York, 1937), II, 28. See also Aristotle, *De partibus animalium* 686a; Cicero, *Nat. D.* II, 56; Ovid, *Met.* I, 84–88. The idea that man was *homo erectus* was thought to be contained in the very word for man in Greek. See Arnold Williams, *The Common Expositor* (Chapel Hill, N.C., 1948), p. 231.

13. St. Basil, *Hom. in Hex.* IX, ii, PNF VIII, p. 102. See also St. Augustine, *De Gen. Contra Manichaeos* I, xvii, 28; Gregory of Nyssa, *De Hominis Opificio* VIII, i; Ambrose, *Hexaemeron* VI, ix, 55–58; Minucius Felix, *Octavius* XVII; and Lactantius, *Div. Inst.* II, i, 15–18.

14. Curtius, *European Literature*, pp. 57f, and G. Paré et al., *La Renaissance du XIIe siècle: les écoles et l'enseignement* (Paris and Ottawa, 1933), pp. 147f.

15. Conrad of Hirsau, *Dialogus super Auctores sive Didascalon*, ed. R. B. C. Huygens (Brussels, 1955), pp. 20, 22, 24, 26, 28, 30, 31, 32, 34, 36, 38, 41, 47, 49, 51, 54, 55, 56, 43.

16. Paré, p. 92.

17. Paré, p. 118.

18. Paré, pp. 115f.

19. Hugh of St. Victor, in his manual on the art of teaching, explains this system clearly. "Expositio tria continet: litteram, sensum, sententiam. Littera est congrua ordinatio dictionum, quam etiam constructionem vocamus. Sensus est facilis quaedam et aperta significatio . . . Sententia est profundior intelligentia." *Didascalion* III, 9, *PL* 176, 771. See also C. Spicq, *Esquisse d'une histoire de l'exégèse latine au Moyen Age* (Paris, 1944), and H. de Lubac, *Exégèse médiévale* (Paris, 1959–1962).

20. Mythographers also wrote conventional commentaries. The Second Vatican Mythographer, for example, has been identified with Remigius of Auxerre, who wrote standard school commentaries on Boethius, Martianus Capella, and other Latin authors. See M. Manitius, *Geschichte der lateinischen Literatur des Mittelalters* (Munich, 1923), II, 656–660, and, more recent, Courcelle, *La Consolation*, p. 247. Arnulf of Orléans not only wrote the allegories on Ovid's fables discussed below, but also some glosses *ad litteram* on Ovid and some on Lucan. See B. M. Marti, ed. *Arnulfi Aurelianensis Glosule super Lucanum*, in *Papers and Monographs of the American Academy in Rome*, vol. 18 (1958).

21. See H. Stewart, "A Commentary by Remigius Autissiodorensis on the *De Consolatione Philosophiae* of Boethius," *JTS*, 17 (1916): 23–24, and P. Courcelle, "La Culture antique de Remi d'Auxerre," *Latomus*, 7 (1948): 248–254.

22. See Cora E. Lutz, ed., *Remigii Autissiodorensis Commentum in Martianum Capellam Libri I-II* (Leyden, 1962), pp. 12–16, for this list and bibliography.

23. Trèves MS 1093 (eleventh century), discussed by Courcelle, "Etude," pp. 12–16. This commentary was at one time thought to be the work of John the Scot and was edited and printed as such by E. T. Silk in his *Saeculi Noni Auctoris in Boetii Consolationem Philosophiae Commentarius*, in *Papers and Monographs of the American Academy in Rome*, vol. 9 (1935). Quotations from Remigius' commentary on the *Consolation of Philosophy* will be drawn from this edition. In "Pseudo-Johannes Scottus, Adalbold of Utrecht and the Early Commentaries on Boethius," *Mediaeval and Renaissance Studies*, 3 (1954): 1–40, Silk abandoned his attribution of this commentary to John the Scot. His original arguments are discussed by Courcelle, "Etude," pp. 21f, who gives further bibliography on the problem.

24. Lutz, ed. *Remigii Autissiodorensis Commentum*, p. 310. I have translated *profunda inventio* as "profound thought" because that is how Eurydice's name is almost always etymologized. When other words are substituted, as in the anonymous gloss on Theodulus in B. N. Lat. 7537 A, "per Euridicen intelligimus discretionem," fol. 61v, they are close to thought or judgment. *Inventio's* connotations from medieval rhetoric make the equivalent English words "invention" or "inventiveness" confusing. Rhetorical *inventio* did have the sense of profound thought or judgment applied to the writer's subject, and that is how Geoffrey of Vinsauf uses it in his *Poetria Nova*. See Margaret F. Nims, tr., *Poetria Nova of Geoffrey of Vinsauf* (Toronto, 1967), I, 55, p. 17. Remigius' interpretation of Orpheus in his Martianus commentary is to be found virtually word for word, in a commentary on Martianus by John the Scot. See Cora E. Lutz, ed., *Johannis Scotti Annotationes in Marcianum* (Cambridge, Mass., 1939), pp. 192–193. For Martianus and his commentators see William H. Stahl, "To a Better Understanding of Martianus Capella," *Speculum*, 40 (1965): 102–115. Remigius' Fulgentian interpretation was also used by musical theorists like Hucbold of St. Amand, c. 920. See his *Musica enchiriadis* in PL 132, 981. Orpheus is the champion of the *ars musicae* because he learned about music from the harmonies produced by the movements of the spheres. See the *Tractatus de musica* in Edmond de Coussemaker, ed., *Scriptorium de Musica Medii Aevi* (Paris, 1864), III, 476, and Dunchad (Martin of Laon) in Cora E. Lutz, ed., *Dunchad Glossae in Martianum* (Lancaster, Pa., 1944), p. 12. One anonymous Carthusian musicologist tells us that Orpheus was among those who invented music. His list of co-inventors provides some examples of the way in which pseudo-historical characters developed from medieval misunderstandings of Greek and Latin words. In his long list of inventors, Tubal, Nicomachus of Gerasa, Mercury, and so on, we find the names "Savius Licaon" and "Phrix," which seem to be personifications of the interval lichanos and the

Phrygian mode. This passage may be found in the *Varia* published by Coussemaker, II, 460.

25. St. Augustine, *On Christian Doctrine*, tr. D. W. Robertson, Jr. (New York, 1958), IV, 5, p. 121. On this subject generally, see Gabriel Muhelmans, "Philologia et son mariage avec Mercure jusqu'à la fin du XIIe siècle," *Latomus*, 16 (1957): 84–107, and for specific examples of the topos, Bernard Silvestris, *Commentum Bernardi Silvestris super sex libros Eneidos Virgilii*, ed. G. Riedel (Greifswald, 1924), pp. 2–3, and John de Foxton, *Liber cosmographiae*, Trinity College, Cambridge, MS R. 15. 21, Cap. 22, d. 2.

26. Paul Piper, ed., *Die Schriften Notkers und seiner schule* (Freiburg and Tübingen, 1882), I, 224 lines 11–12. Page numbers refer to this edition.

27. See Raymond Klibansky, *The Continuity of the Platonic Tradition during the Middle Ages* (London, 1939), pp. 24, 33.

28. In William's lifetime, Boethius' commentaries on and translations of Aristotle's *On Interpretation* and the possibly spurious *Categories* and his revision of Porphyry's *Isagoge* were available, as well as Jacob of Venice's Latin translation of the *Prior* and *Posterior Analytics* and *Topics*. He may also have known the Latin version of the Neoplatonist Nemesius' *On the Nature of Man*, and Gerard of Cremona's version of the pseudo-Aristotelian *Liber de causis* which made some of Proclus' thought available to Latin readers. On the knowledge of Greek and Greek texts in the Middle Ages, see the cautious estimate of R. Weiss, "The Study of Greek in England during the Fourteenth Century," *Rinascimento*, 2 (1951): 209–239, and the same author's *Humanism in England during the Fifteenth Century* (Oxford, 1957), pp. 9–11, as well as J. T. Muckle, "Greek Works Translated Directly into Latin before 1350," *Mediaeval Studies*, 4 (1942): 32–42, and 5 (1943): 102–114.

29. *Glosae super Platonem*, ed. Edouard Jeauneau (Paris, 1965).

30. The text of William's commentary used here is that of MS Troyes 1331, printed in part by Edouard Jeauneau in his "L'Usage de la notion d'*Integumentum* à travers les gloses de Guillaume de Conches," *Archives d'histoire doctrinale et littéraire du Moyen Age*, 32 (1957), pp. 45–46. A microfilm of William's Boethius commentary, B. N. Lat. 14380, is available from the Library of Congress as MLA rotograph 99 (1929).

31. I borrow the phrase "drama of the soul" from J. Hatinguais, "En Marge d'un poème de Boèce: l'interprétation allégorique du mythe d'Orphée par Guillaume de Conches," *Association Guillaume Budé: Congrès de Tours et de Poitiers, actes du Congrès* (Paris, 1954), p. 286.

32. Courcelle, "Etude," p. 97.

33. Beryl Smalley, *English Friars and Antiquity in the Early Fourteenth Century* (Oxford, 1960), pp. 58–59. See also R. Weiss, "Notes on the Popularity of the Writings of Nicholas Trevet, O.P., in Italy during the First Half of the Fourteenth Century," *Dominican Studies*, 1 (1948): 261–265.

34. Boethius, *Consolation of Philosophy*, tr. Jean de Meun, commentary by Nicholas Trivet, B. N. Lat. 18424, folio 101v. The English translation of the tag from *Aeneid* VI, 128–131 is that of H. R. Fairclough, ed. and tr., *Virgil* (Loeb Library ed., London and Cambridge, Mass., 1950). E. T. Silk promised a critical edition of Trivet's commentary on the *Consolation* in *Scriptorium*, 9 (1955): 278.

35. Bernard Silvestris, *Commentum*, p. 54.

36. Peter's commentary has been edited by Antoine Thomas, "Notice sur le manuscrit Latin 4788 du Vatican, contenant une traduction française, avec commentaire par Maître Pierre de Paris de la *Consolatio Philosophiae* de Boèce," *Notices et extraits des manuscrits de la Bibliothèque Nationale et autres bibliothèques*, 41 (1923): 69–70. In much the same mode as Peter's work is the French prose translation of Boethius attributed to the Florentine Alberto della Piagentina, B. N. Fr. 7209. Here Orpheus, called Olfeus in the manuscript, meets a demon perched on the tomb of Eurydice. At his behest, Orpheus goes to the underworld and the devils, amused by Orpheus' frantic joy at the sight of his wife, plot how to make a game of his love. They present him with the familiar covenant and at the same time plan to make a frightful noise behind his back which will force him to turn around and so break the pact. This they do and Orpheus loses his wife once more. See Paulin Paris, *Les Manuscrits François de la Bibliothèque du Roi* (Paris, 1845), VI, 343–346, for the relevant passage. Worth noting here also is the gloss on a thirteenth-century French translation of Ovid's *Art of Love* from MS Modena, B. Estense, Campori 42 (Γ. G. 3.20), fol. 85v. "Orpheus, nez de Trace, par la grant melodie de sa harpe, faisoit *dansser* les pierres . . . les bestes sauvages, et encor plus il faisoit *dansser les laz, c'est a dire lacus infernaulx, et Serberus* . . . et tant fist que Parserpinne lui rendi Erusdissen, sa femme, laquelle il ramena d'enfer et eüst esté sauvee, *s'elle ne se fut tournee ou regardee derrier elle*." Book III, 321–324, my emphasis. I am indebted to Bruno Roy, of the Institut d'Etudes Médiévales of the University of Montreal for this reference.

37. E. F. Jacob, "Some Aspects of Classical Influence in Mediaeval England," *Vorträge der Bibliothek Warburg*, vol. 9 (1930–1931), offers some exceptions to this statement, most notably Bede (p. 5).

38. Ovid's *Metamorphoses* and other poems are mentioned as school texts in the curricula of Conrad of Hirsau (c. 1150), Alexander Neckam (c. 1175), and Eberhard the German (c. 1250). For a complete list of such curricula see Curtius, *European Literature*, pp. 49–50.

39. For a handlist and discussion of these commentators, see L. K. Born, "Ovid and Allegory," *Speculum*, 9 (1934): 362–379, as well as the articles by J. D. Cooke, "Euhemerism: A Mediaeval Interpretation of Classical Paganism," *Speculum*, 2 (1927): 396–410, and Fausto Ghisalberti, "L''Ovidius Moralizatus' di P. Bersuire," *Studj Romanzi*, 23 (1933): 5–136, who prints excerpts from Bersuire's moralization of Ovid.

40. Fausto Ghisalberti, ed., "Arnolfo d'Orléans, un Cultore di Ovidio nel Secolo XII," *Memorie del Reale Istituto Lombardo di Scienze e Lettere*, 24 (1932): 157–232; my citations from Arnulf are from pp. 207 and 222 of this edition.

41. Fausto Ghisalberti, ed., *Giovanni di Garlandia: Integumenta Ovidii, poemetto inedito del secolo XIII* (Milan, 1933), X, p. 67. The gloss that follows is also printed on p. 67 of this edition.

42. It is in his capacity as civilizer that Orpheus makes his appearance in Robert Holcot, *In Librum Sapientiae* (Basel, 1586): "Orpheus in rei ueritate sapientes designat, quorum est homines uitiosos & à se inuicem per passiones uarias discordantes in unam ciuilitatem recolligere, & eos per leges & rationes sapientiae castigare" (Ch. I, lec. ii, p. 8). On Holcot, see Beryl Smalley, *English Friars and Antiquity*, pp. 133–202. She prints a portion of one of his sermons containing a passage on Orpheus from the pseudo-Palaephatius which is merely an account of his legend, Appendix II, p. 360.

43. Fausto Ghisalberti, ed., "Giovanni del Virgilio Espositore delle 'Metamorphosi'," *Il Giornale Dantesco*, 34 (1933): 89.

44. C. De Boer, ed., *Ovide Moralisé* (Amsterdam, 1915–1938), X, 220–243. See on this work, J. Engels, *Etudes sur L'Ovide Moralisé* (Groningen, 1945), especially Ch. II, pp. 23f, which treats the poem's relation to Bersuire's *Metamorphosis Ovidiana* discussed below, and Born, "Ovid and Allegory."

45. C. De Boer, ed., *Ovide Moralisé en prose* (Amsterdam, 1954), VII, 264.

46. Pierre Bersuire, *Metamorphosis Ovidiana, moraliter explanata* (Paris, 1509), fol. LXXIIIv. This text has recently been re-edited by J. Engels as *Petrus Berchorius, Reductorium morale, Liber XV, cap I: De Formis Figurisque Deorum* (Werkmateriaal: Utrecht, 1960) and *cap. II–XV: "Ovidius Moralizatus"* (Werkmateriaal 2: Utrecht, 1962). Engels published a critical edition of the *De Formis Figurisque Deorum* as Werkmateriaal 3 (Utrecht, 1966). "Child of the sun" is my conjecture. The Paris, 1509, version reads *folis*, leaf, or poetically a Sibyl, but the compositor or scribe may have taken f for long s, and Orpheus was known as the son of Apollo. On Bersuire's life and works see Charles Samaran, "Pierre Bersuire," in *Histoire littéraire de la France*, 39 (Paris, 1962): 259–450, and F. Stegmüller, *Repertorium Biblici Medii Aevi* (Madrid, 1950–1959), IV, 235f, as well as Ghisalberti, "L''Ovidius Moralizatus'," pp. 5–86, referred to above, who prints the passage from the *Reductorium* in which Bersuire thanks Philippe de Vitry for the *Ovide Moralisé*, p. 89. A bibliography of books and articles relating to Bersuire and of articles on various medieval subjects making use of his works is given by J. Engels, "Berchoriana I," and "Berchoriana I: suite," *Vivarium*, 2 (1964): 62–124.

47. François Rabelais, Prologue to *Gargantua* in Jacques Boulanger, ed., *Oeuvres complètes* (Paris, 1955), p. 27.

48. A similar interpretation of Orpheus is offered in the *Fulgentius*

metaforalis, a mythographic treatise by the English Minorite John Ridevall. For him, Orpheus' "instrumentum musicum intellegitur communitas ecclesie et omnium electorum." Hans Liebeschütz, ed., *Fulgentius metaforalis* (Leipzig and Berlin, 1926), p. 108. See the important discussion of Ridevall in Beryl Smalley, *English Friars and Antiquity,* pp. 109–132.

49. G. H. Bode, ed., *Scriptores rerum mythicarum Latini tres Romae nuper reperti* (Celle, 1834, reprinted Hildesheim, 1968). For the identity of Albericus, see Eleanor Rathbone, "Master Alberic of London, Mythographus Tertius Vaticanus," *Mediaeval and Renaissance Studies,* 1 (1941): 35–38, and K. O. Elliot and J. P. Elder, "A Critical Edition of the Vatican Mythographers," *TAPA,* 78 (1947): 205.

50. Robert A. Van Kluyve, ed., *Thomae Walsingham, De Archana Deorum* (sic)(Durham, N.C., 1968), X, ii, p. 149. In my translation of this passage, I have added a few words from the text of the Third Vatican Mythographer in the interest of clarity.

51. Reginus of Prüm, *De Harmonica Institutione,* ed. Martin Gerbert in *Scriptores Ecclesiastici de Musica* (San Blas, 1784), I, 246. Manfred F. Bukofzer, "Speculative Thinking in Mediaeval Music," *Speculum,* 17 (1942): 174–175, discusses this passage from Reginus.

52. W. M. Lindsay, ed., *Isidori, Etymologiarum sive Originum Libri XX* (Oxford, 1957), I, ii, 7.

53. See Albertino Mussato, *Epistolae* (Venice, 1636), pp. 72–74. See also A. Zardo, *Albertino Mussato* (Padua, 1884), pp. 302–310. The treatise of Salutati's antagonist has been edited by E. H. Hunt, *Iohannis Dominici lucula noctis* (Notre Dame, Indiana, 1940); for the humanist's reply see F. Novati, *Epistolario di Coluccio Salutati* (Rome, 1905), IV. On the matter generally, see D. W. Robertson, Jr., *A Preface to Chaucer* (Princeton, 1962), pp. 352–355, and Richard H. Green, "Classical Fable and English Poetry in the Fourteenth Century," in D. Bethurum, ed., *Critical Approaches to Medieval Literature* (New York, 1960), pp. 114–122. For Boccaccio's references to the friars, see his *Genealogia deorum gentilium libri,* ed. Vincenzo Romano (Bari, 1951), II, xiv, 5, pp. 695–697. For bibliography on the secular-mendicant controversy and some examples of secular arguments and epithets, see my article "Henryson, the Friars, and the *Confessio Reynardi,*" *JEGP,* 66 (1967): 550–561.

54. *Colucii Salutati de laboribus Herculis,* ed. B. L. Ullman (Zurich, 1951), I, i, 2, p. 10.

55. Servius had glossed *Aeneid* VI, 127: "This earth where we live is seen as hell because it is the lowest of the nine spheres . . . The souls of those who live well remount to the upper circles—that is, to their place of origin—those of evil doers remain in the body by various transformations and thus remain forever in hell." G. Thilo and H. Hagen, eds., *Servii Grammatici qui feruntur in Vergilii carmina Commentarii* (Leipzig, 1878–1902), II, 27–28.

56. *Disputatio de Somnium Scipionis,* ed. R. Van Weddingen (Brussels, 1957), XIV, 4, p. 36.

57. Bernard, *Commentum,* p. 30. On the intellectual background of Bernard's commentary, see J. R. O'Donnell, C.S.B., "The Sources and Meaning of Bernard Silvester's Commentary on the *Aeneid,*" *Mediaeval Studies,* 24 (1962): 233–249. For an example of Bernard's use by Dante commentators, see Pietro di Dante's *Commentarium,* pp. 11–17.

Chapter V

1. E. Langlois, ed., *Recueil d'arts de seconde rhétorique* (Paris, 1902), II, 39–40.

2. B. N. Fr. Sign. Rés. R. 89, fol. g3v: "Mais la loy d'amour est si fort/qu'elle [ne] crainct peine ne mort./Dont c'est fole peine e errour/ De bailler loy a fin amour./Car Orpheüs fut amans fins." According to Michault Taillevent, "Ainsy comme fist Orpheüs/Jadis, maint amans ne font mie." See P. Champion, *Histoire poétique de XVe siècle* (Paris, 1925), I, 325.

3. A Latin lyric from MS Auxerre 243 tells us of "Orpheus, whose habit was to research into the spirits of the sun, the monthly orbit of the moon, the numerically established courses of the stars in heaven." The lyric was edited and translated by Peter Dronke, *Medieval Latin and the Rise of the European Love Lyric* (Oxford, 1966–1967), II, 404. In a curious comment on Psalm 38, John Fisher remarks: "Almyghty god commaundeth lyght to shyne out of derkenes. The clerke Orpheus meruayled gretely of it sayenge. O nox que lucem emittis. O derke nyght I meruayle sore that thou bryngest forth lyght." *The English Works of John Fisher,* ed. J. E. B. Mayor (London, 1876), *EETS:ES* 27, pp. 47–48.

4. Cassiodorus, *An Introduction to Divine and Human Readings,* tr. L. W. Jones (New York, 1946), II, 195. See also his *Expositio in Psalterium* 49 (50), *PL* 70, 352.

5. *Hexaemeron, PG* 92, 1438–1439.

6. John Tzetzes, *Historiarum Variarum: Chiliades,* ed. T. Kiessling (Leipzig, 1826), II, 54, 11. 843–857, p. 73. All quotations from Tzetzes are drawn from this text.

> Ἡ Εὐρυδίκη σύζυγος ὑπῆρχε τοῦ Ὀρφέως.
> Ταύτην ὑπ' ὄφεως φασὶ δηχθεῖσαν τεθνηκέναι,
> Ἀνενεχθῆναι δὲ πρὸς φῶς πάλιν ἐκ τῶν νερτέρων,
> Ὀρφέως Ἅιδην θέλξαντος καὶ Κόρην μουσουργίαις.
> Τὸ δ' ἀλληγορικώτερον· ἢ λύπῃ βεβλημένην,
> Λειποψυχοῦσαν νόσῳ τε δεινῇ, περικαρδίῳ,
> Ἅπερ καὶ χείρω δήγματος τυγχάνουσι δρακόντων,
> Τέρψας Ὀρφεὺς ἐξήλασε τῇ μουσικῇ τὸ πάθος·

Ἤ ὑπὸ ὄφεως αὐτὴν τῷ ὄντι δεδηγμένην
Καὶ κινδυνεύουσαν θανεῖν ταῖς ἐπῳδαῖς αἷς οἶδε,
Καὶ ἀγχινοίᾳ, μούσῃ τε καὶ τῇ πολυμαθείᾳ,
Ὡς πρὶν Δαβὶδ τὸ τοῦ Σαοὺλ δαιμόνιον ἐκεῖνο,
Αὐτὴν ἐζωοποίησεν . . .

7. B.N. Lat. 8115, fifteenth-century, fol. 36v: "concordancia est in hoc quod sicut Orpheus citharizavit in inferno, sicut David coram Saule; et sicut Orpheus mitigavit deos infernales cum sua cithara, sic David malignum spiritum Saulis."

8. Edited by Ernst Sieper (London, 1901–1903), I, 147, ll. 5603–5611.

9. See H. Buchthal, *The Miniatures of the Paris Psalter* (London, 1938); and Kurt Weitzmann, "Der Pariser Psalter," *Jahrbuch für Kunstwissenschaft,* 6 (1929): 178–194. The portrait of David in the psalter reminds us of the portraits of classical authors sometimes with their muses, to be found at the beginnings of illustrated classical MSS. On this point, see A. M. Friend, "The Portraits of the Evangelists in Greek and Latin Manuscripts," *Art Studies,* 5 (1927): esp. pp. 138–147 and figs. 151–168. For a review of the controversy surrounding the dating of the miniatures of the Paris Psalter, see C. R. Morey, "Castelseprio and the 'Byzantine Renaissance,'" *Art Bulletin,* 34 (1952): 173–201. Morey calls for a date "at the latest ca. 700" on page 200. His article recapitulates much of what he said on the subject in "The Byzantine 'Renaissance,'" *Speculum,* 14 (1939): 139–159. A recent study of the miniatures in the various Byzantine psalters is that of Suzy Dufrenne, *L'Illustration des psautiers grecs du Moyen Age* (Paris, 1966).

10. The pose copies that of the well-known sculpture of the Nile god in the Vatican Museum. It would seem that the man who drew the figure of Orpheus in the pose of the sleeping river god in the cosmological miniature from Reims Mun. Bib. 672 sometime during the thirteenth century may well have seen one of the Byzantine psalters and, dimly remembering the pose of Orpheus-David or confusing it with the pose of the mountain god of Bethlehem, arranged his Orpheus in this unlikely position. The miniature (p. 86, fig. 4) is published by Charles De Tolnay, "Music of the Universe," *The Journal of the Walters Art Gallery,* 6 (1943): 82–104. There is some evidence for the movement of Byzantine ideas and painters westward as early as the thirteenth century, as instanced by the frescoes from Castelseprio and St. Maria Antiqua, which are of even earlier date. In manuscript illustration one sees the clear influence of Alexandrian illusionism by way of Byzantium in the miniatures of the Utrecht Psalter. A gospel title page bound into the Utrecht MS and written about 700 in Northumbria contains the inscription "Holy Mary help the Scribe," in perfect Greek. For a picture and discussion of this gospel leaf, see E. A. Lowe, "The Uncial Gospel Leaves attached to the Utrecht Psalter," *Art Bulletin,* 34 (1952): 237–238, fig. 1.

11. David is nimbed in the nearly contemporary western psalter portrait of him in Cotton MS Vespasian A. i, fol. 306, an eighth-century psalter from the Augustine Abbey at Canterbury. Orpheus was nimbed in the late antique mosaic from Ptolemais published by Harrison.

12. Vat. Cod. Barb. Gr. 320, fol. 2r, published by Kurt Weitzmann, *Greek Mythology in Byzantine Art* (Princeton, 1951), fig. 85.

13. This codex is sometimes called the Vatican Psalter. It is Vat. Pal. Gr. 381 B. fol. 1v, published by Goodenough, *Jewish Symbols*, vol. XI, fig. 83, among others, and discussed by N. P. Kondakov, *Histoire de l'art byzantin* (Paris, 1886–1891), II, 31.

14. These miniatures have been discussed by Kurt Weitzmann, *Greek Mythology*, pp. 67–68.

15. *Lavision-Christine*, ed. Sister Mary L. Towner (Washington, D.C., 1932), p. 120.

16. Strabo, *Geography*, ed. and tr. H. L. Jones (Loeb Library ed., Cambridge, Mass., 1917–1933), VII, 18.

17. See H. D. Austin, "Artephius-Orpheus," *Speculum*, 12 (1937): 251, whose translation of Ristoro I have used here. Ristoro's view of Orpheus is close to that of Alfonso X, *General estoria, Segunda parte*, ed. A. Solalinde et al. (Madrid, 1957), I, 320: "Et trauaios por esta razon por su saber de philosophia, e por su magica, e por sos encantamientos e sus coniurationes de desçender a los infiernos, e fizo lo." A somewhat similar attribution of the wizard's powers to Orpheus is made by John Lathbury in his commentary on Lamentations. Orpheus piped so sweetly that "feras domesticavit, serpentes pertractavit, hostes immolitavit, et ventus silere imperavit." MS Oxford, Lincoln College Lat. 66, fol. 102r–v. I am indebted to Judson Allen for this reference, whose forthcoming study of the "classicizing" friars will treat Lathbury's role in the medieval mythographic tradition. See also Beryl Smalley, *English Friars and Antiquity*, pp. 221–239.

18. Pseudo-Albericus, *De Deorum imaginibus libellus*, Vat. MS Lat. Reg. 1290, fol. 5r. On the authorship of this work, see Seznec, *The Survival of the Pagan Gods*, pp. 170–179. The miniatures are published by Liebeschütz, pls. XVI–XXXII.

19. Tr. Helen Waddell, *Mediaeval Latin Lyrics* (London, 1951), p. 121.

20. *Les Oeuvres poétiques de Baudri de Bourgueil*, ed. Phyllis Abrahams (Paris, 1926), CCXLIV, 24.

21. *Viaticum* (Leyden, 1515), XX, fol. CXLVI. There is an informative article on Constantine Africanus, perhaps best known for his work *De Coitu*, by Maurice Bassan, "Chaucer's 'Cursed Monk,' Constantinus Africanus," in *Mediaeval Studies*, 24 (1962): 127–140.

22. *Ars Musica*, Gerbert II, 392. "Orpheus dixerit 'imperatores ad convivia me invitant, ut ex me se delectent, ego tamen condelector ex ipsis, cum quo velim, animos eorum flectere possim, de ira ad mansuetudinem.'"

23. *Musica*, Gerbert III, 334. "Orpheus per suam musicam mutasse

corda principium de tristitia in laetitiam; nam excitat dormientes, dormitare facit vigilantes & sanat melancholiam."

24. Dorothy Everett discusses the typicality of these conventions in her article "A Characterization of the English Medieval Romances," *Essays and Studies,* 15 (1929): 98–121.

25. A curious blending of the Orpheus legend with a romance motif occurs in the fourteenth-century *La Treselegante hystoire du tresnoble et excellentissime roy Perceforest* (Paris, 1528), II, 70, fol. 73r: "et par tel tour il [Orpheus] recouvra sa femme par telle maniere qu'il ne la devrit regarder tant qu'elle viendroit en sa maison, mais luy desirant de la veoir regarda par derriere soy et lors fut muee en pierre."

26. *King Alfred's Version of the Consolation of Boethius,* tr. W. J. Sedgefield (Oxford, 1900), pp. 116–117.

27. *Orat.* X, cited in C. S. Baldwin, *Medieval Rhetoric and Poetic* (Gloucester, Mass., 1959), p. 18.

28. Sidonius had cited the authority of Horace's *Ars Poetica* for the elaboration of the poem by purple passages (Carmen XXII, 6). The elaborate portraits of the virtues and vices in Prudentius' *Psychomachia* and the static though extremely vivid descriptions of the martyrs and the tortures they underwent for their faith in his *Peristephanon* are the results of recasting the sophistic *ekphrasis* for the purposes of Christian rhetoric.

29. Isidore of Seville, *Etymologiae,* ed. Lindsay, II, ii, 2.

30. Roger B. Parr, ed. and tr., Geoffrey of Vinsauf, *Documentum de modo et arte dictandi et versificandi* (Milwaukee, Wisc., 1968), II, B. i, ii, pp. 45–46. Brunetto Latini in his *Li Livres dou Trésor,* ed. F. J. Carmody (Berkeley, 1948), tells the would-be author how to expand his work by "aornemens": "tout çou que on poroit dire en .iii. mos ou en .iiii. ou a mout poi de paroles, il l'acroist par autres paroles plus longues et plus avenans ki dient ce meismes" (III, xiii, p. 330).

31. *Poetria Nova,* ed. Nims, III, 3, 624–633.

32. A ballade by Jean le Mote offers an interesting example of this sort of classicizing school exercise using Orpheus. The poem is about a love-sick lady, modeled on one of the heroines of Ovid's *Heroides.* She says that she is so unhappy in love that she can hear nothing, no, not even "Dyodonas a ses cleres buisines,/Ne Orpheüs li dieux de melodie,/Ne Musicans a ses chançons divines,/Ne Dedalus od sa gaye maistrie." She concludes her rather unusual list of musicians with this sad rhetorical question, "Je suis avec Dido a compagnie!/Ovide, ou sont remedes femenines?" This poem was printed by E. Pognon, "Ballades Mythologiques," *Humanisme et Renaissance,* 5 (1938): 408. Jean was a member of the circle of Philippe de Vitry, who was honored as "Orphealis heres . . ./Cuius nomen vivat per secula" in a witty classicizing poem by Jean de Savoie. The passage is printed and discussed by D. W. Robertson, Jr., "The 'Partitura Amorosa' of Jean de Savoie," *PQ,* 33 (1954): 1–9.

33. Printed by Wilhelm Meyer, "Zwei mittellateinische Lieder in Florenz," *Studi letterari e linguistici dedicati a Pio Rajna* (Milan, 1911), p. 149f.

34. The text of Thierry's poem is printed in full in F. W. Otto, *Commentarii critici in codices Bibliothecae Academicae Gissensis Graecos et Latinos* (Giessen, 1842), pp. 163f, ll. 1009–1024. I have used the translation of Peter Dronke, "The Return of Eurydice," *Classica et Mediaevalia,* 23 (1962): 199.

35. "Imperioque dei redditur uxor ei." The text of Gautier's poem has been published by M. Delbouille, "Une Mystérieux ami de Marbode: le 'Redoubtable Poète,' Gautier," *Le Moyen Age,* 6 (1951): 229.

36. Text published by A. Boutemy, "Trois Oeuvres de Godefroid de Reims," *Revue du Moyen Age Latin,* 3 (1947): 357. "Et rediviv[a] fores Herebi fugit atque furores." The sense requires that Boutemy's "redivivus" be changed to "rediviva."

37. Published by Dronke, *Medieval Latin,* II, 341–343. F. J. E. Raby, "*Amor* and *Amicitia*: A Mediaeval Poem," *Speculum,* 50 (1965): 599–610 gives a rhetorical analysis of this poem.

38. See A. Boutemy, "Une Version médiévale inconnue de la légende d'Orphée," *Hommages à Joseph Bidez et à Franz Cumont* (Brussels, 1949), pp. 53f and ll. 649f.

39. Published by Dronke, *Medieval Latin,* II, 404.

40. E. Langlois, *Recueil,* II, 39.

41. Orpheus' loss of his wife and death at the hands of the Bacchantes gets only a sentence in Boccaccio's *De casibus virorum illustrium* (Paris, 1520), I, fol. viii. Lydgate, however, in his *Fall of Princes,* ed. H. Bergen (London, 1924), expands the story, making Orpheus an exemplum for the perfidy of women and the evils of marriage. In Lydgate's portrait, curiously, Orpheus is "ful ougli on to see" and "gaff counseil ful notable/To husbondis that han endurid peyne,/To such as been prudent and tretable:/Oon hell is dreedful, mor pereilous be tweyne;/And who is onys boundyn in a cheyne,/And may escapen out off daunger blyue—/Yiff he resorte, God let hym neuer thryue!" (5779, 5832–5838). Needless to say, the Thracian women were enraged at Orpheus' view of marriage and accordingly killed him for his words.

42. The standard edition of the poem is that of A. J. Bliss (2d edition, Oxford, 1966). He discusses manuscript problems and gives a bibliography for the poem through 1964, to which should be added D. M. Hill, "The Structure of 'Sir Orfeo,'" *Mediaeval Studies,* 23 (1961): 136–153; A. M. Kinghorn, "Human Interest in the Middle English *Sir Orfeo,*" *Neophilologus,* 50 (1966): 359–369; John Block Friedman, "Eurydice, Heurodis, and the Noon-Day Demon," *Speculum,* 41 (1966): 22–29; K. R. R. Gros Louis, "The Significance of Sir Orfeo's Self-Exile," *RES,* 18 (1967): 245–252; J. K. Knapp, "The Meaning of *Sir Orfeo,*" *MLQ,* 29 (1968): 263–273. All quotations from *Sir Orfeo* will be drawn from Bliss.

43. See Albert C. Baugh, "The Middle English Romance: Some Questions of Creation, Presentation, and Preservation," *Speculum,* 42 (1967): 1–31.

44. A variety of sources, all conjectural, have been suggested for the narrative of *Sir Orfeo.* Those positions advanced before 1964 are summarized and discussed in Bliss's introduction. Bliss, however, does not mention J. B. Severs' paper "Antecedents of *Sir Orfeo,*" *Studies in Honor of Albert Baugh* (Philadelphia, 1961), pp. 187–207, which sees influence mainly from Alfred's Boethius translation, Celtic legend, and Walter Map's tale of the Knight of Little Britain in *De Nugis Curialium.*

45. *The Poems of William Dunbar,* ed. W. M. Mackenzie (London, 1950), p. 116. In the thirteenth-century poem *Li Tournoiemenz Anticrit* by Hugo de Méry, ed. G. Wimmer, *Ausgaben und Abhandlungen aus dem Gebiet der romanischen Philologie,* 76 (1888), Pluto and Proserpine are the king and queen of hell with a court made up of classical gods and demigods, biblical devils, and evil Christians (ll. 552–601).

46. Vat. Lat. 1593, 3v, in Ghisalberti, "Arnolfo d'Orléans," p. 222, n. 1.

47. *Anal. Hymn.* LI, 216, p. 275.

48. Ginzberg, *The Legends of the Jews,* I, 40. An account of the relations between medieval Jewish and Christian exegetes, and more particularly of the use of Midrashic material by Christians like Hugh of St. Victor and Nicholas of Lyra, is given by Herman Hailperin, *Rashi and the Christian Scholars* (Pittsburgh, 1963), pp. 15–28 and 103–108.

49. Vincent of Beauvais, *Speculum Naturale* (Douai, 1624), XX, 33, p. 1478. See J. Bonnell, "The Serpent with a Human Head in Art and Mystery Play," *AJA,* 21 (1917): 255–291, who offers a handlist of the figure in medieval art. Bonnell is in error when he makes Vincent a primary source for the draconopede, for Vincent indicates his own indebtedness to Thomas of Cantimpré, *De Naturis Rerum,* VIII, xvi.

50. Mortimer J. Donovan, in an interesting article, "Herodis in the Auchinleck *Sir Orfeo,*" *Medium Aevum,* 27 (1958): 162–165, argues that Heurodis is to be associated with the evil Herodias who helped to bring about the death of St. John the Baptist.

51. Ginzberg, *Legends of the Jews,* I, 105.

52. *The Book of Enoch,* tr. R. H. Charles (London, 1962), VI–VII, pp. 34–35. For knowledge of the Book of Enoch in the Latin West, see H. J. Lawlor, "Early Citations from the Book of Enoch," *Journal of Philology,* 25 (1897): 164–225. See also the fragmentary Latin translation of the work, of eighth-century British provenance, edited by M. R. James, *Apocrypha Anecdota* (Cambridge, Engl., 1893), pp. 146–150.

53. Solomon of Basra, *The Book of the Bee,* ed. E. A. Wallis Budge (Oxford, 1886), XVIII, 27, n. 3.

54. *Clementine Homilies,* VIII, 13, *ANF,* VIII, 273.

55. The Jews had long believed this of the lesser demons. See *The Babylonian Talmud,* ed. I. Epstein (London, 1938): Hagigah II, 16a, pp. 101–102.

56. *The Midrash on Psalms,* tr. William G. Braude (New Haven, 1959), II, iv, p. 102.

57. Background on man's susceptibility to supernatural influence at noon has been collected by R. Caillois, "Les Démons de midi," *RHR,* 115 (1937): 142–173, and 116 (1937): 54–83, 143–186. Rudolph Arbesmann, O.S.A., discusses the idea in the works of the Fathers in "The 'Daemonium Meridianum' and Greek and Latin Patristic Exegesis," *Traditio,* 14 (1958): 17–31.

58. *Tractatus sive homiliae in Psalmos,* ed. G. Morin, *Anecdota Maredsolana* (Maredsous, 1897), III, pp. 115–117. For Hugh of St. Cher, noon "ut jam reveletur homo peccati, filius perditionis, Antichristus, daemonium non modo diurnum, sed & meridianum . . ." *Opera omnia in universum Vetus et Novum Testamentum* (Venice, 1732), II, 241v. See also Bernard of Clairvaux, *PL* 183, 199.

59. Richard of St. Victor, *Adnotationes mysticae in Psalmos, PL* 196, 395.

60. *Enarrationes in Psalmos, PL* 131, 626.

61. M. D. Anderson, *Drama and Imagery in English Medieval Churches* (Cambridge, Engl., 1963), has stressed the importance of carved rafter bosses and other such works as sources of biblical imagery for medieval authors.

62. See Howard Rollin Patch, *The Other World* (Cambridge, Mass., 1950), pp. 27f, and Theodore Spencer, "Chaucer's Hell: A Study in Mediaeval Convention," *Speculum,* 2 (1927): 177–200, for discussion and bibliography.

63. Marie de France, *Lais,* ed. A. Ewert (Oxford, 1960), ll. 355–364.

64. G. R. Woodward and H. Mattingly, ed. and tr., *Barlaam and Ioasaph* (Loeb Library ed., London and New York, 1914), XXX, 280, 282.

65. John MacQueen, *Robert Henryson, A Study of the Major Narrative Poems* (Oxford, 1967), pp. 16–17.

66. H. Harvey Wood, ed., *Robert Henryson, Poems and Fables* (London and Edinburgh, 1958), p. xi. All quotations from Henryson's poetry are drawn from this text.

67. See Plato, *Laws* XII, 964f, and, on the ennobling character of virtue, Colucio Salutati, *De nobilitate legum et medicinae,* ed. E. Garin (Florence, 1947), p. 8: "Vera tamen nobilitas, non in . . . sanguine, sed in virtutibus est."

68. John Hollander, *The Untuning of the Sky* (Princeton, 1961), pp. 85f, and Sydney J. Harth, "Convention and Creation in the Poetry of Robert Henryson: A Study of *The Testament of Cresseid* and *Orpheus and Eurydice,*" unpublished dissertation (University of Chicago, 1960), pp. 136–147, discuss Henryson's musical lore.

69. This detail occurs with an Aristaeus at once lustful and a symbol of virtue in *Ovide Moralisé,* X, 26–33. John MacQueen interprets the "beistis" of Aristaeus as "the carnal passions" which virtue keeps in check (*Robert Henryson,* pp. 34–35), but there is little evidence to support this in either the Orpheus tradition or in Henryson's poem itself.

70. For example, St. Paul's famous visit to Paradise is described in Poem Number 16, ll. 236–260, of *The Poems of John Audelay,* ed. E. K. Whiting (London, 1931), *EETS:OS,* 184.

71. James had been reading Boethius' *Consolation* to give himself comfort with regard to his own imprisonment when he decided to write his poem. He refers to the *Consolation* as "Compilit by that noble senatoure/Off rome," while Henryson begins his *moralitas* with a reference to "Boece, that senatour." Both authors give similar lists of the Muses, though it must be admitted that such lists were not uncommon—Chaucer, for example, names the Muses in a like fashion in *Troilus.* James I, *The Kingis Quair,* ed. W. Skeat (Edinburgh, 1884), ll. 16–19.

72. This detail appears in Trivet, folio 102r.

Index

241